TAKEN AT THE FLOOD

Ancient Warfare and Civilization

SERIES EDITORS:

RICHARD ALSTON   ROBIN WATERFIELD

In this series, leading historians offer compelling new narratives of the armed conflicts that shaped and reshaped the classical world, from the wars of Archaic Greece to the fall of the Roman Empire and the Arab conquests.

Dividing the Spoils: The War for Alexander the Great's Empire
Robin Waterfield

By the Spear: Philip II, Alexander the Great, and the Rise and Fall of the Macedonian Empire
Ian Worthington

Taken at the Flood: The Roman Conquest of Greece
Robin Waterfield

TAKEN AT THE FLOOD

The Roman Conquest of Greece

Robin Waterfield

OXFORD
UNIVERSITY PRESS

OXFORD
UNIVERSITY PRESS

Oxford University Press is a department of the University of Oxford.
It furthers the University's objective of excellence in research, scholarship,
and education by publishing worldwide.

Oxford   New York
Auckland   Cape Town   Dar es Salaam   Hong Kong   Karachi
Kuala Lumpur   Madrid   Melbourne   Mexico City   Nairobi
New Delhi   Shanghai   Taipei   Toronto

With offices in
Argentina   Austria   Brazil   Chile   Czech Republic   France   Greece
Guatemala   Hungary   Italy   Japan   Poland   Portugal   Singapore
South Korea   Switzerland   Thailand   Turkey   Ukraine   Vietnam

Oxford is a registered trademark of Oxford University Press
in the UK and certain other countries.

Published in the United States of America by
Oxford University Press
198 Madison Avenue, New York, NY 10016

© Robin Waterfield 2014

Library of Congress Cataloging-in-Publication Data
Waterfield, Robin, 1952–
Taken at the Flood : the Roman Conquest of Greece / Robin Waterfield.
pages cm.—(Ancient Warfare and Civilization)
Includes bibliographical references and index.
ISBN 978–0–19–991689–4
1. Illyrian Wars.   2. Rome—History—Republic, 265–30 B.C.   3. Illyria—History.   I. Title.
DG246.W37 2014
939.'87—dc23
2013019020

1 3 5 7 9 8 6 4 2
Printed in the United States of America
on acid-free paper

This is for two sets of friends, two wonderful families,
the Snowdons and the Stanfords

There is a tide in the affairs of men
Which, taken at the flood, leads on to Fortune.
William Shakespeare,
Julius Caesar, Act 4, scene 3

CONTENTS

PREFACE

"Is there anyone on earth who is so narrow-minded or uninquisitive that he could fail to want to know how and thanks to what kind of political system almost the entire known world was conquered and brought under a single empire, the empire of the Romans, in less than fifty-three years—an unprecedented event?" So wrote the Greek historian Polybius of Megalopolis at the beginning of his monumental work.[1] The 53-year period he had in mind (counting inclusively) stretched from the start of the Second Punic War in 219 BCE until 167, the year of the overthrow of the Macedonian monarchy by Rome and the division of Macedon into four independent republics.

The period I cover in this book includes Polybius's fifty-three years, though I start a little earlier and end a little later. I start with the First Illyrian War of 229 and a final chapter looks ahead past 167 to the destruction of Corinth in 146. The importance of the period lies fundamentally in the clash of the superpowers—Rome, Macedon, and Syria. But I start with the so-called Illyrian wars (they hardly deserve the name), not least because I believe that their contribution to the eventual clash of the superpowers has not been fully appreciated, or has at least been underestimated by recent historians.

This was a period of extraordinary activity and expansion by Rome, but, as the subtitle of the book implies, my focus is limited to the Greek east, and chiefly the Greek mainland. Roman imperial expansion into Hellenized lands further east than the Balkan peninsula took place later, though the foundations were laid in my period. Roman expansion in the west was happening more or less simultaneously, by means of a series of wars with the wealthy North African trading city of Carthage (the Punic wars), and then with Spanish tribes. These events, critical for Mediterranean history, will play a part in the book chiefly and merely in the sense that Roman experiences in the west conditioned their responses to opportunities and events in the east—reaction to Hannibal and depletion of resources being the most telling factors. In any case, the titanic struggle with Carthage has tended over the years to distract attention from the equally critical events that were happening further east.

I have broken up the (largely military) narrative of events with commentary, and with "asides" on social and cultural matters, that illuminate and add depth to our understanding of the period. For instance, when the conquest of Greece began, Rome was still relatively poor and simple, and so when it came into more constant contact with its older neighbors, with their long cultural history and urbane reputations, insistent questions arose: How much of this culture can we adopt without losing our identity? Would it matter? What *is* our identity? The Romans were forced to define themselves by contrast with Greeks, and the beginning of that process of self-definition is a fascinating aspect of the history of the period—fascinating, but hard to grasp. At the same time, of course, the Romans were also refining their impressions of the Greeks. There is just enough evidence to give us tantalizing glimpses of what the Romans thought of the Greeks, and vice versa.

This book is part of a series designed for consumption not only by scholars, but also by undergraduates and anyone interested in ancient history. Apart from the addition of aids such as a glossary and a timeline, this consideration has shaped the book mainly in that I have avoided going in any depth into the controversies that abound. I should take this opportunity, therefore, to say something about a few broad conclusions to which my reading and thinking have led me.

First, and most importantly, where Roman imperialism is concerned, I fall closer to the camp of William Harris than I do to that of Maurice Holleaux or his later allies. That is, I believe that the Romans were more aggressive imperialists in this period than used to be commonly held before the first edition of Harris's *War and Imperialism in Republican Rome* in 1979—that they did not go to war only when they were truly threatened (though they might pretend they were), nor were they dragged into entanglement with the east by accident or a series of accidents (Gruen, simplified), nor were their eastern wars purely the result of factors systemic to the Mediterranean world of the time (Eckstein, simplified).

The difficulty in appreciating this, and the reason that redoubtable scholars can look at the same body of evidence and arrive at contradictory conclusions, is that Roman imperialism, at this stage, took on a peculiar form. For a long time, there was no actual annexation—no taxation, no army of occupation, no imperialist administrative structures. Every time the Romans came, they also withdrew, in a tidal pattern that lasted several decades. But, in my view, each time they withdrew, they left more of the Greek world under a form of indirect, extralegal rule. It was an economical and effective system, requiring only deference from their subjects, and little in the way of commitment of resources by Rome. However, it did require the Romans to display enough resolution, and even ruthlessness, while they were there, to command deference while they were absent even from those who had not already been weakened by the previous round of brutality.

To argue that Rome was compelled to war for moral reasons, such as obligations toward friends, or because in a condition of Mediterranean "anarchy" (lack of international law or a strong central authority) war was inevitable, fails to give the whole picture. Even supposing that there was some external compulsion, the level or kind of response the Romans delivered was not fully determined by it. The evidence shows, I believe, that they often chose war of their own accord, that the discourse of "compulsion by external factors" is an echo of their very potent justificatory propaganda, and that, thanks to the militaristic nature of their culture, they relished the opportunity to expand their power.

Second, I find it difficult to see that there was a "party" of "Greek experts" in Rome who influenced senatorial policy. There were, of course, men who had more experience of the Greek language and Greek affairs than others, and the senators, not being stupid, made use of them; in the narrative that follows, we will often find men chosen by lot to command an army in Greece or Asia Minor, and then repeatedly used after that for diplomatic missions in the east or as advisers to subsequent generals. Then again, one of the novel practices forced upon Rome by the Second Punic War was the introduction of annual extensions of the field commands of men who were doing a good job, and this simple and effective measure was applied to the eastern wars as well; it was a way of counteracting the negative effects of the inevitable short-termism of Roman political life, with its annual elections and other hedges against individual power. But, although pressure groups undoubtedly existed within the Senate, and although personal relationships counted for a great deal in the political life of Rome, it goes beyond our evidence to see these Greek experts as a pressure group.

Third, I am not convinced that there was much in the way of a class struggle in Greece in the first half of the second century. What little evidence there is fits the idea that it was propaganda rather than actual fact: knowing the Roman preference for administration by the rich, factions portrayed their enemies as fostering popularist constitutional reforms. There were undoubtedly financial and social crises in a number of Greek states, but they seem to have affected all strata of society.

Fourth, some will find similarities between the imperialism of Republican Rome and that of the United States today. Cultural historian Thomas Bender pinpoints the peculiar nature of U.S. imperialism since the Second World War in the following terms: "Indirect rule and influence replaced colonialism; military bases, client states and financial aid replaced pith helmets, jodhpurs, and rajas."[2] With the appropriate terms changed, this could almost be a description of Roman policy, as portrayed in this book. I do not deny the similarities, then, but it would take a different kind of book to bring them out in detail—and a different author, one more steeped in modern history and political analysis. Still, I would not deny that familiarity with the modern version of empire-creation by bullying, bribery, and judicious intervention may have helped to open my eyes to the nature of its ancient cousin.

In short, for the purposes of this book, I have avoided the finer details of all scholarly controversies. My first aim has been no more than to explicate a complex, important, and relatively unknown period of European history, and I have hardly strayed from that goal. But I have used the notes not just for referencing, but to alert the reader to the major scholarly controversies as they arise. By the same token, I have included a generous bibliography to aid further research.

And there are indeed many topics that invite further reading. This was a unique period of European history, filled with world-changing events. The two cultures whose intermingling would come to create what we think of as "the Classics," the foundational culture of Europe, made their first enduring contact. Of the great Macedonian kingdoms that had emerged from the wars of Alexander the Great's Successors, one was destroyed by the Romans (Macedon) and another was severely weakened (Syria); Egypt was already weak, and Pergamum was aligned with Rome anyway. At the start of my period, there were five superpowers in the Mediterranean; less than sixty years later, there was only one. Above all, we witness large parts of Greece thrown into turmoil and then devastated so thoroughly that they did not recover for centuries. It is tempting to end this preface as it began: with the same challenge to the reader that Polybius issued over two thousand years ago.

ACKNOWLEDGMENTS

WHILE PREPARING FOR OUR trip to northern Greece, Albania, Montenegro, and Croatia in April 2012, my wife Kathryn and I received enthusiastic advice from John Papadopoulos, Sarah Morris, and Alda Agolli of the University of California at Los Angeles, from Saimir Shpuza of the Albanian Institute of Archaeology, from Jack Davis of the American School of Classical Studies at Athens, and from Oliver Gilkes— Albanian experts all. In Albania itself we were given a personal tour of the museum of the Albanian Institute of Archaeology by Shpresa Gjongecaj, Director of Antiquities, and Ilir Zaloshnja, the curator of the museum. We were shown all the visitable antiquities of Hvar Island, Croatia, by Aldo Čavić and Vilma Stojković of the Stari Grad museum, good people. In Ioannina, Georgia Pliakou of the Ioannina Archaeological Museum shared some of her views, and the former (but scarcely "retired") director of the 12th Ephorate of Prehistoric and Classical Antiquities, Kostas Zachos, showed us Passaron (if it is Passaron) and a delightful lakeside restaurant. Almost everywhere we went, we were conscious of following the footsteps of N. G. L. Hammond. For live directions, we are in the debt of passersby everywhere (particularly in Albania, where signs are few), but especially 90-year-old Izet Selman Baba of Klos, Albania, and Kostas Korkizogoulou of Zoodokhos Pigi, Thessaly, both of whom instantly dropped what they were doing to steer us around the antiquities of Nicaea and Cynoscephalae respectively.

This book completes at least one cycle of my life, since I was first seized by love of ancient history through studying the Roman Republic at school and university. Since then, my specialization has been in Greek matters. But one of the many pleasures of writing this book was the chance to get back in touch with John Briscoe, who had taught me as an undergraduate, and ask him to read the typescript. He agreed, and his comments proved, of course, immensely useful. By my elbow throughout the writing of this book have been his commentaries on Livy, alongside Walbank's on Polybius. I also owe profound thanks to my other readers, lay and specialist: Richard Alston, Andrew Erskine, Tim Hucker, Andrew Lane, and Kathryn Waterfield. Stefan Vranka, exemplary commissioning editor, was as always a pleasure to work with for his skill and knowledge. Naturally, none of them is responsible for any blemishes that remain.

I wrote to many academics around the world asking for offprints of articles, and as usual met with nothing but kindness. I communicated over details with Professors Jean-Paul Descoeudres, Jerzy Linderski, Bill Murray, Nathan Rosenstein, and Tony Woodman—thank you, one and all. Professor Adrian Anastasi of the Department of Antiquity, Albanian Institute of Archaeology, University of Tirana, kindly made available the photograph of the Labeatan coin. I spent peaceful days reading for the book in the library of the Institute of Classical Studies in London, and in the Blegen Library in Athens. It is always a pleasure to thank the staff of these institutions for their patience, kindness, and efficiency.

LIST OF ILLUSTRATIONS

MAPS

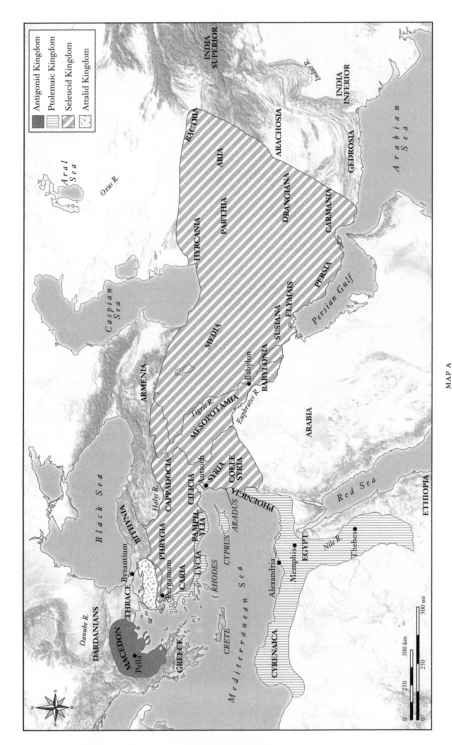

MAP A

The Hellenistic Kingdoms, c. 230 BCE

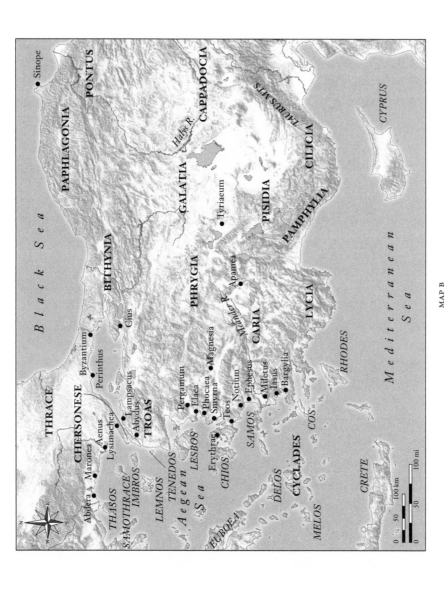

MAP B

Asia Minor and the Aegean

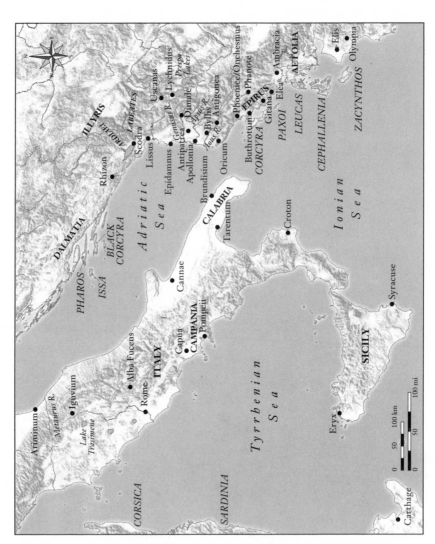

MAP C
The Central Mediterranean

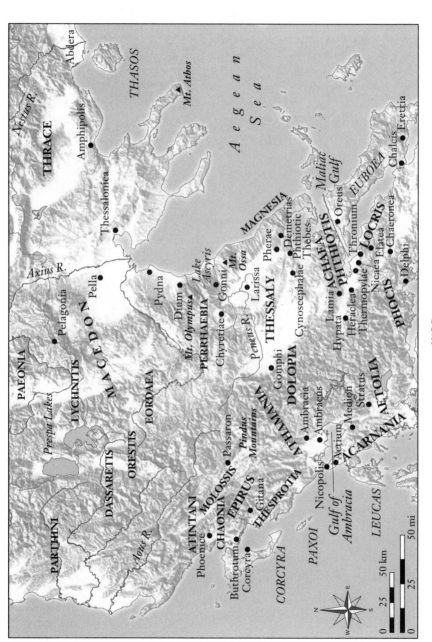

MAP D

Northern Greece, Macedon, and Thrace

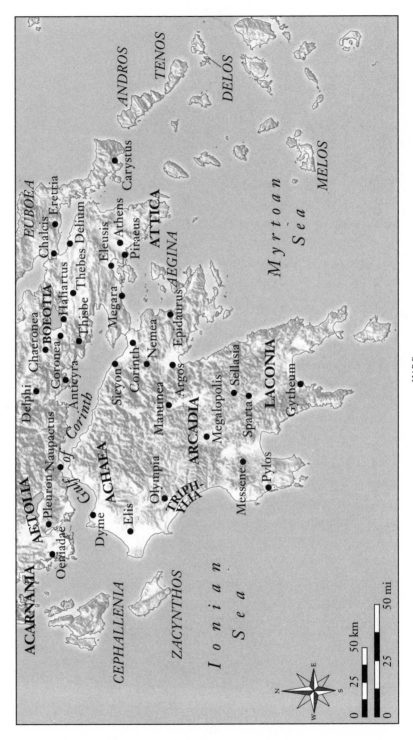

MAP E
The Peloponnese and Central Greece

PRELUDE: CLOUDS IN THE WEST

IT CAME TO HIM, I suspect, like a flash of lightning—the bold insight that prompted Polybius of Megalopolis to put pen to paper in the 150s BCE and compose one of the greatest works of history ever written in the West, the story, in forty books, of Rome's rapid rise to imperial power in the Mediterranean. He had lived through much of the turmoil of this transformative period himself, and what he saw was that, after a certain point, all Mediterranean history became an organic whole (his metaphor), in the sense that the various histories of the various parts of the Mediterranean world all became subsumed under the history of Rome. Rome became the center, and *everything* else was on its peripheries. He also believed that he could pinpoint the moment when the process began: the summer of 217 BCE, at a convention attended by representatives of all the most important Greek leagues and states at Naupactus, near the entrance to the Gulf of Corinth.[1]

The only speech Polybius recorded from this convention, though unlikely to be accurate in all its details,[2] was delivered by a dignitary of the Aetolian League, Agelaus of Naupactus. Agelaus urged the assembled Greeks to stop making war on one another, not just as a matter of principle, but also as an urgent expediency. "If you ever allow the clouds now gathering in the west to loom over Greece," he said, "I deeply fear that all the games we now play with one another, our truces and our wars, will be so thoroughly denied us that we shall find ourselves imploring the gods to grant us this right, to make war and peace with one another as we wish, and in general to manage our own internal disputes." Agelaus was right: the peace negotiations at Naupactus were the last the Greeks would ever conduct on their own, without Roman interference. Whether he was also right in his further implication that, if the Greeks united, they could keep the Romans at bay, we will never know, because that did not happen.

Strictly, a speaker at that moment in time could not know that it would be the Romans who would come. Polybius has Agelaus imply, correctly, that it would be either the Romans or the Carthaginians. Whichever of them won the war then raging in Italy would control the whole of the civilized western Mediterranean, and the rich resources of Spain, Sicily, Italy, and Tunisia would only serve to increase its power and its greed. Whichever side won the war was bound, before long, to turn its attention east. That was the way of the ancient Mediterranean. But, of course, Polybius knew, and his readers knew, that it would be the Romans.[3] The speech is a piece of prophetic irony.

But the advent of the Romans was not the only reason why Polybius chose this moment as critical for Mediterranean history. When Agelaus said that the Greeks should stop making war on one another, he actually had chiefly in mind a Macedonian, rather than a Greek, strictly speaking. He dared to rebuke King Philip V of Macedon and tell him to stop stirring up war among the Greeks. If he was ambitious, he said, he should look to Italy. Whoever won there was going to be exhausted and vulnerable. An imperialist idea that had been no more than a seed in Philip's mind at once blossomed (or so Polybius claims). The western and eastern halves of the Mediterranean were set on a collision course.

Agelaus's speech reflects the fact that in 217 some Greek statesmen were aware of the possibility of a threat from Rome. Now here is a second anecdote, a famous story, set fifty years later, in 168. Antiochus IV of Syria was poised to take Alexandria, overthrow the tottering dynasty of the Ptolemies, and gain all Egypt, but a Roman troubleshooter, Gaius Popillius Laenas, demanded that he call off the invasion and come to terms. When Antiochus prevaricated, Popillius (acting with the plenipotentiary freedom commonly granted Roman legates and commanders abroad) drew a circle around him in the dust and told him not to step outside it until he had given his answer. Antiochus caved in.[4]

The question is unavoidable: how did the eastern Mediterranean get from A to B? From a position where Rome was no more than a cloud looming in the west, to a position fifty years later—only fifty years—where it was able to threaten the most powerful king in the known world and deny him the right to pursue a foreign policy of his own choosing? This is the question this book sets out to answer.

1.

ROME TURNS EAST

THE CONFERENCE DID NOT go well. The Roman envoys told Teuta, the Illyrian queen, why they were there and itemized their overt complaints: piracy by her subjects in the Adriatic, the sea that lay between Illyris and Italy, had been worsening for some years, until a number of Italian traders had been killed and complaints had been received in Rome. They had come, they explained, to ask the queen to rein in her subjects, and to make sure that no such incident ever happened again. These were not the first such complaints the Romans had received, and with piracy rampant in the Adriatic (as elsewhere in the Mediterranean at the time) there must have been deaths before, but in 230 the Romans chose to act.

As often in diplomatic exchanges, as much was left unsaid as was heard aloud. For the Romans had also been approached for help by the people of the Adriatic island of Issa, and the envoys, the brothers Gnaeus and Lucius Coruncanius, in fact found the queen busy with the siege of Issa town. The purpose of the visit by the Roman envoys, then, was not just what it seemed to be. They were there to gauge the level of threat Teuta represented not just to Adriatic shipping, but to the region more generally. These undercurrents in the queen's pavilion escalated the tension.

As Teuta listened, she made no attempt to disguise her contempt. After the envoys had finished speaking, there were a few minutes of silence while the queen consulted with her advisers. Then she turned back to the Romans. Despite maintaining the facade of politeness that was proper to diplomatic occasions, her rejection of the envoys' petition was total. "Of course," she said, "I would never provoke Rome at an official level. But the incident you're talking about is no business of Rome's as a state, and rulers of Illyris are not in the habit of preventing their subjects from privately profiting from the sea."

This was indeed an arrogant reply. Normal diplomatic practice might have recommended a denial that the alleged killers had been Illyrians, with an accompanying promise to look into the incident and do her best to curb piracy by her subjects. The delay would have defused the immediate tension. Instead, while fully accepting that piracy was an established way of life among her subjects,[1] she simply refused to do anything about it. But Queen Teuta's tactlessness was matched by the Romans. The younger Coruncanius lost his temper, as diplomats should not, and warned Teuta that, if her refusal to curb her subjects was normal Illyrian practice, maybe the Romans should come and change the way things were done there. The undercurrents in the meeting, as much as the deaths of Italian traders, caused the outburst. From what they had seen and heard at Issa, the Coruncanius brothers had already decided that Teuta was an enemy of Rome.

The meeting broke up in rancor, with this threat of armed retaliation hanging in the air. It is not clear what happened next, but as the envoys were getting ready to sail back home, one or possibly both of them, and the Issaean dignitary whose appeal to Rome had triggered the Roman mission, were killed. Whether or not these murders were officially sanctioned, the Romans, no doubt agreeing with the report they heard from the survivors of the diplomatic mission, took them as an act of war.[2] The Romans were committing themselves to their first overseas military venture eastward, to lands where the language and culture were Greek.

THE ILLYRIAN BID FOR LEGITIMACY

The region known as Illyris (Albania and Dalmatia, in today's terms) was regarded at the time as a barbarian place, only semi-civilized by contact with its Greek and Macedonian neighbours. It was occupied by a number of different tribes, linked by a common culture and language (a cousin of Thracian). From time to time, one of these tribes gained a degree of dominance over some or most of the rest, but never over all of them at once. Contact with the Greek world had led to a degree of urbanization, especially in the south and along the coast, but the region still essentially consisted of many minor tribal dynasts with networks of loyalty. At the time in question, the Ardiaei were the leading tribe, and in the 230s their king, Agron, had forged a kind of union, the chief plank of which was alliances with other local magnates from central Illyris, such as Demetrius, Greek lord of the wealthy island of Pharos, and Scerdilaidas, chief of the Illyrian Labeatae.

In the late 230s, the Illyrians' Greek neighbors to the south, the confederacy of Epirote tribes and communities, descended into chaos following the republican overthrow of a by-then hated monarchy. Agron seized the opportunity. Following a significant victory over the Aetolians in 231—they had been hired by Demetrius II of Macedon to relieve the siege of Medion, a town belonging to his allies, the Acarnanians—the Illyrians, confident that they could stand up to any of their neighbors, expanded their operations. The next year, they raided as far south as the Peloponnesian coastline, but, more importantly, they seized the northern Epirote town of Phoenice (see Fig. 1.1).

The capture of Phoenice, the strongest and wealthiest city in Epirus, and then its successful defense against a determined Epirote attempt at recovery, were morale-boosting victories, but the practical consequences were uppermost in Agron's mind. Phoenice was not just an excellent lookout point; it was also close to the main north–south route from Illyris into Epirus. More immediately, the town commanded its own fertile (though rather boggy) alluvial valleys, and access to the sea at Onchesmus. There was another harbor not far south, at Buthrotum (modern Butrint, one of the best archaeological sites in Europe), but for a ship traveling north up the coast, Onchesmus was the last good harbor until Oricum, eighty kilometers (fifty miles) further on, a day's sailing or possibly two. And, even apart from the necessity of havens in bad weather, ancient ships had to be beached frequently, to forage for food and water (warships, especially, had room for little in the way of supplies), to dry out the insides of the ships (no pumps in those days), and to kill the teredo "worm" (a kind of boring mollusk). Phoenice was a valuable prize.

FIGURE 1.1

Phoenice. The capture by King Agron of this strategic northern Epirote city in 230 BCE gave the Illyrians the confidence that made them a threat to the region—and so brought them into collision with Rome.

Agron died a short while later, reputedly from pleurisy contracted after the over-enthusiastic celebration of his victories. He was succeeded by his son Pinnes—or rather, by his wife Teuta, who became regent for the boy.[3] Teuta inherited a critical situation. Following the loss of Phoenice, the Epirotes had joined the Aetolian–Achaean alliance, and their new allies dispatched an army north as soon as they could. The Illyrian army under Scerdilaidas moved south to confront them, numbering perhaps ten thousand men. The two armies met not far north of Passaron (modern Ioannina).[4]

The fate of the northwest coastline of Greece hung in the balance. But before battle was joined, the Illyrian forces were recalled by Teuta to deal with a rebellion by one of the tribes of her confederacy (we do not know which), who had called in help from the Dardanians. The Dardanian tribes occupied the region north of Macedon and northeast of Illyris (modern Kosovo, mainly), and not infrequently carried out cross-border raids in considerable force, with several tribes uniting for a profitable campaign. Scerdilaidas withdrew back north, plundering as he went, and made a deal with the Epirote authorities whereby he kept all the booty from Phoenice and received a handsome ransom for returning the city, relatively undamaged, to the league.

The Dardanian threat evaporated, and in 230 Teuta turned to the island of Issa, a neighbor of Pharos. This was a natural extension for her: Issa (modern Vis), along with Corcyra (Corfu) and Pharos (Hvar), was one of the great commercial islands of this coastline, wealthy from its own products,[5] and as a result of the convenience of its harbors for the Adriatic trade in timber and other commodities; in fact, at ten hectares, Issa town was the largest Greek settlement in Dalmatia. Teuta already had Pharos and its dependency, Black Corcyra (Korčula); if she could take Issa and Corcyra, her revenue would be greatly increased and she would become a major player in the region. Teuta put Issa town under siege; in those days, each island generally had only one large town, the main port, and so to take the town was to take the island.

When the campaigning season of 229 arrived,[6] Teuta (who still had Issa under siege) launched a major expedition. Her forces first attacked Epidamnus, a Greek trading city on the Illyrian coast, with an excellent harbor and command of the most important eastward route towards Macedon, the road the Romans began to develop a century later as the Via Egnatia. The attack was thwarted by the desperate bravery of the Epidamnians, but the Illyrians sailed off and joined up with the rest of their fleet, which had Corcyra town under siege. The people of Corcyra, Epidamnus, and Apollonia (another Greek colony, eighty kilometers [fifty miles] down the coast from Epidamnus, and certain to be the next target) naturally sought help from the Aetolians and Achaeans, who had already demonstrated their hostility toward the Illyrians, and the Greek allies raised a small fleet and sent it to relieve Corcyra. But the Illyrians had supplemented their usual fleet of small, fast *lemboi* with some larger warships loaned by the Acarnanians, who were pleased to thank them for raising the siege of Medion. Battle was joined off Paxoi, and it was another victory for the Illyrians.

The Corcyraeans surrendered, and a garrison was installed under Demetrius of Pharos, while the remainder of the Illyrian forces returned to besiege Epidamnus again. Success breeds success, and the Illyrians' position was hugely strengthened when the confused and frightened Epirotes abandoned the Aetolian–Achaean alliance they had only just joined, which had demonstrated its ineffectiveness off Paxoi, and entered into an alliance with the Illyrians instead. In return, they ceded Atintanis, the district around the critical pass at Antigonea (see Fig. 1.2), on the border between Illyris and Epirus. The Epirote alliance gave the Illyrians control of 650 kilometers (400 miles) of coastline, from Dalmatia to the Gulf of Ambracia, and as a result of their success as Demetrius II's mercenaries in 231, they had the friendship of Macedon, usually the most powerful state in Greece. They were now a force to be reckoned with. Their alliances with Epirus and Acarnania put these coastlines out of bounds

FIGURE 1.2

The Drin valley at Antigonea. This vital pass, the main route from Illyris to Epirus, fell within the original Roman sphere of influence in Illyris, but remained a bone of contention until Antigonea was utterly destroyed by the Romans in 167 BCE.

for their piracy—but then, Teuta was fast evolving from pirate queen to empress of a mini-empire.

This campaign of Teuta's in 229 was not, or not just, expansionist aggression. In 230, as we have seen, the people of Issa had appealed to Rome for help. To whom else could they turn? They were surrounded by enemies; the Aetolians and Achaeans had just been beaten by the Illyrians; the Macedonians had just lost one of their most important outlying districts, Paeonia, to a Dardanian invasion, and their king to inopportune illness. Their new king, Philip V, was no more than a boy, who needed a regent. (In that, the Macedonians were lucky, because Philip gained the very competent Antigonus Doson, who soon became king. But at the time he had his hands full trying to recover Paeonia.) The two great powers currently in Greece, the Macedonians and the Aetolian–Achaean alliance, were therefore out of the picture, so the Issaeans turned to the nearest known power, the Romans. Their appeal was probably mediated by Hiero II, king of Sicilian Syracuse. Issa was a Syracusan foundation and retained strong links with the mother city, and Hiero was currently one of Rome's most critical allies.

The outcome of the appeal was the official visit of the Coruncanius brothers, and after that fiasco Teuta knew the Romans were coming. Her moves in the early part of 229 were therefore defensive, designed to secure the landing places that were not yet under her control. Pharos and Corcyra were hers, Epidamnus and Issa were under siege, and if she could get Apollonia as well, that would sew up a nice little domain and make it hard for the Romans to land a force anywhere nearby.

THE COMING OF ROME

The meeting between Queen Teuta and the Coruncanius brothers climaxed with the younger Coruncanius's threat. Even though this was delivered in the heat of the moment, it was clearly meant to be a credible threat—one that conformed not only to whatever image Teuta had of Rome, but also to the image Coruncanius himself had of Rome at this moment in history, the Rome he was representing. He must have known that his and his brother's mission would have the backing of the Roman army if needed. He must have known that Roman interest in a region could easily be a prelude to armed intervention.

Rome had been demonstrating its aggression and belligerence for the past 200 years. In the course of the fifth century, the city came to dominate its immediate neighbors in Italy.[7] By the end of the first decade of the third century, much of central and northern Italy was in Roman hands. The new territories were secured by supporting the dominance of local elites, and by planting colonies of Roman citizens (nineteen by the year 290), which repressed the inhabitants by the simple expedient of depriving them of some of their land. In the far north of modern Italy, Celtic tribes occupied the fertile Po valley from southern France to the head of the Adriatic, and in the south long-established Greek settlements and native tribes lived uneasily side by side.

Lacking the administrative apparatus to govern its growing Italian empire directly, the Romans developed a unique system whereby they left conquered cities free to govern themselves, in return for alliances (which came in various forms, but always asserted or affirmed Roman dominance), backed up by wholesale grants of Roman citizenship rights in various degrees. The allies in return were obliged to provide Rome not with tribute, but with manpower. The system worked brilliantly. By 225 BCE the Romans could, in theory, field over 600,000 men: no one in the Mediterranean could come close.[8] But this pool of men, gained by expansion in Italy, was almost bound to feed further expansion abroad: since Rome took no money from its Italian allies, the only way it could benefit from their alliance was by using them as soldiers, to gain more territory. The system would therefore fuel any other cultural factors that might incline the Romans towards aggressive expansionism.

The Romans next turned their attention to the troubled south of Italy, which had been settled by Greeks for so long that it was known as Magna Graecia, Greater Greece. Ostensibly to help the Greeks there in their prolonged struggle against resentful hill tribes—the Greeks had, after all, carved out an existence in their aboriginal territory—in the late 280s the Romans decided to install garrisons in several Greek cities. The citizens of Tarentum, the greatest city in Italy after Rome, correctly regarded this as an imperialist move: the garrisons would be followed by a more permanent Roman presence and accelerated Romanization. An anecdote suggests that the issue was very much Greeks versus Romans. As a conciliatory gesture, a Roman envoy delivered a speech in Greek, and the Tarentines mocked his errors; one man, drunk, even defecated on the wretched Roman.[9] A 10-year war began.

Knowing that they could not resist the Romans on their own, the Tarentines asked for help from Pyrrhus, the king of Molossis. The Molossians were currently the dominant tribe in Epirus, just across the Ionian Sea, and so Pyrrhus was effectively the king of northwestern Greece, with Ambracia (modern Arta) as his capital city.[10] He had a military reputation second only to that of his late cousin, Alexander the Great. Pyrrhus arrived in 281 with stunning force, and his initial successes alarmed the Romans. After all their efforts, it looked as though they could lose southern Italy to a Greek king. But then the Carthaginians offered Rome an alliance, specifically against Pyrrhus:[11] they occupied the west of Sicily and were concerned about his effect on the Sicilian Greek communities, which had long been vying with the Carthaginians for more complete control of the island.

The Carthaginians were right to be alarmed, because in 278 Pyrrhus landed in Sicily and soon overran almost the entire island. However, his regal ambitions did not sit well with his allies, and at the same time the Romans were threatening the garrisons he had left in Italy. Pyrrhus abandoned Sicily and returned to Italy, but was soon forced to withdraw: however often he defeated the Romans, they gathered further armies and returned (so a "Pyrrhic" victory is a futile victory, one that amounts to a defeat). In 275 he returned to Greece, abandoning the southern Italian cities in their turn to the mercy of the Romans. He died three years later, in the course of yet another adventure.[12]

The long and bloody war against Pyrrhus scarred the Romans, and Pyrrhus's ghost (later boosted by Hannibal's 16-year presence in Italy) became a key factor in Roman foreign policy: invasion became their worst nightmare, and an easy pretext for aggression.[13] But following their defeat of Pyrrhus, they had little time to lick their wounds, because in 264 they became involved in one of the longest and most brutal wars of the ancient world, the First Punic War against the Carthaginians (*Poenus*, from which we get the English "Punic," means "Phoenician" in Latin, and Carthage was a Phoenician foundation). The war dragged on for twenty-three appalling years, but in the end the Romans were victorious. The Carthaginians were compelled to evacuate Sicily, and then Sardinia, and the two great islands became the first overseas possessions of Rome. The Romans took their first steps in managing an overseas empire, gained enormous naval experience, and learnt a lot about keeping armies in the field overseas.

As Coruncanius knew, then, Rome had long shown its determination to rule Italy and, having created a firm foundation for itself there, had more recently shown that it would and could expand abroad as well. Circumstances meant that Rome's first aggressive steps abroad were taken in Sicily. But if Sicily was an obvious target because it lies only a few miles off the Italian peninsula, Illyris and western Greece were scarcely less obvious: at the narrowest point, the heel of Italy is separated from western Greece by only 72 kilometers (45 miles) of water.

Moreover, Rome was gradually taking over and securing the eastern coastline of Italy. Over the preceding fifty or sixty years, six colonies had been founded down the east coast of Italy, from Ariminum in the north to Brundisium in the south, and Adriatic trade had increased exponentially.[14] Then again, Rome's ally, the Sicilian city of Syracuse, was also heavily engaged in Adriatic trade; it seems very likely that Hiero had suffered from Illyrian piracy himself and had put extra pressure on the Senate. At any rate, at the end of the First Illyrian War, the Romans dedicated some of their spoils in the great temple of Olympian Zeus in Syracuse.[15] And then there was a third factor: at the time of the invasion of Illyris, Rome was involved in hostilities with the Celts of the Po valley, and there was always the possibility that its troops there would need to be transported and supplied from the Adriatic. They had good reasons for responding to a perceived threat from Illyris, and that is why the impression we get of the Coruncanius brothers' mission is that they were almost looking for a *casus belli*.

THE ROMAN OLIGARCHY

Politically, Rome was an oligarchy.[16] The Senate, the ruling body of Rome, consisted at this period of about 300 men, in a city where the overall population was at the time perhaps 275,000. In order to become a senator, a man had to have held high political office, but in order to hold high office he had to be a member of the highest wealth class. It was an oligarchy of the rich. Membership of the Senate was then for life, provided he did not disgrace himself too badly.

It was a paradox that the Senate was the ruling body because it was the only assembly in Rome that did not in itself have executive powers. The sovereign body was the people, meeting in various assemblies, so that from this perspective Republican Rome might seem a democracy. But, along with the passing of laws, the main power wielded by the people was the annual election of officials, and in so doing they effectively handed power over to these officials. And the forum of power for Republican officials was the Senate.

The Senate was a deliberative council, responsible for all the most important public issues: it met to debate all future legislation, and it controlled the state's finances and relations with foreign powers. It was the only semi-permanent council, since it met forty times a year, at least, while the popular assemblies were convened irregularly, by particular officers for particular purposes. A debate in the Senate led to a resolution, a *senatus consultum*, which in many cases was then presented to the appropriate assembly for ratification or passage into law. In theory, the assembly could alter or even vote against the proposal, but in practice that rarely happened (at this phase of the Republic), and so the Senate ruled largely by *auctoritas*, roughly "authority": its proposals had done everyone good so far, elected officials generally listened to its advice, and so it was allowed to continue. Every time they voted in favor of a senatorial proposal, the people were legitimizing the dominance of the aristocracy in Roman society.

So the Senate either presented its resolutions to an assembly, or it instructed the appropriate officer (consul, praetor, etc.),[17] who had previously been elected for the year by assembly vote, to put the proposal into effect. After that, the officer was more or less on his own, although he took into account the advice of his senatorial peers in future debates on whatever matter he was responsible for. Each officer had different responsibilities: if it was a matter of food supply to the city of Rome, the Senate would turn to an aedile; if it was a matter of making war, it would turn to a consul.

Rome was governed, then, by an elite, with a relatively small number of families repeatedly holding a proportionately large number of senior offices. They even kept all the most important priesthoods to themselves, to prevent the emergence of a powerful priestly estate. They fought together, dined together, shared cultural interests, intermarried, adopted one another's sons, and loaned one another money. They were almost obsessively concerned with maintaining the status of their ancestors, revealing an assumption that there would be a continuity of status over the generations. Nevertheless, it was a permeable elite: "new men" (*novi homines*), or men whose families had not produced a high officeholder for some generations, could rise to the very top, and old families could fall by the wayside, if in any generation they did not produce male offspring, or at any rate suitable or willing male offspring, or could not afford to take part in the competition for office. But there was an inner core of about 40 percent of the senators of consular rank whose fathers and grandfathers had also been consuls, the highest political and military office.[18] They were consulted first in all debates, and they formed a self-perpetuating oligarchy, in the sense that their prominence and wealth gave them opportunities to influence voters that were denied to others.

THE SWORD OR THE SHADOWS

There were no hereditary ranks in the Roman aristocracy, no "dukes" to rank per se above "earls": position in the hierarchy depended on prestige, and that was a precarious commodity. There were very few top jobs per year, and a man could not bet that his position would be extended past that year. After an interval of ten years (or so: such matters were more fluid in the middle Republic than later), he could stand again for the same office he had held before, or aim higher; but, as far as he knew, he had just that one year to shine. Competition was understandably intense.

The best way for a man to add glory to his own and his family's name was on the battlefield. In fact, in Rome most civic posts were simultaneously military positions. A consul, for instance, whatever civic duties he may have had, was first and foremost the general of an army, which was assigned to him, along with his "province" (theater of operations), immediately after his election.[19] The preeminence of military service was enshrined in the regulation (which was hardly ever broken) that a young man could not even embark on the lowest rungs of a political career until he had served for ten seasons in the field. An adult male could expect to enter the army at the age of seventeen, and spend a sixth of his life under arms; he was, first and foremost, a soldier. He had been brought up with tales of noble Roman warriors of the past; by the time he was thirty or so, his indoctrination into military values was complete.

During his initial ten years in the army, a promising young aristocrat would most likely have risen to become a military tribune. There were only six of these in each legion, so it was a middle rank of some importance, and he would begin to learn the delicate art of command. Then, later in his career, with his foot now on the ladder, he might become a quaestor, an aedile, a praetor, or even a consul. If he had the talent for command, he had plenty of chances to develop it; if he did not, his peers had plenty of time to notice it before he became too senior. The Senate contained, then, a pool of experienced militarists, and this was reflected in the fact that provinces were assigned by lot: it could be assumed that even the random method would throw up in sufficient quantity generals who had at least the limited level of competence required for ancient battles.

The Senate was known for its warmongering—at any rate, Livy has a tribune of the people accuse the senators in 201 BCE of constantly stirring up fresh wars as a way of keeping the ordinary people occupied and in their place[20] —and it is easy to see why: it was driven not just by its desire as a body to extend Rome's power and influence (and hence its own *auctoritas*), but also by the desire of its members for fields of glory. Of course, very few could hope to gain the very top jobs, but even so the general impetus of the Senate was warlike. Public service was a kind of sacred trust for these elite families, so at the same time as increasing his personal glory, a successful young man was serving his family, the state, and the gods—a heady mix.

The first two Punic wars raised the bar in a number of respects. Most importantly, individual commanders showed future generations what was possible in the way of personal glory, and the spoils of past Italian wars paled beside the riches of Carthage and the Greek cities of Sicily and southern Italy. Military success had always led to enrichment, but not on this scale. As until recently in European history, systematic plundering was part of every military campaign. Soldiers were poorly paid, and were expected not only to supplement their stipends with booty, but also to forage in the field if the season was right. Allied troops were treated no differently from citizen soldiers; even Rome's allies learnt to see fighting for Rome as a way of improving their lot. At the outset of the Third Macedonian War in 171, volunteers rushed to join up because they had seen how their neighbors' lives had improved as a result of earlier wars in the east.[21]

A share of the booty belonged, naturally, to the general, but he also had greater responsibilities—and other sources of profit. The state had bankrolled the war, and so had wealthy Romans, and they needed to be repaid. It was the general's responsibility to decide how much of the booty to extract for state purposes—how much he could reserve before angering his men, should they think he had left them too little. But in addition to his generous share of the booty, a Roman general also got rich from what went on before and after battle. Communities that were affected or likely to be affected would approach him to see if they could steer the action away from their land, or reduce the quantity of grain they were supposed to provide; in the time-honored Greek way, they would pay him either to settle their affairs or to stay out of them altogether. Antiochus III of Syria paid Lucius Cornelius Scipio Asiagenes 18,000,000 *denarii* for the maintenance of the Roman army in Asia Minor after his defeat in 190, and some of it certainly ended up in Scipio's own pockets.[22] There were always ways for a general to make money, by fair means or foul.

Later, we find senators using their own or their colleagues' conquests to advance their commercial interests, but that is hardly relevant to the first period of expansion covered in this book: such interests had not yet taken root to a significant degree.[23] But a benign cycle was beginning to form—benign for the military aristocracy, that is: the riches they brought back from their wars enabled them to buy up increasingly large estates (incorporating land left vacant by the death or impoverishment of farmers on military service, or their removal to towns and cities), which then needed huge numbers of slaves, which further wars would supply; more slaves enabled greater productivity and profits. Agricultural profits were not as great as those to be gained by warfare, or even commerce, but they were steady and reliable.[24] Besides, commerce was felt to be a less dignified occupation than farming.[25]

There was a very obvious and very direct connection: military success gave a general the resources he needed to fuel his ongoing quest for glory, retire forever, or at least recoup the considerable expenses he had already laid out in canvassing for election and fulfilling the obligations of office, for which he was not paid by the state. The quickest and surest way to get ahead was warfare; the sword was a man's best route out of the shadows. A successful general might even crown his career with a triumph, the most visible form of glory. And the state benefited too; even if not every war covered its immediate costs, conquered foes were often heavily indemnified, and war was, in general, an enormous source of revenue for the state. It has been estimated that between 200 and 167, the state gained, from indemnities and official booty, 250,000,000 *denarii* (perhaps $25 billion).[26] If everyone profited, everyone was inclined to go to war more readily than they would otherwise have been, and those who made policy were those who profited most. Rome was a militarized and warmongering society, and the Senate led the way.

MEDITERRANEAN ANARCHY

Republican Rome was a warrior society, then, from the aristocracy downwards (except that the very poorest citizens were not allowed, yet, to serve

18

in the army). Every year between 10 and 15 percent of the adult male population was under arms, and in times of crisis more: an incredible 29 percent at the height of the Hannibalic War in 213.[27] And everyone benefited, not just from the booty and spoils, but from the intangible benefits of security and the city's increasingly formidable reputation. Over time Rome became adorned with visible reminders of military victories: temples built in fulfillment of a vow taken in wartime; elaborate statues of conquerors, inscribed with blunt reminders of their victories. "I killed or captured 80,000 Sardinians," boasted one general on a prominently displayed inscription,[28] and this was not untypical. Most monumental inscriptions dating from the middle Republic—and by the end of the second century the city was crowded with them—focused largely or wholly on military achievements. The qualities the Romans most admired in a man were best developed and displayed in warfare.

In short, a state of war was not only considered "business as usual" in Rome by the entire population, but was not considered undesirable, especially by Rome's aristocratic leaders. It is far harder to recover the motives of the ordinary soldier, but several of Plautus's plays (third/second centuries) suggest that the attraction of warfare for them too was profit.[29] It was bound, then, to be relatively easy for the Romans to go to war; and it was equally easy to present the wars as justified self-defense or protection of weaker neighbors. Slight pretexts could be taken as serious provocation. This is not to say that Rome was the aggressor in every war it fought, but the facts remain: Rome was almost continuously at war in the early and middle Republic (500–150 BCE, in round numbers), every opportunity for war that the Senate offered was accepted by the people of Rome, and the benefits were recognized by all. The report the Coruncanii, or the survivors of their mission, brought back to Rome fell on receptive ears. There can be little doubt that there were voices in the Senate pushing for eastern expansion too.

But Rome was not the only militant community in the Mediterranean. We have only to think of Agron's and Teuta's desire to forge Illyris into a Mediterranean power. The ethos of the Hellenistic kings was always one of aggressive expansion.[30] Royal status was gained by war and maintained by war, and all Hellenistic kings presented themselves, just as much as individual senators, as men of war. In a never-ending bloody cycle, military success brought wealth (from plunder and indemnities) and increased territory, which enabled a king to create more revenue, to pay for more troops, and hence to gain further military successes. The Greek leagues and cities were scarcely less belligerent, just on a smaller scale: they were constantly trying to filch territory from neighbors, and the Aetolian and Achaean leagues disputed for decades the position of leader of central and southern Greece. The annually elected leaders of both these leagues, and of many others, were called "generals"; as with Roman consuls, war was their first and chief priority.

Warfare was accepted as a regular and normal event all over the Mediterranean. Aggression was loudly denounced in one's enemies and widely practiced by oneself. Roman culture was more militarized than any other, but it was only a matter of degree. Add to this mixture a distinct lack of international law and the general conviction of expansionist states that "might is right," and clashes become more or less inevitable. In theory, it is always possible to avoid warfare by negotiation, but in the ancient world it is undeniable that, while diplomacy was often effective for small-scale disputes, it usually did no more than delay major wars. In any case, as we shall see, Roman belligerence often precluded successful negotiation, and Roman arrogance often made Romans reluctant to accept the mediation of third parties. Belligerence and arrogance: the Romans were natural imperialists.

2.

THE ILLYRIAN WARS

T HE ROMANS' FIRST EXPEDITIONS to the Balkan peninsula were extremely brief. Two wars were fought, but neither of them lasted for more than a few weeks. And in both cases, after they had done what they came to do, the Romans immediately withdrew their forces. But they did not, of course, leave things unchanged, and the extent and significance of those changes will demand our attention. Even though the Romans' goals in these wars were limited, these were their first overseas expeditions eastward, and the changes they introduced inevitably altered the previous status quo. By their very presence, however brief, the powerful newcomers impinged on others' interests and set up an edgy dynamic for future relations with political entities in Greece.

THE FIRST ILLYRIAN WAR

It is not always easy to guess why the Romans acted as they did, but the reason they went to war in 229 genuinely seems to lie on the surface. The killing of their ambassador was an extra spur, but their primary reasons were economic. Why else help the Issaeans, with whom the Romans had no relationship? They may have been touched by their appeal, the first from a Greek state,[1] but they acted pragmatically, not out of sentiment. Nor was it just that Italian traders had been killed; the future threat was just as potent. The Romans did not want a powerful neighbor; they wanted the Adriatic for themselves.

They came late in the season of 229, but in large numbers. Both consular armies assembled at Brundisium and crossed the Adriatic, 22,000 men transported in 200 ships. Nothing should be read into this massive force beyond the fact that the Romans had a large stretch of territory to conquer, and they had no way of knowing how strong the resistance would be. The Illyrians had been performing well in battle recently.

The consuls for 229 were Gnaeus Fulvius Centumalus and Lucius Postumius Albinus. While Fulvius led his men against Corcyra, Postumius made Apollonia the Roman base camp. Demetrius of Pharos, Teuta's general in Corcyra, surrendered to Fulvius even as he approached, and was taken on as an adviser by the Romans for the remainder of the war. Presumably Pharos island went over with him, as well as Corcyra. With Corcyra, the Romans cut the Illyrians to the north off from their Acarnanian allies to the south, whose naval abilities had already been proved off Paxoi earlier in the year.

But it is unlikely that the Acarnanians could have made any difference. The Romans swiftly relieved the sieges of both Epidamnus and then Issa, and that was the end of the war. The Romans had easily defeated the Illyrians, who had terrorized the coastline of western Greece. Teuta, Pinnes, the royal court, and the royal treasury retreated to Rhizon, on the Bay of Kotor (in Montenegro, nowadays), a fjord with both an inner and an outer bay, each with a narrow entrance. The place was virtually impossible to assault by sea, and even more impossible by land, since the fjord ends abruptly in sheer mountains. Teuta chose her refuge well, but the Romans were content: it would be easy to keep an eye on her there. Perhaps the fact that she was confined in one of the most stunning locations in Europe was some consolation.

A number of communities in the area, whether or not they had surrendered to Rome (as Corcyra had), chose to "entrust themselves to Roman good faith."[2] To do this was not to make oneself entirely dependent on Rome, but it was an acknowledgment of inferior status: the people were trusting first the Roman commander in the field, and then Rome itself once the relationship had been officially ratified, to determine their fate and look after their interests. And each time a state accepted Roman protection, the Romans declared it free—that is, free to regulate itself without outside interference. There was no doubt a register in Rome of all the states which agreed to this arrangement, but otherwise it was an informal relationship, and Rome simply thought of them all as its *amici*, "friends."

Fulvius returned to Italy with most of the troops, while Postumius wintered in Epidamnus to make sure the situation was secure, and to conclude negotiations with Teuta. The negotiations resulted in a formal agreement whereby Pinnes would pay whatever indemnity the Romans saw fit to impose, renounce his claim to the places that had entrusted themselves to Roman protection, and remain in his reduced kingdom, without sailing south of Lissus with more than two ships, and even then they had to be unarmed. Lissus was chosen because it was the northern neighbor of Epidamnus, and so lay on the edge of the large chunk of Illyris that had accepted the protection of Rome.

Then, leaving Demetrius of Pharos, who on his surrender had become a "friend of Rome," in overall charge of the new Illyrian dispensation, Postumius sailed back to Italy with all his forces. The Romans were pleased enough to award both consuls triumphs. It was the start of a series of dazzling triumphs awarded for eastern victories.

ROMAN INTENTIONS

As wars go, this was very slight. Nevertheless, its outcome was important in that by 228 the Romans had established a zone of influence in Illyris, or rather, since it is not clear that all the lands involved were contiguous, a number of zones of influence. The most important elements were the Greek cities of Epidamnus, Apollonia, and Oricum; the islands (Corcyra, Pharos, Issa); and two tribes, the Parthini (in the Genusus valley) and the Atintani (around Antigonea and Byllis). Large parts of Illyris were now free to govern themselves in their own ways, as they had before, but now under the oversight of Demetrius of Pharos and the promise of protection by Rome.[3]

The nature of the zone of influence (to continue with the singular for convenience) is significant; a glance at a relief map shows why. Epidamnus, Apollonia, and Oricum were not just fine harbors,[4] but controlled about 90 percent of the Illyrian lowlands—all the best land for cereals and pasture. It is hardly surprising, then, that neighboring tribes also recognized their dependency on Rome: as largely mountain-dwelling transhumant pastoralists, they needed the fertile lowlands for their winter pasturage. Then the rest of the zone consisted of the wealthiest Greek islands of the Adriatic. The Romans effectively gave control of southern Illyris to the Greeks who lived there, and removed it from the Illyrians themselves; hence, again, Lissus was the cut-off point, because it was a specifically Illyrian town, not a Greek colony. The purpose was to allow southern Illyris to develop into a civilized, Greek confederacy of communities, initially under Demetrius of Pharos, perhaps in much the same way that Epirus had recently been modernized by Pyrrhus.[5]

This result was always part of the Roman plan: as soon as they came, they began to issue the invitation of friendship. They wanted to enter into a long-term relationship with the southern Illyrian states, but understanding their reasons for doing so is difficult and requires the rigorous elimination of hindsight. On the one hand, one might argue that nothing was going on apart from what appears on the surface: the Romans' intention was to quell the Illyrians. To think anything else is to use hindsight, because the Romans did eventually come as conquerors of Macedon, and control of the Illyrian ports was indeed critical for that enterprise. But for the time being they came as friends, making use of their superior strength and leaving their new friends the right to call on them if they needed to.

On the other hand, the friendship that the Romans offered the Illyrians was a familiar aspect of their relations with others. The conquest and subjugation of Italy had proceeded only partly by establishing formal treaties, but largely on the basis of similar kinds of informal relationship.[6] Southern Illyris was basically an extension of the same system that was in force in Italy, and that system was a means of subordination. That is what the Romans intended in southern Illyris as well—not out of sinister motives, but just because that was the way they acted. That was the only kind of relationship with lesser states that they felt was possible. Illyris at a stroke became a place where the Romans were interested in establishing and maintaining dominance.

For Polybius (as a Greek), the Romans' first military contact with the Greek world was highly significant. He was right: it would indeed lead to catastrophic changes for Greece. But they were a long way off. Annexation was not yet on the Romans' minds. They withdrew this time, and they would do so again. But each time they left a greater degree of dependency behind them. They were a small state rapidly learning to think big, learning to adjust their view of themselves to the vastly increased horizons the First Punic War had afforded them. Only when they had regained their focus—in the first flush of appreciation of the benefits of empire—would they be ready to expand their horizons again. In the meantime, they had established in Illyris a sphere of influence.

A SNUB TO MACEDON

What of Macedon? The question is not generated merely by the hindsight knowledge that Macedon would become Rome's main enemy in Greece. There is a genuine puzzle here, in that the Romans did not send an embassy to Macedon to announce and explain their actions, while they did to the Aetolians and Achaeans (naturally, since before the Romans they had been the champions of those threatened by the Illyrians), and then to Corinth and Athens. Perhaps this was only a tactless breach of diplomacy, but it looks like an insult; at any rate, it would likely have been understood as such. Macedon was weak at the time, and the Romans had undertaken a task which might very well have fallen to the Macedonians themselves if they had had the strength; for over a hundred years, since the time of Philip II, they had held hegemony in Greece. The Romans had, in a sense, drawn attention to Macedon's weakness and tarnished its standing among the Greek states. They should have made diplomatic contact.

There seems no good reason for the Romans to have explained themselves to the Corinthians and Athenians (who were not involved at all and were presumably chosen because of their illustrious pasts, as "representative Greek cities"), and not to have sent a delegation to Pella, the main city of Macedon, even if the situation there was uncertain following the death of Demetrius II earlier in 229. Certainly, they wanted to present themselves as the benefactors of the Greeks—as having rid Greece of the Illyrian menace—but they could have presented themselves this way in Pella as well. The Macedonians might on the whole have been pleased by what the Romans had done, since curbing piracy was good for them too. Perhaps the Romans ignored the Macedonians because the Macedonians were currently friends with the Illyrians, or with some of them.

But the Macedonians were certainly interested in what was going on, even if they were preoccupied at the time by warfare with the Dardanians. It was not just that they had long earned the right to think of themselves as the power-brokers of Greece, but there had also been, since prehistoric times, many links, friendly and hostile, between them and the west coast. In times of peace, Macedonian trade passed through the western ports, as did everyone else's. The west coast was well within the sphere of Macedonian interests, even if they had never exercised control there, and the Romans must have known it. They should have made contact, and their failure to do so was bound to set up an uneasy dynamic for the future.

WARFARE IN GREECE

The Roman evacuation took place early in 228; they did not return until the summer of 219. In the intervening period, significant changes took place on the Balkan peninsula. The 20-year alliance between the Aetolians and Achaeans broke down. Macedon, under Antigonus Doson, at first supported the Aetolians but soon changed over to the Achaeans. It was Achaean policy to incorporate every community of the Peloponnese into their league, and this brought them into conflict with Cleomenes of Sparta and his Aetolian allies. The Achaeans became so hard pressed in the war that they turned to Macedon for help, for which the cost was the cession of the superb fortress of Acrocorinth.

Antigonus Doson reneged on his pact with the Aetolians. He already had alliances with the Epirotes and Acarnanians, dating from 228; the detachment of these confederacies from Illyris by the Romans had compelled them, in their weakness, to look elsewhere for a protector. Now Doson formed all the rest of the Greek leagues into a Common Alliance, under the leadership of himself and his heirs forever.[7] The immediate pretext was the Cleomenean War (229–222), but it was clearly intended to outlast that affair; the common enemy of all the members of the alliance was Aetolia, not Sparta. Once Cleomenes had been defeated at the Battle of Sellasia, Macedon was once again firmly the power-broker of Greece.

But tuberculosis-ridden Doson died in 221. He bequeathed 16-year-old Philip V hegemony of Greece by means of the Common Alliance, and the enmity of the Aetolians. Was the new king a callow youth, vulnerable to exploitation from within and without? If anyone thought that, he soon proved them wrong by purging his court and beating back successive Dardanian and Illyrian raids over the next few years. And then, as we shall see, he became the chief obstacle to the Roman takeover of Greece, a fiery Macedonian patriot who was determined to guide Macedon once more to greatness.

Philip marched south late in 220. Greece was once again riven by war, only two years after the defeat of Cleomenes. In the Peloponnese, Aratus of Achaea had been encouraging Messene and Elis, who with Sparta were effectively the only holdouts, to join the Achaean League. Aetolia intervened in Messene, and the Common Alliance, provoked also by Aetolian raids the previous year, voted for war at a summer meeting in Corinth. The war to curb the Aetolians, which lasted from 220 until 217, is known as the Social War, or "war fought by the allies" (Latin *socii*).

The course of the war need not concern us.[8] Messene did indeed join the Achaean League, but the war was fairly inconclusive because Philip brought it to an abrupt end. The action took place not just in the Peloponnese, but on the west coast further north. Philip ravaged Aetolia (and stuck to the task even though the Aetolians were doing the same to his territory) and improved the position of his Acarnanian and Epirote allies, in particular recovering Oeniadae for the Acarnanians, where he paid for improvements to the harbor town's facilities and fortifications (see Fig. 2.1). At the same time, by taking the fortress town of Ambracus for the Epirotes, he secured one of the important routes from Macedon to the west coast. The Aetolians still retained Epirote Ambracia, but it was of less use to them now.

FIGURE 2.1

The remains of the shipsheds at Oeniadae, part of the facilities that made the town an important prize. The ramps are visible for only about half of their length, sloping down into what is now bog. Some of Philip V's fortifications can be seen on top of the rock from which the rear of the sheds was carved.

REBEL DEMETRIUS

By the end of the Social War, then, Philip had increased the loyalty of his allies on the west coast, facing Italy, and made it easier for a Macedonian army to travel there. He also took the island of Zacynthos, though he failed with Cephallenia. He was already on good terms with Demetrius of Pharos, who had fought by his side at Sellasia, though possibly as a mercenary general. It seems to have been important for Philip to make the west coast secure. But his plans were interrupted by a typically Illyrian hiccup, when Demetrius and Scerdilaidas resumed piratical activities.

Demetrius's actions in the 220s are hard to fathom. First, in about 228, he married Triteuta and thereby became the guardian of the young king Pinnes, Triteuta's son.[9] But the Romans had specifically divided Illyris, confining Pinnes to the mountainous north, and putting Demetrius in charge of the fertile south. Did Demetrius, then, become de facto king of a reunited Illyris? Apparently not, for, next, "he began pillaging and destroying the Illyrian communities that were subject to Rome."[10] So Demetrius must have completely disassociated himself from his Roman overlords, and moved north, abandoning the mainland part of the Roman zone of influence, but presumably retaining some or all of the islands. Then, from his bases in north Illyris, he began raiding the southern Illyrian communities. This was a direct attack on Rome, and our sources guess that he was taking advantage of the fact that the Romans were pre-occupied by war with the Celts in northern Italy;[11] it took them four years, 226–222, to crush the threat.

Perhaps Demetrius was just hugely ambitious; the rewards of friend-ship with Rome were great, but he thought he could do better, and so responded positively to an appeal from Pinnes' court at Rhizon. After Teuta's death, the northern Illyrians were faced with an unacceptable queen in Triteuta, and with increasing poverty. They had few sources of income, especially in bad years, and needed to resume piracy.[12] Perhaps they appealed to Demetrius on these terms: lead us again to greatness, as Agron did; you are no Roman puppet. In the final analysis, Polybius's assessment of him is probably sound: "He was a man of courage and dar-ing, but completely lacked the ability to think clearly or to make reason-able assessments of situations."[13] Certainly, he underestimated the Roman reaction to his defection.

In the summer of 220, accompanied by some of their Istrian neighbors, Demetrius and Scerdilaidas took a fleet of ninety *lemboi* (light galleys) south and joined the Aetolians for a raid on Pylos, a Messenian town that was now a member of the Achaean League. The attack failed, and Demetrius sailed on for some piracy among the islands of the Aegean (piracy on a grand scale, as befitted a king), while Scerdilaidas headed back home. On the way, however, he was persuaded to join an Aetolian expedition to the Peloponnese, in return for a share of the booty.

Scerdilaidas did not long remain an enemy of Macedon. He joined the Aetolians for their raid, but, feeling that they had cheated him out of his share of the spoils, he transferred his allegiance to Macedon when Philip offered him an annual retainer generous enough for him to main-tain a small fleet for use on the west coast against the Aetolians (and no doubt to keep himself in style as well). But this arrangement was also short-lived: in 217, claiming that Philip had not kept his promises, Scerdilaidas resumed independent activity as a brigand and buccaneer for a few months, against Philip chiefly, before seeking the protection of Rome in 216.

The Macedonians hired Demetrius as well, paying him to join Scerdilaidas in harassing the Aetolians on the west coast. With the knowledge that he had the backing of Macedon, Demetrius returned to southern Illyris, detached the Atintani from Rome and persuaded the Parthinian fortress town of Dimale to join him—a very useful addition, since the town was virtually impregnable and guarded the future Via Egnatia east of Apollonia. A man who had just occupied the past few years demonstrating his hostility to Rome was accepted as a friend by Macedon.

ROME REACTS

Demetrius began raiding Rome's southern Illyrian friends perhaps in the late 220s. For some years Rome did nothing, but kept watch. They were, as already mentioned, preoccupied with fighting the Celts in the Po plain. In 221 both consuls were sent against Istrian pirates at the head of the Adriatic; in 220 there were further campaigns against the Celts in the Alps. But in the summer of 219 both consuls, Lucius Aemilius Paullus and Marcus Livius Salinator, were sent to Illyris.

The timing is significant. The Romans knew that trouble was brewing in Spain—the trouble that would lead to the Second Punic War—and in fact Hannibal was poised to march on the Spanish city of Saguntum, a Roman ally,[14] even as the consuls were preparing to campaign in Illyris. The Romans must have had a very good reason to commit both armies to this campaign. No reason could have been more compelling than the imminent resumption of war with Carthage. They knew from their previous encounter with the Carthaginians that they could not afford to tie troops up elsewhere. That is why both armies went to Illyris again; overwhelming force was needed to get the job done quickly.

Clearly, by 219 they had decided that Demetrius now posed the same threat to the security of the Adriatic as Teuta had in 229; from this perspective, going to war against Demetrius was part of the campaign they had fought two years earlier against the Istrians and had the same motives as in 229: fear of strong neighbors and protection of commercial interests in the Adriatic. Clearly, however, there was also a more particular point to this second war: they wanted to punish Demetrius for having accepted Roman friendship and then failing to behave like a friend. That is why Demetrius was severely punished—his home town razed, personal exile, and family and friends interned in Italy—while Scerdilaidas was soon accepted within the Roman fold.[15]

What of Macedon? The Romans might have ignored it at the end of the First Illyrian War, but in the intervening years Macedon had regained influence in Greece, and the Romans must have known that any action they took, even in Illyris, would have wider implications. Moreover, at exactly the same time that the Romans were campaigning in Illyris, Philip was campaigning further down the west coast, in southern Epirus. The Romans knew that Demetrius of Pharos, if not an ally exactly, was on good enough terms with the Macedonians to be hired by them. They could now see that Philip was intending to improve his own and his allies' positions on the west coast, as indeed he did, by the end of the Social War. If they lost Illyris, almost all the western Greek coastline would be in potentially hostile hands. That is why Demetrius's challenge demanded a response. It was not just a matter of curbing piracy this time. Macedon was now on the Romans' horizon.[16]

To deny that the Romans were thinking of Macedon in the slightest is to attribute great short-sightedness to them. They knew of Macedon's formidable reputation; they could see that, under Doson and now Philip V, Macedon was well on the road to full recovery of its hegemony in Greece. Philip could call on almost all the leagues of Greece for military support under the terms of their Common Alliance, and by the end of the Social War he was the "darling of Greece."[17] If checking Demetrius hampered Philip at the same time, that was all to the good. But for the moment the Romans needed to do no more than that because Philip had become entangled with the Social War.

THE SECOND ILLYRIAN WAR

The Second Illyrian War was very brief—as brief as the Romans wanted, given the Carthaginian threat. Demetrius prepared for their coming by placing a garrison in impregnable Dimale, and another force, 6,000 strong, in his home town of Pharos. He had clearly been intriguing politically in the communities of southern Illyris, because at the same time he replaced as many pro-Roman administrations there as he could with his own friends. But it was all futile. Dimale fell after being besieged for only seven days, presumably terrified just by the sheer numbers of their enemies, and the rest of the pro-Demetrius towns and communities in southern Illyris immediately capitulated: they probably had minimal garrisons, if any.

The Romans moved on to Pharos island. The town (modern Stari Grad) was going to be a difficult nut to crack; it was well fortified, strongly garrisoned, and its long, narrow harbor made it difficult to approach (see Fig. 2.2). They sent a squadron of twenty ships forward as if to attempt a landing near the entrance to the harbor, and Demetrius sallied out from behind his fortifications to prevent it. But, the night before, the Romans had hidden the bulk of their army in some woods behind the town. As soon as Demetrius's forces had left the protection of their walls, these troops advanced and the Illyrians found themselves trapped outside their fortifications, with enemies to their front and rear.

Demetrius had some *lemboi* hidden in a cove and escaped, abandoning his family to imprisonment in Italy and his men to death at the hands of the Roman troops. It was all over; it had taken no more than a few weeks. Demetrius found his way to Philip's fleet at Actium and was made welcome. He joined Philip's court and, in rivalry with Aratus, became one of his closest advisers. He died in 214, still fighting for Philip.

If the war was followed by any kind of settlement, we do not hear about it. Pinnes was probably required to pay a further indemnity; at any rate, we hear of a Roman mission in 217[18] to remind the young Illyrian king (or whoever was now his guardian) that he was late in paying a tranche of his indemnity, but this may refer to the original indemnity of 229. The Romans added Dimale to their zone of influence in southern Illyris. With

FIGURE 2.2

Pharos town (modern Stari Grad, "Old Town," Hvar Island), the scene of Demetrius's last stand, showing the narrow approach to the harbor which foiled a direct assault.

Roman support, Scerdilaidas was now the de facto ruler of northern Illyris, and his rule marks a change of dynasty, from the Ardiaei to the Labeatae.

Again, despite the relative ease of the campaign, both consuls were awarded triumphs on their return. Again, the Romans withdrew all their troops, leaving no military presence in Illyris and displaying little further interest in Greek affairs for some years. They withdrew their troops partly to avoid the expense of maintaining an army abroad, and partly because they would soon be needed elsewhere—Italy, as it turned out, when Hannibal marched from Spain and invaded in 218. In any case, the Romans had achieved what they intended to do: remove Demetrius and improve conditions for traders in the Adriatic. But they had also demonstrated, to Philip above all, that they had the will to intervene in the east, just as they had in the west, to protect their and their friends' interests.

TRIUMPH

The best way, as we have seen, for a young Roman aristocrat to enhance his own and his family's standing in Rome, and to convince the voting public that he had the devotion to the Republic that made him a suitable leader, was by displaying prowess on the battlefield. A man who was successful at this, and who survived, would rise through the ranks and hope to become a praetor, or even a consul, and thereby gain command of an army for a year or perhaps longer, if his command was extended. Then, if he was successful at that too—if he killed enough of the enemy he had been assigned, took prisoners and plunder, and increased Rome's dominion—he might petition the Senate for a triumph.

Not all such petitions were granted, but the attempt had to be made, because nothing set the seal on a man's career like a triumph. It was one of the ultimate accolades from the Senate (though there was usually one about every eighteen months, in this period of the Republic),[19] but, more importantly, it was a unique opportunity for a man to lodge himself securely in the minds of his fellow citizens, and therefore served as a stepping-stone to further glory. This was also helped by the fact that the victorious general would give every single man in his army a bonus, commensurate with his status, which, if generous enough, would ensure his loyalty in the future. And there is no doubt that a triumph did help political careers: fifteen out of nineteen praetors who we know triumphed between 227 and 79 BCE went on to crown their careers with consulships.[20]

There was a sensible regulation in Rome that made it illegal for a general to enter the city with his army. A general seeking a triumph, then, brought his army, or however much of it he had not yet dismissed, up to the *pomerium* of Rome—the boundary beyond which he was not allowed to bring armed men. A special meeting of the Senate was convened outside the *pomerium*, usually in one of the sanctuaries on the Field of Mars, to consider whether he deserved a triumph. We hear of various rules supposedly governing a triumph—such as that the general had to have killed at least 5,000 of the enemy—but it seems that they were only guidelines because no rule was consistently applied. It had to be a significant victory, and even the Illyrian wars counted, because they significantly extended the power of Rome, even if otherwise victory had been easy.

And so the senators debated the case—and the debate could get heated, not just because of conflicting desires (the general's desire to triumph versus his political opponents' desire to stop him from triumphing) and the flexibility of the guidelines, but because the Senate did not want to find, some time in the future, that it had awarded this great distinction to an unsuitable man. Finally, if they decided to award a triumph, the petition was presented to the people of Rome for ratification, which always went through on the nod. The general was then permitted to cross the *pomerium* with as much of his army as was needed for the parade, and the preparations could begin.

A triumphing general was supposed to find a balance between boasting and humility. He did not want to lay himself open to charges of extravagance, but at the same time he had been offered a unique occasion for boastful display (see Fig. 2.3). Dressed in purple, as a king or even a god, he would ride in an ornate chariot, followed by his men carrying plunder in their arms or on stretchers, carts laden with spoils and exotic items, captured slaves and prisoners of war (preferably including high dignitaries such as kings or notorious chieftains), members of the Senate, paintings showing the towns and cities he had captured for the honor of Rome, and sacrificial animals. All these were concrete reminders of the growing power of Rome; the triumph was a jingoistic display of brutal militarism.

The rowdy entourage—especially noisy if the general had laid on musicians—processed through the city, the streets lined with cheering crowds tossing flowers, to the temple of Jupiter on the Capitoline Hill, where the general dedicated his purple robes and other accoutrements, and performed a magnificent thanksgiving sacrifice to the god. To offset the rush of pride that all this was bound to induce, a slave might ride in the chariot beside him, whispering in his ear: "Remember: you're only human."

This was an expensive procedure, but if the Senate decided to award a general a triumph, it would also cover the costs—knowing, of course, that the treasury would soon be more than compensated from the general's plunder. However, if the Senate refused to award and finance a triumph, there were two lesser possibilities: the Senate might award an *ovatio*, or

FIGURE 2.3

Triumph! This detail from a lost monument of Marcus Aurelius (second century CE) shows the emperor at the moment of entering Rome for a triumph on a gorgeous chariot, preceded by a trumpeter and with a winged Victory on his shoulder.

the general could pay for the triumph at his own expense. An *ovatio* was similar to a regular triumph, except that the general processed with considerably less splendor, on foot or horseback, and was crowned with myrtle rather than the victor's laurel. An *ovatio* was rather rare—for obvious reasons it was considered not to enhance one's dignity as much—and a general refused a triumph by the Senate might consider holding his own on the Alban mount (now Monte Cavo, about 25 kilometers southeast of the city), whose splendor was limited only by the general's personal financial situation and the willingness of crowds to make the journey out of Rome.[21] Not only did the Senate not disapprove of this, but, in terms of personal glory, such a triumph hardly counted as less distinguished; it was entered in the official registry alongside Senate-financed triumphs. It seems that the triumph—the display—was more important than who financed it.

MOUNTING TENSION

After the two Illyrian wars, there was no Roman army in Illyris, no permanent Roman presence further east than Italy. On the face of it, Roman interest so far had been tentative and defensive. There is no sign that at an official level an imperialist policy towards Greece had crystallized. And yet four consuls had triumphed for relatively insignificant wars, and enough booty had been brought back to arouse resentment: Livius Salinator was accused of retaining more than his fair share of the profits.[22] Recent history told the Romans a lamentable tale of disunity and inter-Greek warfare, and now that Rome had demonstrated even a slight degree of interest in the Balkan peninsula, Greek states began in gradually increasing numbers to appeal to Rome for arbitration and mediation, as well as to fellow Greeks. Given the competitive dynamics of the Senate, there were those who began to see that responding to these appeals could combine altruism with a quest for personal and familial glory.

By acting so decisively for the second time in Illyris, the Romans confirmed that they accepted overall responsibility for their Greek and Illyrian friends there. But it is almost inevitable that the intervention of a greater state in the affairs of a smaller will lead in due course to some degree of control being exercised by the greater over the smaller. The seeds had been sown for a higher degree of Roman involvement on the Greek mainland, and since the level of tension between Rome and Macedon had undoubtedly been raised by the Second Illyrian War, the seeds of Philip's determination to resist Rome had also been sown. Macedonian kings thought of themselves as protectors of Greece against barbarian incursions,[23] and the Roman invasion was just one more barbarian incursion. The Romans were barbarians to the Greeks in the literal sense that they were not Greek-speakers (to the Greeks all such speech sounded like *bar-bar-bar*, hence the word), and, as we shall see, their brutality allowed them to be portrayed as barbarians in the ethical sense too. But Philip's determination to resist would lead directly to Rome's permanent intervention in Greek affairs.

It is also likely, however, that Philip was beginning to formulate grander plans than mere resistance. I have already mentioned that he brought the Social War to an abrupt end in 217, before the allies had achieved even the limited goals they had set themselves.[24] This needs explanation, and Polybius makes it quite clear why, in his view, it happened: Philip had received news of the terrible Roman defeat by Hannibal at Lake Trasimene and had become tempted by the idea, proposed to him by Demetrius of Pharos, of subduing Illyris as a launch-point for an invasion of Italy.[25] Demetrius was in the first instance undoubtedly just trying to get Scerdilaidas booted out of Illyris and himself re-installed with Philip's help, but the idea took root in Philip's mind. And this is where our story properly begins, for the Naupactus conference which occupied us in the Prelude was the conference that brought the Social War to an end and encouraged Philip in his grand design.

Recently, the trend among historians has been to cast doubt on Polybius's idea. There is no way that Philip could have entertained such designs, they say: he had only just emerged from the Social War; he lacked the resources (especially an adequate fleet); thanks to Scerdilaidas, he lacked good access to the west coast. Polybius himself says that Philip kept his ambitious plans to himself, so how did anyone get to know about them?[26]

These are mostly good reasons, but they do not take account of Philip's character. Rather than being exhausted by the Social War, our evidence suggests that its ending freed him to think of himself as a player on a larger scale. He was young and energetic; he had already shown that he was willing to take military gambles; and he saw himself as a conqueror in the mold of Alexander the Great, whom he claimed, falsely, as an ancestor.[27] He was a dyed-in-the-wool Hellenistic monarch, and their ethos was militaristic, belligerent, and expansionist; his coin portraits show him as strong, intelligent, and determined (see Fig. 2.4). Like all Hellenistic kings, his economy depended crucially upon continuing warfare, which absorbed vast amounts of revenue and demanded a return. The king's status before his people depended on conquest. It would be foolish to deny that Philip was thinking big, or that Italy could have been what he was thinking about.

A contemporary poet, Alcaeus of Messene, wielding a nice ironic pen, had no doubt about the hubristic extent of Philip's ambitions:[28]

> Better build defensive walls, Zeus of Olympus!
> There's nothing Philip cannot scale.
> Close the bronze gates of the gods' abode,
> For earth and sea have been tamed by Philip's sceptre
> And all that is left him is the road to Olympus.

FIGURE 2.4

Philip V on a silver didrachm, Pella or Amphipolis mint, c. 180 BCE. Note the simple diadem on his head, the mark of Macedonian kingship since Alexander the Great. The club is the club of Heracles, from whom the Macedonian kings claimed descent.

I am not suggesting that Philip felt capable of invading Italy immediately, but all his actions over the next few years are consistent with the hypothesis that he was trying to gain sufficient control over the west coast, and Illyris in particular, to launch an invasion of Italy if the occasion arose, or to cooperate with a Carthaginian re-invasion of Italy. For the time being, however, the possibility of such a mighty confrontation was remote, and Philip's primary goal was to banish the foreign interloper. Given that he saw the Romans as probable future enemies, he was bound to see the Roman zone of influence not just as an affront, but as a possible future bridgehead for action against himself. By the end of the Second Illyrian War, Rome and Macedon were aware of each other as potential enemies and were circling around each other like fighting dogs, not yet engaging, not yet even probing, but eyeing each other's strengths and weaknesses.

3.

BARBARIANS, GO HOME!

B Y THE TIME OF the Naupactus conference in 217 and the end of the Social War in Greece, the Romans and Macedonians were aware that, given the right circumstances, they might come to blows. The next few years were marked by increasing tension, caused entirely by Philip. It is tempting to say that the withdrawal of the Roman forces after the Second Illyrian War might have duped him into thinking that Macedon could continue to act with impunity, as it had for decades, as though Greece were its playground and its interests were all that mattered. But Philip did not merely strengthen Macedon's position in Greece: on both the military and the diplomatic fronts he took steps that were plainly acts of aggression against Rome, above all by allying himself with Hannibal—a move to which the Romans were bound to respond.

As far as Philip was concerned, the Romans constituted a threat to Macedonian hegemony in Greece and would have to be dealt with. In the first instance, they would have to be driven out of Illyris. However much some recent historians downplay the importance of the Roman zone of influence in southern Illyris, Philip took it very seriously and was determined to put an end to it, first by installing Demetrius of Pharos there as his puppet or ally. In this war, Philip was the aggressor, in the sense that he was responding to a perceived threat. He was reclaiming Greek cities for the Greeks, driving out a foreign invader.

For a while, he got away with it: the Romans were too bound up with the Hannibalic War in Italy to react. In 214, however, they reached breaking point and the long process of humiliating Macedon began. But the First Macedonian War was scrappy and indecisive, largely because the

Romans were unable to commit themselves to it as fully as they wished. The will was there: they were not half-hearted, but overcommitted. And as a result of the First Macedonian War, the Romans found themselves far more involved in the Greek world, and with far more authority there, than they had at the beginning. Given the indecisive nature of the war, then, it was only a matter of time before trouble with Macedon was renewed.

THE SECOND PUNIC WAR

Hannibal's crossing of the Alps in 218 left his forces quite severely depleted. But his invasion of Italy had always been predicated on the cooperation of the Celts of the Po valley, where the brutal Roman campaigns of the late 220s had left a deep reservoir of resentment. In fact, Hannibal was hoping for help not just from the Celts: he suspected that the more he succeeded, the more Rome's disgruntled allies in Italy, especially the southern Greeks, would flock to his banner. His success, on foreign soil, depended largely on his winning such support.

The Hannibalic War was being fought in Italy at the same time that the Romans were engaged in Greece. Its course therefore has the greatest bearing on events further east. Hannibal first met the Romans in Celtic territory at the Trebia river, in December 218. His victory there secured him the loyalty of the Celts and the rich Po valley as a supply base. He then marched into Italy and, in June 217, led a Roman army into a trap at Lake Trasimene. Thirty thousand Roman soldiers died or were taken prisoner in the course of a few hours, and Hannibal proceeded down the east coast of Italy unopposed.

After these disasters, the Romans made Quintus Fabius Maximus responsible for the war, and he adopted the evasive tactic that famously earned him the epithet "Cunctator," the Delayer. He shadowed Hannibal, to make sure he did not break out and advance on Rome itself, but never gave battle. The fewer victories Hannibal gained, the less likely it was that Rome's allies would go over to him, and the more disgruntled Hannibal's Celts and North African mercenaries would become: all they wanted was a quick victory and opportunities for plunder.

In Rome, however, Fabius's opponents argued that he was simply being ineffective, and pushed for battle. When it came, at Cannae in August 216, it secured Hannibal's reputation forever as a brilliant general. About seventy thousand Roman soldiers lost their lives, almost the entire army.[1] Seventy thousand! The Romans were terrified, and resorted to human sacrifice—a very rare event indeed[2] —to ward off further disaster. Two Greeks and two Celts were buried alive. And then the Romans fought on.

Cannae taught the Romans how right Fabius had been, and from then on they fought a war of attrition. It was almost too late. Following Cannae more and more Sicilian and southern Italian Greeks came over to Hannibal's cause, including the great cities of Tarentum and Capua. Southern Italy was effectively lost to the Romans, while in the north the Celts were once again flexing their muscles; in 215 Hannibal formed an alliance with Philip V of Macedon, and in the following year with the new young ruler of Syracuse, Hieronymus. These were devastating blows for Rome.

Gradually, however, very gradually, the tide began to turn; it is hard for an invader to win a war of attrition. Syracuse was recovered in 211, after a long siege, by Marcus Claudius Marcellus, five times consul of the Roman Republic, and Hannibal's other international ally, Philip of Macedon, was preoccupied in Greece. Hannibal was on his own and losing ground. His allies in southern Italy consisted almost entirely of the Greek cities; he had not been able to win over the Latin colonies, the "ramparts of the empire," as Cicero was to call them.[3] And he consistently failed to penetrate the Roman lines and win his way through to central Italy, to threaten Rome itself.

In 211, after a long siege, the Romans also regained Capua, Hannibal's most northerly outpost and the principal city of fertile Campania. Capua, which had wanted little more than the recognition by Rome of its dignity, was virtually annihilated: its administrative apparatus was demolished and its fertile farmland became the property of Rome. The message to Rome's wavering allies was reinforced in 209, when Tarentum was recaptured by Fabius and sacked so terribly that it too never fully recovered.

In Spain, the other theater of the war, after near disaster in 211, the Romans took the unorthodox step of sending out Publius Cornelius

Scipio, only twenty-five years old and therefore surprisingly young for high office. It was an inspired choice: by 206 he had driven the Carthaginians out of Spain, putting an end to their overseas empire. Back in Rome he pushed for taking the war to Carthage itself in Africa rather than focusing on Hannibal in Italy, whom he saw as a spent force, now confined almost entirely to Croton. He got his way, and was proved right.

After a difficult beginning, in 203 he forced the Carthaginians to sue for peace. Hostilities were renewed when Hannibal returned home from Italy with his army, before the peace had been signed, but Hannibal and the final army the Carthaginians could field were defeated at Zama, southwest of Carthage, in 202. The terms imposed were naturally ferocious, with enough of an indemnity to swell Rome's depleted coffers and keep Carthage quiet for the foreseeable future. Publius Cornelius Scipio took the extra *agnomen* Africanus in honor of his great victory and was acclaimed in Rome almost as a god. He was the first in the long line of charismatic leaders who would eventually undermine the Republic, but he did not take undue advantage of the adulation he received or the loyalty of his troops. He was no Sulla, Caesar, or Octavian

A NEAR MISS

While Rome was engaged in the war with Carthage, Philip was actively pursuing a strategy to expand and strengthen the Macedonian sphere of influence, especially in the west. As soon as he had extricated himself from the Social War, he began, late in 217, with a brilliant campaign against Scerdilaidas in Dassaretis, where he quickly re-established command of the main road between Macedon and southern Illyris north of the Prespa Lakes, the road that would later become the Via Egnatia. In combination with his capture, earlier in the year, of Bylazora in Paeonia, he could worry less about his northwestern and western borders.

Earlier in the year, the Romans had at last made official contact with Philip—but only to ask him to surrender Demetrius of Pharos to them. This would have been a perfectly normal request if the Romans had ever been in touch before, but it was a somewhat presumptuous first contact.

Philip seems to have ignored it, and the request remained hanging, ratcheting up the tension between the two nations a notch or two. But it gave Philip an extra reason to be pleased at his successful recapture of Dassaretis: it was the perfect snub to Rome. So far from surrendering Demetrius, Philip was determined to install him in Illyris.

His campaigns the next year were a continuation of the same policy. In the spring of 216, he took a newly constructed fleet of 100 *lemboi* around Greece, but, just as they approached Apollonia, some Roman warships appeared on the horizon. Scerdilaidas had written to the authorities in Rome, warning them that Philip was planning a campaign against their friends in southern Illyris and asking for help. The Romans sent only ten warships, but Philip took it to be the vanguard of a large fleet and chose a prudent withdrawal back to Cephallenia.⁴ He was not ready for a confrontation with Rome, but the clash that many must have seen as inevitable was edging closer.

ENTER HANNIBAL

It edged a lot closer in 215. Philip was looming as a second Pyrrhus (as some in Rome saw it) on the Romans' eastern flank; at Cannae Hannibal had just inflicted one of the worst defeats ever on a Roman army. And now, with Rome at its most vulnerable, these two enemies entered into a treaty of cooperation. Throughout their history, the Romans had enjoyed the good fortune of never having faced more than one major enemy at the same time. This treaty was a shocking blow for them.

The first moves could have been scripted in Hollywood, and probably did receive some embellishment in the telling. Philip sent his agent, Xenophanes of Athens, to Hannibal in Italy. Xenophanes boldly bluffed his way through the Roman lines by pretending that his mission was to arrange a treaty between Philip and the Romans, and surreptitiously made his way to Hannibal's camp instead. They agreed to terms and Xenophanes left, but the ship on which he and Hannibal's representatives were sailing back to Greece was intercepted. Xenophanes tried the same bluff again, but the presence of the Carthaginians gave the game away.

TAKEN AT THE FLOOD

A search brought to light both a letter from Hannibal to Philip, and the text of the draft treaty which Philip was to return, ratified, to Hannibal.

The draft treaty was read out in the Roman Senate. To their horror, it was a general treaty of mutual cooperation for the future, which especially committed Philip (along with the Greek Common Alliance) to help Hannibal defeat the Romans in Italy. In return, Hannibal undertook to force the Romans, once he had defeated them, never to make war on Macedon, and to renounce their authority over their southern Illyrian friends, all of whom were specified.[5]

But the treaty had been intercepted before its formal ratification, so there was no reason to panic, and all the Romans did in the short term was reinforce the Adriatic fleet under the command of Publius Valerius Flaccus. Flaccus now had enough warships to prevent or hold up an invasion of Italy from the east and to leave the Romans free to concentrate on Hannibal in Italy; his instructions were to patrol the coastline off Illyris and "to gather intelligence on the likelihood of war with Macedon."[6] If the intelligence he received was sufficiently worrying, the praetor Marcus Valerius Laevinus was to proceed with the fleet to Illyris and contain Philip within the borders of Macedon. Philip's alliance with Hannibal made obvious strategic sense, but it would bring the might of the Romans down on him. It aroused their worst fears, and the ghost of Pyrrhus was especially poignant because Laevinus's grandfather had suffered defeat at his hands in 280, in the first battle Pyrrhus fought on Italian soil.

The initial reports were not enough to prompt Laevinus to action. There was no immediate threat because, as usual, Philip was preoccupied. We are reminded once again how constant minor warfare was on the Greek mainland. Macedonian military intervention was needed in the Peloponnese to help their Achaean allies, in both 215 and 214. Sparta had cooperated with the Aetolian League during the Social War, and it looked as though Messene was about to secede from the Achaean League. There was nothing to be done about Sparta for the time being, but Messene was bludgeoned into submission. It was during this campaign in 214 that Demetrius of Pharos died; he would not, after all, be the beneficiary of Philip's policy for southern Illyris.

THE SUPERPOWERS COLLIDE

With the Romans naturally focused on the more immediate threat of Hannibal, Philip went to work as soon as he had sufficiently settled Peloponnesian affairs. In the three years 214–212, he repeatedly and successfully attacked Roman friends in southern Illyris, until he had extended Macedonian sway for the first time in history to the west coast of Greece and reduced the number of communities with whom Rome had relations. He was bidding fair to achieve his aim of expunging the Roman presence, and it was only a question of when the Romans would be able to do something about it.

The campaign in 214 was undoubtedly coordinated with Hannibal; their treaty must in the meantime have been ratified, this time without anyone in Rome getting to hear about it. While Philip's land army marched through Epirus and up towards Illyris, his fleet sailed around Greece, so as to attack Apollonia by sea and land at once. The naval maneuver would have been out of the question had Rome's Adriatic fleet been free, but Hannibal tied it up with a simultaneous attack on Tarentum. Obtaining no quick result against the formidable fortifications of Apollonia, and in urgent need of a secure coastal base, Philip ordered his fleet down the coast to attack Oricum instead, which soon fell. He left a small garrison there, and returned to try again at Apollonia, but the inhabitants of Oricum had managed to get an urgent message off to Laevinus.

Philip was not expecting the Romans to come. They should have been reeling, not just because of Hannibal's attack on Tarentum, but because earlier in the year Hieronymus of Syracuse had broken with Rome and thrown in his lot with Hannibal, after Syracuse had been Rome's most important ally in the region for decades. But Laevinus, given command of the eastern war as propraetor, set sail with most of the fleet, made Corcyra his base, and easily recovered Oricum. The smoothness of the operation should not disguise the importance of the moment: this was the first clash between Roman and Macedonian troops, and though there had been no formal declaration of war, this was its beginning—the start of the Romans' first war against Macedon.

After securing Oricum, Laevinus sent his lieutenant up the coast to defend Apollonia. The Roman fleet managed to trap Philip's ships in the mouth of the river, and he was forced to burn his fleet, to prevent it from falling into enemy hands, and escape overland. Afterwards, the Romans spread the rumor that Philip had been taken by surprise and had fled ignominiously from his camp only half-dressed, but that was sheer propaganda: if he had time to order the destruction of his fleet, he had time to get dressed. The Romans had demonstrated that the Adriatic was theirs, Laevinus duly wintered with the fleet at Oricum, and the Senate extended his command and aggressively awarded him "Greece *and Macedon*" as his field of operations for the next year.[7]

Philip's underestimation of the Roman response cost him dearly. He lost his fleet, and was therefore confined to land operations until he could build another one; three thousand men had died in the fiasco at Apollonia; and the Romans now had a presence in Illyris, with the fleet at Oricum. But he more than made up for the losses of 214 in the following year. At the start of the season, he advanced by land to the edge of the Illyrian mountains, detached the Parthini and Atintani from Rome, and captured Dimale. From there, he at last achieved his goal of breaking through to the coast by capturing the Illyrian port town of Lissus (see Fig. 3.1).

The capture of Lissus was important not just for giving Philip, for the first time, a good harbor on the coast facing Italy, for use by himself and/ or the Carthaginians, and shipyards in which a fleet undoubtedly began to be built straight away. It was important also for the fertile farmland in the region. Now Philip would more easily be able to supply an army on the west coast. And immediately after the capture of Lissus the local tribesmen could not wait to surrender to him. Scerdilaidas was now confined to the northern lake shore, from Scodra (his chief city) up to Rhizon, and separated from his Roman friends in southern Illyris by a Macedonian wedge at Lissus. Philip's remorseless pressure on Illyris had finally paid off.

With Philip at Lissus and the Roman fleet at Oricum, a stalemate occurred, with no significant action for several months outside of Italy. The Romans were still fighting for their lives in Italy and Sicily, and the loss of Tarentum in 212 was a major blow, not just in itself, but in feeding Roman fears of an invasion: Tarentum would make an excellent port of

FIGURE 3.1
Lissus, one of the main strongholds of the Labeatae. Its occupation by Philip V from 213 to 197 was the realization of a long-held Macedonian dream, an overt threat to Roman interests in the region, and a possible threat even to Italy.

arrival from Lissus. If they could not negate the threat of Philip by themselves, they needed someone to do it for them. Laevinus turned to the Aetolians—not surprisingly, because they were the only Greek state with any military muscle that was not on good terms with Philip. In theory, they were bound to friendship with Macedon by the peace treaty that had ended the Social War in 217, but they could never be happy with a treaty that left them no room for expansion, or even raiding. They were very open to Laevinus's approach.

ALLIANCE WITH THE AETOLIANS

The Roman alliance with the Aetolian League—the first formal, written agreement between Rome and a Greek state—was probably concluded in the autumn of 211, after earlier approaches.[8] The division of labor was that the Romans would have authority over the war at sea, and the Aetolians over the war on land. Any town that was captured by the Romans alone would be handed over by them to the Aetolians, while the Romans kept the booty; any town that was captured in a joint operation would belong to the Aetolians, and the booty would be divided. But the limit of operations to the north was to be Corcyra: the Romans did not want Aetolian freebooters in the Adriatic any more than their Illyrian counterparts; so, essentially, the Aetolians were let loose on Acarnania, which had, after all, sided against Rome in the Illyrian wars. In an attempt to create a Greek alliance to rival Philip's Common Alliance, the Eleans and Spartans, and Pleuratus and Scerdilaidas of northern Illyris were invited to become partners; King Attalus of Pergamum (a small but wealthy kingdom carved out of former Seleucid territory in Asia Minor), a friend of the Aetolians, was also invited to join this new alliance, extending Roman friendship for the first time to Asia Minor.

Laevinus was offering generous terms to make sure of winning the Aetolians. The state would profit also, not just from the booty, but from not having to commit men who were needed in Italy to the occupation of any town or city in Greece. The Romans could continue to avoid serious embroilment in the affairs of Greece, while the majority of their resources were being put to more critical use elsewhere. The Aetolians would do their fighting for them.

The Aetolians must have had strong reasons to take on such a role. They saw the alliance in the first instance as a way to recover the losses they had suffered in the Social War—chiefly territories in Acarnania and their cherished forward post against Macedon, Phthiotic Thebes (see Fig. 3.2). But their long-term goals remained the defeat of Macedon and achieving hegemony in Greece; the alliance would help them on the way—as long as the Romans chose not to gain authority themselves in Greece on the back of the Aetolians' indebtedness to them.

Philip's first response to the news of the treaty was to raid Apollonia and Oricum, and he further secured his northern border against the Dardanians. But now, late in 211, the Aetolian army was massing at full strength on the borders of Acarnania. The Acarnanians, knowing that

FIGURE 3.2
Phthiotic Thebes. Little remains of this hillside town overlooking the Gulf of Pagasae, but its strategic importance made it a valuable prize, and it was for some years the forward outpost of the Aetolian League against Macedon.

they would not survive, came up with a desperate expedient. They sent their non-combatants to safety in Epirus, and took a solemn oath to fight to the death. At the same time, however, they sent an urgent message to Philip, and this caused him to break off his operations in the north and race south. Even the rumor of his approach caused the Aetolians to abort their invasion, but the Roman plan was working. Philip had been diverted from Illyris and was fighting to keep his alliance intact.

LURCHING TOWARD THE NEGOTIATING TABLE

Over the next couple of years, all those invited in the Roman–Aetolian treaty to join the anti-Macedonian alliance did indeed commit themselves. No doubt they had various reasons: the Spartans, for instance, were likely motivated more by their ongoing conflict with the Achaeans than by any particular love for the Romans or Aetolians. It was a natural move for the Illyrians, Scerdilaidas and his son Pleuratus, who seems to have been acting now as joint ruler.[9] The Messenians too, who had remained conflicted since Philip's savage reprisals there in 214, seceded from the Achaean League and joined the Aetolians. The Eleans were old friends of the Aetolians.

But why did Attalus of Pergamum join, adding a piquant international flavor to the coalition? He had a long friendship with the Aetolians, and enmity with his expansionist neighbor Prusias of Bithynia, who, with Philip's sister as his wife, was on good terms with Macedon. Constrained by an agreement with Antiochus of Syria, Attalus could not risk expansion in Asia Minor, and he may have been persuaded to join by the promise of some or all of Philip's Aegean possessions in the event of their capture. What the Aetolians most wanted from him—the reason that he was asked to join—was an Aegean fleet, forcing Philip to look east as well as west. Philip's weakness at sea was critical. He was busy making up the loss, but for the time being there was nothing he could do against Attalus in the Aegean, or the Romans and Scerdilaidas in the Ionian and Adriatic. And Laevinus's primary purpose was clearly to use his naval superiority to secure stretches of coastline for himself and his allies.

In fact, however, the Romans and Aetolians achieved little over the next few years: gains were invariably offset by losses. Laevinus almost retook the island of Zacynthos, but it survived and remained in Macedonian hands. He seized some places in Acarnania, but Philip had recovered most of them within a few years. Oeniadae, however, fell back for a while into Aetolian hands, and early in 210 Laevinus also managed to take Anticyra by naval siege. Anticyra was a strategically placed town on the north side of the Corinthian Gulf, with an excellent, sheltered harbor. Since it lay at the terminus of the land route south from Macedon, it was a useful port for Philip, and Laevinus made sure of it by plundering the town and selling its inhabitants into slavery, before handing it over to the Aetolians.

Meanwhile, even as Laevinus had Anticyra under siege, Philip marched down the east coast of Achaea Phthiotis, securing this land route as far as the Maliac Gulf. The Romans, now commanded by Publius Sulpicius Galba, who had just come out as proconsul to replace Laevinus, counterattacked to no avail.[10] Philip was now close to the vital pass at Thermopylae, by far the best land route south into central Greece (and hence the site of many battles over the centuries, not just the famous clash of 480 BCE between the invading Persians and the "three hundred" Spartans). But Thermopylae had for decades been garrisoned by the Aetolians.

Galba's expedition—the first appearance of a Roman fleet as far east as the Aegean—was not entirely wasted, for on the way back he took the island of Aegina from the Achaeans. After raising money by ransoming wealthy citizens, he handed the island over to the Aetolians, in accordance with their treaty, but they sold it to Attalus for 30 talents—a meagre sum of money for a whole island, and clearly intended as a kind of bribe to secure Attalus's services for 209.[11]

In the summer of 209, the Carthaginian fleet was driven from Tarentum by the city's impending fall. Presumably by arrangement with Philip, to make up his weakness at sea, they sailed into the Ionian Sea and challenged the Romans, who were based on Corcyra, to give battle. This was clearly intended to be a major effort, to decide control of the west coast of Greece. But the Romans refused to rise to the challenge, having learnt from the Cunctator that in war less may well be more. They stayed safe in their harbors, and the Carthaginians could do nothing except sail away in frustration. The next year they were equally useless, failing to link up with Philip because they were afraid of the Roman and Pergamene fleet. Perhaps, after all, the Romans had overestimated the danger of the treaty between Philip and Hannibal.

By land, in 209 Philip edged closer to Thermopylae, but he was open to the suggestion of a group of states that perhaps a peaceful solution could be negotiated. He arranged a truce with the Aetolians, and a meeting later in the year to talk terms and conditions. Then he marched on to relieve the Achaeans, who were hard pressed by the Spartans, and left them sufficient troops to turn the tide in the Peloponnese in their favor. Philopoemen, the most prominent man in the Achaean League since the death by poisoning of Aratus in 213 (perhaps by Philip),[12] was also in the process of overhauling the Achaean army, turning it (at last: the

Boeotians and the Spartans had made the change some decades earlier) into a formidable fighting machine along Macedonian lines.

The peace conference was a farce, thanks to Roman gunboat diplomacy. Galba ordered his fleet close to where the conference was being held, as if to threaten the proceedings; with their resolve thus stiffened, the Aetolians made demands that were especially outrageous because the premise of the negotiations was that they were in the weaker position (speaking for the Romans, they demanded that Philip cede Lissus and the Atintani); and just then Attalus's troops and fleet reached Aegina from Asia Minor—Attalus responding not just to the gift of Aegina, but also to his honorary election as joint commander of the Aetolian League for the year. It was clear that the Roman–Aetolian alliance was not serious about peace.

At the beginning of 208, then, everything was ready for a major offensive from the Roman coalition. While Scerdilaidas and Pleuratus made nuisances of themselves on Macedon's western borders, the Romans were to continue the campaign, begun with the capture of Anticyra, of attacking Philip's communication and supply lines. The main event was to be an assault on Euboea, which was of great importance to Philip. As long as the Aetolians held Thermopylae, Philip's best route south was to transport his army from Demetrias to Oreus, and march them across the bridge at Chalcis to the mainland.

The Romans achieved little on Euboea, however, thanks to a storming response by Philip. And, since Fortune favors the brave—unless Philip had been in touch with Prusias—at this point Attalus learnt that the Bithynians had invaded his territory. He returned home to meet the danger and took no further part in the war. This was a major blow to the Roman coalition. Philip spent the rest of 208 in a successful campaign against the Aetolians, in the course of which he recovered Anticyra and ravaged deep into the Aetolian heartland. All Galba managed to do was sack the Achaean town of Dyme and raise money by selling the inhabitants into slavery.

By the beginning of 207, the advantage clearly lay with Philip. Philopoemen seemed capable of keeping the Peloponnese fairly quiet—and, indeed, in its first test his reformed army thoroughly defeated the Spartans at Mantinea later in the year. In any case, Philip felt free to deal with the Aetolians—but, first, delegates arrived from neutral states to try once again to arrange a comprehensive peace.[13] Two meetings followed, but again Galba deliberately derailed them both. This was a significant moment: the Romans could have accepted Philip's terms, which were not unreasonable, and if their motives had been purely defensive, they would have done so. They may have started the war to distract Philip from Italy, but now they wanted the war to continue so that they could punish him. And that desire would outlive the unsatisfactory conclusion of the war.

Philip responded to the failure of the peace talks with another lightning strike into Aetolia, via Athamania: he paid for passage through Athamania by giving Amynander, the king, the island of Zacynthos. As a result, Philip achieved the considerable coup of recovering Ambracia for his Epirote allies. In fact, he did not hold the city for long—but long enough to force the Aetolians to think seriously about peace once more. Rome had promised them reinforcements, but the Aetolians could not realistically expect much in the way of help from that quarter. After all, not only was Hannibal still in southern Italy, but another Carthaginian army had just arrived in the north, under Hannibal's brother Hasdrubal. As it happened, Hasdrubal was soon defeated and killed in northeast Italy at the Battle of the Metaurus River, bringing the Carthaginians' Italian adventure effectively to a close; but the Aetolians could not foresee that.

TWO PEACE TREATIES

So the Aetolians were ready for peace; they were fed up with being stalking horses for the Romans. Philip seized the opportunity to break up the enemy coalition and humiliate the Aetolians with terms of his own choosing. Most importantly, he got to keep all the places in Achaea Phthiotis that he had taken from them in 210 and 209; it was a reduced Aetolia that emerged from the First Macedonian War.

The Aetolians ratified this peace at their 206 spring general meeting. Ironically, the Aetolian collapse was accompanied by a rise in Rome's fortunes, since they had forced the Carthaginians onto the defensive in both Spain and Italy. But when Galba's replacement, the proconsul Publius Sempronius Tuditanus, arrived in Epidamnus with fresh forces, he was faced with the fait accompli of Aetolian surrender. From now on, there was a distinct cooling in Roman–Aetolian relations: the Romans were furious that, contrary to the explicit terms of their 211 agreement, the Aetolians had made a separate peace with the enemy. They did not understand that, in the Greek world, alliances were routinely made or broken according to expediency.

But there was nothing Sempronius could do, and the Epirotes seized the opportunity to broker a peace conference. Both Philip and the Romans had reasons to feel that their resources might be put to better use elsewhere: Philip had the usual border troubles with Dardanians, and the Romans needed to finish off the Second Punic War. If the treaty Philip eventually ratified with Hannibal was the same as the intercepted draft, whose contents we know, he was not supposed to make a separate peace with Rome; but by now the treaty with Hannibal was a dead letter.

The terms of the peace treaty that was hammered out in Phoenice in 205 concerned only Illyris: Greece had been taken care of by the peace with the Aetolians. Philip returned Dimale and recognized Roman control over the Parthini, but he kept Lissus and, since the Atintani also remained attached to Macedon, he retained control of the most important land link between Illyris and Epirus. As long as his good relations with the Epirotes lasted, he could always move an army swiftly into southern Illyris. And the cession of Dimale was no great loss because he kept Dassaretis, and therefore Antipatrea (modern Berat, a UNESCO World Heritage Site for its Ottoman-period architecture), which lay only a little east of Dimale and had much the same strategic importance. Pleuratus—the old pirate Scerdilaidas had recently died—had to continue to accept a reduced kingdom based on Scodra and Rhizon (see Fig. 3.3).

The treaty shows that the protagonists already regarded the Greeks as falling into two camps, depending on their allegiance. Although the signatories were Philip and the Romans, in an appendix their respective associates were also considered to be co-signatories. The associates are listed:[14] on the Roman side were Ilium (that is, probably, the whole Troad League of northwest Asia Minor, allies of Attalus since 226),[15] Attalus, Pleuratus, Nabis of Sparta, the Eleans, the Messenians, and the Athenians; on Philip's side were Prusias of Bithynia and the Greek leagues: Achaean, Boeotian, Thessalian, Acarnanian, and Epirote. In other words, Rome was now

FIGURE 3.3

A rare contemporary coin of the Labeatae tribe of Illyris, to which Scerdilaidas, Pleuratus, and Genthius belonged. The crudely engraved ship is presumably a *lembos*, the type of galley that is particularly associated with Illyris.

asserting hegemony in Greece alongside Macedon, on the basis of the coalition they had put together with the Aetolians, and the number of Greek states that looked to Rome for protection had increased and widened in geographical extent.

Nevertheless, this was a humiliating peace for the Romans to sign: the balance of the gains was well on Philip's side, and they had failed to punish him. Not the least of Philip's gains was immaterial: in their very first intervention on Greek soil the Romans acquired a reputation for brutality that they were never able to shake off. When Laevinus took Anticyra, he sacked it and sold the inhabitants into slavery. When Galba took Aegina, he threatened enslavement of the entire population, but ended by ransoming only the wealthier citizens. When Galba and Attalus took Oreus on Euboea, the city was sacked. When Galba took Dyme, the town was plundered and the inhabitants sold into slavery. Zacynthos and other places were merely plundered. In general, the Romans were seen as barbarians.[16]

What was involved when the Romans sacked a town? The *locus classicus* is Polybius's description of the sack of New Carthage (the Carthaginian capital in Spain, modern Cartagena) in 209:[17]

> When Scipio thought there were enough troops inside the city, he let most
> of them loose on the inhabitants—this is normal Roman practice—with

orders to kill everyone they met without exception, but not to start pillaging until the order had been given. I think that the reason they do this is to inspire terror. That is also why often, when a place falls to the Romans, one can see not only slaughtered human beings, but dogs cut in half and the dismembered corpses of other animals.

To a certain extent, cultural factors lay behind the Romans' ability to perpetrate such horrors in cold blood: it was possible for them to feel utter contempt for those who surrendered in war, as if they were less than human.[18] But when Polybius implies that Roman practices were more barbaric than those of other peoples, he is stretching a point. To give just two examples out of very many: in 416 the Athenians, the heroes of western Classical culture, massacred the men and sold into slavery the women and children of the Aegean island of Melos, just because they did not want to join the Athenian alliance, and repopulated the island with their own settlers; in 217, when Philip V took Phthiotic Thebes from the Aetolians, he sold the surviving inhabitants into slavery, repopulated the town with Macedonians, and changed its name to Philippi.[19] In part, the problem was that these kinds of practices had not been seen on the Greek mainland for several decades, but what these ripples in the historical record really reflect is the spin of ancient propagandists: depending on your politics, Romans could be portrayed as brutal barbarians, seeking to enslave Greeks, or as liberators of Greeks from the tyranny of Macedon. If the Romans were transgressing the conventions of ancient warfare, it was only because they were more consistently brutal than their opponents.

If the Romans had good reasons to resent the peace, Philip cannot have been too happy with it either. He had intended to remove the Roman presence altogether. The peace was in fact a temporary measure, a stop-gap. Future friction was almost guaranteed by the protagonists' dissatisfaction with the peace, and by the fact that Philip was now, in both Lissus and Dassaretis, an immediate neighbor of Rome's friends in southern Illyris. His military reputation had peaked again and, as a Hellenistic king, he was likely to want to continue while the gods were blessing his ventures. The only reason for the peace was that the protagonists had other fish to fry. This is explicit in Livy's account of the peace: he says that the Romans wanted to focus on Africa and therefore to be released "for the time being" from other wars; they saw their concessions to Philip as temporary.[20] They withdrew their troops as usual at the end of 206, because there was no longer any immediate danger, but they would be back. There was a defeat here to be avenged.

GREEK REACTIONS TO ROME

Before the Romans landed on Greek soil, the Greeks had few preconceptions about them. Rome's appearances in earlier Greek literature are rare and trivial;[21] the city had not yet created substantial ripples in the wider Mediterranean world. After their arrival in Greece, a wide range of views began to be canvassed, as reflected in Polybius: some (including Polybius himself) saw them as aggressive imperialists, but others as bringers of peace and freedom. Yet others pragmatically went along with Roman wishes, fearful of the consequences of opposition. All of these are responses to aggression and greed, since brutality inspires both loathing and, from cowards or pragmatists, deference. Already in the 190s, Titus Quinctius Flamininus, in an open letter to the small Thessalian town of Chyretiae, felt he had to defend the Romans against the "slanderous" charge of greed. He returned property to the city that had been confiscated by Rome "so that in these matters too you may learn of our nobility and realize that we absolutely never intended to be avaricious."[22]

Surprisingly, Greek writers seem (most of the literature is lost) rarely to have had anything to say about Rome even during the sixty or so years of the conquest of Greece.[23] A poem has been preserved by the poetess Melinno, from the island of Lesbos. Written perhaps in the middle of the second century, it is in effect a hymn to Rome, punning on the coincidence that the word "Roma" in Greek means "strength" as well as "Rome." The poem has five stanzas; here are the first two:[24]

Hail, Roma, daughter of Ares,
Warlike mistress with a girdle of gold,
Whose abode on earth is holy Olympus,
Forever unshaken.

To you alone, honoured lady, Fate has given
The royal glory of eternal rule,
So that you may govern with the might
Of sovereignty.

At much the same time, the historian Agatharchides of Cnidus commented bitterly on Roman rapacity, by attributing an Arabian people's prosperity to their distance from Rome.[25] This is little enough to be going on with, but it reflects the same range—deference to loathing—that we might have expected.

By contrast, as we shall see later in the book, Roman writers thought a great deal about their encounter with the Greeks and its consequences for Rome, with reactions to Greek culture ranging from enthusiastic acceptance to stubborn resistance. If there are fewer mentions of Rome by Greeks, that is due, in the first place, simply to the fact that resistance or deference were about the only choices the Greeks had, where responses were concerned. In the second place, consider the fact that a pro-Roman Greek historian of the first century BCE, Dionysius of Halicarnassus, felt the need to argue that, since Rome was fundamentally a Greek city, Greeks should not despise Romans. The implication is that many Greeks did despise the Romans as culturally inferior.[26] So perhaps the lack of interest in Rome evinced by Greek writers (apart from historians) was due in part to their not considering the Romans worth thinking about. Their subjugation by these upstart barbarians from the west must have come as a shock.

The shock generated some bizarre reactions. Phlegon of Tralles, writing in the second century CE, preserved a tale set around 189 BCE.[27] In this story, a Roman consul identified only as "Publius" (perhaps Scipio Africanus) went mad, or became possessed, in the sanctuary of Zeus at Naupactus on the Gulf of Corinth. The visions he saw he described, some in fluent Greek verse and some in prose, to a doubtless gaping crowd of soldiers and civilians. The very first vision was that a king would come from the east to take violent revenge for the Roman subjugation of Greece. As proof of the authenticity of his visions, Scipio offered one more: that a red wolf would come and eat him up. And so it did, until only the consul's skull remained, still spouting prophecies of doom for Rome. But such prophecies are wishful thinking, and desperate attempts to reclaim the high ground after defeat by Rome. In the first instance, what impressed itself upon the Greeks was the uncompromising ruthlessness of the Romans.

4.

KING PHILIP OF MACEDON

B Y THE END OF the First Macedonian War in 206, the Romans found themselves in a position of considerable influence in the Greek world, but unable to capitalize on it. For the time being, their attention was necessarily engaged elsewhere, and so that influence was perpetuated sporadically and by indirect means, chiefly diplomacy. The Romans clearly already intended to play a significant role in Greek affairs, despite the fact that this would continue to bring them into conflict with Macedon, but they had as yet no coherent plan for bringing this about. So far their presence in Greece had seemed to them to be demanded, on three occasions, by emerging situations in Illyris, most recently by Philip's threat to their friends there—or, rather, his threat to their hegemony there. But this process of merely reacting to emerging situations came to an end now. Once the Second Punic War was resolved in the Romans' favor in 202, they were free to develop a more aggressive policy, targeting Philip of Macedon.

THE REVIVAL OF THE MACEDONIAN EMPIRE

In the years following the end of the First Macedonian War, those Greeks who feared Macedon, who wanted to ingratiate themselves with Rome, and who saw some advantage in it for themselves, sent a string of embassies to Rome with complaints about Philip's behavior. Clearly, it was widely known that the Romans wanted another opportunity to curb Philip and needed only sufficient reasons for doing so. The Romans listened attentively to these complaints, and sent out a commission to investigate,[1] but when the Aetolians came, early in 201,[2] to appeal for help against Philip and to suggest a renewal of the 211 treaty, they were sharply rebuffed: How dare you turn to us? It was *you* who negotiated a unilateral peace with Philip in 206. But of course it was only the fact that they had already sent out the investigatory commission that enabled the Romans to occupy the moral high ground with the Aetolians.

Philip, for his part, did nothing to allay Roman fears, and hardly slowed the pace of his expansion. In fact, he made it clear that his goal was now to revive and even extend the Macedonian empire first established by his great namesake, Philip II (the father of Alexander the Great), in the middle of the fourth century. He raided in Illyris and further secured his northern border against the Dardanians, but his most important campaigns were overseas. Two blistering campaigns in 202 and 201 netted him critical cities and islands in the Hellespont and along the northern Aegean coastline, until much of what the Greeks called "the Thraceward region" and the Thracian Chersonese was in his hands. He also helped Prusias of Bithynia take Cius, a move that was guaranteed to alarm Attalus in Pergamum.

In the Aegean, where many of the island and mainland coastal cities were Ptolemaic possessions, part of the Egyptian overseas empire, Philip took advantage of Egypt's weakness, caused by the secession of half of the kingdom and power struggles within the court following the accession, in 204 or 203, of the boy king Ptolemy V. He gained several of the Cyclades, and established good relations with cities on the Asia Minor coastline. Philip's successes were made possible by a newly rebuilt fleet, financed in part by raids on Aegean islands by a pirate chieftain in his employ, Dicaearchus of Aetolia—a man with a strange sense of humor: as soon as he touched land on one of his raids, he would set up two altars, one to Impiety and the other to Lawlessness.[3] He seems to have served his gods well.

Philip clearly had no qualms about antagonizing everyone—or everyone except his ally Prusias—not just by what he did, but by how he did it: there were brutal massacres and enslavements at both Cius and Thasos, followed by imposed garrisons. Cius, Lysimachea, and other places he took in the Hellespontine region had been allies of the Aetolian League, and, since the collapse of Egypt, the Aegean islands had looked to Rhodes for protection. The Rhodians were further aggravated by Philip's support of the Cretan pirates, with whom they were at war,[4] and in 201 they declared war on Philip. Attalus of Pergamum soon followed suit.

Undaunted, Philip garrisoned the major Cycladic islands, seized the Ptolemaic fleet in the harbor of Samos, and then moved on to Chios, where he put the town under siege. After defeating a joint Rhodian–Pergamene attempt to relieve the siege, though he took heavy losses, he struck next at Pergamum itself. Despite defeating the Pergamene land army, the city withstood his attack, but he stocked up on provisions before returning to his campaign on the Aegean coastline, where he quickly turned much of Caria, and most of the Rhodian Peraea (the island's extension on the mainland), into an overseas province of Macedon, with its own governor.[5] A Rhodian fleet attacked Philip again off the island of Lade (just off Miletus), but Philip repulsed it and sailed on in triumph to Miletus, which put up no resistance.[6] Philip's progress was incredibly rapid, but Egypt was too torn by internal problems to look after its overseas possessions, and Antiochus of Syria was not inclined to interfere. Anything that weakened Pergamum, which held territory he considered rightfully his, was all right by him.

Philip next captured Iasus and Bargylia (modern Boğaziçi), adding to the number of safe havens he held on the coast of southwestern Asia Minor. But the Rhodians seized the opportunity to bottle him up in the gulf, and forced him to winter in Bargylia, "living like a wolf," Polybius says,[7] meaning that he had difficulty foraging for or begging enough food to survive the winter. He must have been raging with frustration, knowing that his enemies were even then gearing up to make war on him. But in the spring of 200 he managed to trick his way out and escape back to Macedon with the Rhodians and Pergamenes hot on his heels. Bargylia was their third attempt to contain Philip, and their third failure.

Immediately on his return, Philip became involved in a conflict between Athens and his ally Acarnania. There had been bad blood between the two since the previous autumn, when the Athenians had executed two Acarnanians for the sacrilege of attending, uninitiated, the sacred rites of the Eleusinian Mysteries. There had long been a low level of tension between Athens and Macedon because of the Athenians' cordial relations with the Ptolemies, and the tension had risen recently as Philip's gains in the north Aegean threatened Athens' vital grain route through the Hellespont. Philip sent ships, and a joint Acarnanian–Macedonian fleet ravaged Attica until it was seen off by a Pergamene–Rhodian fleet from Aegina. The Athenians were helpless to defend themselves, and expressed their hostility by formally cursing Philip and hysterically rescinding the honors they had awarded his Macedonian predecessors. No longer the international powerhouse it had been a century or two earlier, Athens was fast becoming little more than a university town.

Meanwhile Philip continued his northern Aegean campaign with the bulk of his forces. Towns large and small surrendered to him, but Abydus, a vital Ptolemaic possession on the southern shore of the Hellespont, the main crossing point between Europe and Asia, had been reinforced by contingents of both Rhodian and Pergamene troops. It chose resistance, and was put under siege. Attalus took a fleet from Aegina to the island of Tenedos, just outside the mouth of the Hellespont, but did not dare to confront Philip in the Hellespont itself. It was the late summer of the year 200, and the long-anticipated war was about to break out.

A SECRET PACT

While Philip was stuck in the Gulf of Bargylia in the winter of 201–200, Rhodian and Pergamene envoys arrived in Rome. They had failed to contain Philip on their own, or even prevent him invading Pergamum at will. They needed help, and with the Second Punic War finally over, they could hope for a positive response in Rome to their appeal. In addition to the usual complaints and warnings about the danger Philip's aggressive surge posed to Rome itself—no doubt the envoys stressed Philip's new navy, knowing how vital Roman naval superiority had been in the previous war—they brought some startling news. They claimed that Philip had entered into a secret agreement with Antiochus of Syria to exploit current Egyptian weakness.[8]

Egyptian ineffectiveness certainly presented a unique opportunity for both Philip and Antiochus. Philip was clearly bent on gaining an overseas empire for Macedon, and Egyptian garrisons were bound to be his targets in the Aegean and Hellespont; and Antiochus, who had just returned from several years of fairly successful campaigning in the far east of his empire, was determined also to recover Coele Syria and as much of Asia Minor as he could, and needed Philip not to interfere in those projects. In 203, Philip was approached by the Egyptian court for a marriage alliance. No doubt Antiochus was moved to offer Philip the pact by his desire to scotch such an alliance between Egypt and Macedon.

It was a nonintervention pact, designed to leave each of them free to undermine Ptolemaic influence in Asia Minor and the Aegean where he chose. So, for instance, while Philip was campaigning in 201 in coastal Caria (the pact probably having been agreed to in 202), Antiochus was busy re-establishing his own control a little way inland, but the two great Hellenistic kings avoided confrontation there and elsewhere. Or again, while bottled up in Bargylia, Philip seems to have been supplied, even if reluctantly, by one of Antiochus's generals.[9] It was on the back of this secret agreement, then, that Philip was targeting Ptolemaic possessions in Caria and the Aegean, and Antiochus launched the Fifth Syrian War (201–199), which enabled him to recover Coele Syria once and for all, after a hundred years of intermittent attempts.

THE TIPPING POINT

"Men," said Scipio Africanus before the Battle of Zama (according to Polybius), "you are fighting not just for Africa, but to win for yourselves and your country dominion over the rest of the inhabited world."[10] This is too close to Polybius's "clouds in the west" thesis—that the Romans would follow victory over the Carthaginians with dominance in Greece—for us to believe that we are actually hearing Scipio's voice, but by the end of the First Macedonian War, the Romans clearly had resolved to be a significant presence in Greece. As so often in international politics, their subsequent inactivity was not a sign of indifference, but of different priorities.

They were only biding their time until further opportunities came their way—opportunities they could hope to exploit once the Carthaginian menace had been removed.

So, although the news of the pact between Antiochus and Philip galvanized the Senate to ask the Roman people for a declaration of war against Macedon, this does not represent a change of direction. The news acted as a trigger only because the senators already thought they had a stake in the east, otherwise they would not have felt threatened by Philip's actions in the distant Aegean and would have done no more than protect their Illyrian and Greek friends, as before, while watching Antiochus and Philip destroy Egypt and then, no doubt, each other. They could have ignored the missions from the Rhodians and Pergamenes, but they chose instead to intervene in the kind of explosive situation from which no one emerges unscathed. It was a world-changing moment—the moment when the destinies of the western and eastern Mediterranean became inextricably entangled—but it was also no more than an extension of the course the Romans had been committed to for a while. Despite the short-termism of Roman politics, with annual elections and so on, it was possible for consistent policy to emerge: the Senate was determined for several decades to crush the Celts of the Po valley, and now we see them determined to maintain and extend their influence in the Greek world. All that was needed was a pretext, and alleged fear of a resurgent Macedon provided it.

But when the popular assembly was first presented with the proposal for war, they rejected it. There were good reasons to avoid war. The end of the Second Punic War had left Rome with military commitments in Spain; the Celts of the Po valley were restive; southern Italy had been devastated and urgently needed attention. Rome had a lot of expensive repair work to do and loans to repay. Why, at this point, undertake a huge new venture, and one which, despite the involvement of their Greek allies, would be hugely expensive?

The Senate's response to the assembly's rejection of war was to give one of the two consuls for 200, Publius Sulpicius Galba (one of the generals from the First Macedonian War), who had already gained Macedon as his province in the event of war, the job of winning the assembly over. And

Galba was successful. If we are to believe the speech given him by Livy, he worked on popular fear of Rome's two greatest *bêtes noires*, Hannibal and Pyrrhus, arguing that Philip was as dangerous as Hannibal, and that if they did not fight him in Greece, they would have to do so in Italy.[11] As usual, it is difficult to know if this expression of fear of invasion was sincere, or a belligerent ploy. Galba's argument may have been a factor in changing the assembly's mind, but the Roman people were probably just as impressed by the Senate's committment to war. The Senate had steered them well during the Hannibalic War and seemed sure that this war would benefit Rome as well. In fact, the senators foresaw Galba's success in the assembly: in the short interval between the people's rejection of war and Galba's speech, they had already put Marcus Valerius Laevinus in charge of a fleet and sent him to Illyris to prepare the way and secure supply routes from Italy.

This was a critical moment. Especially given the popular assembly's initial reluctance, the Senate could easily have ignored the news from Greece and chosen peace. Clearly, the Senate did not want peace. So determined was the Senate on war that they backed Galba's persuasiveness with concessions. Knowing the veterans were war-weary, they recruited largely from those with the shortest periods of active service (though veteran volunteers were always welcome); and, knowing that undertaking another war would make it impossible for the state to repay the rich men who had bankrolled the Second Punic War, they gave them land (of which they had plenty to spare after the war, especially as a result of confiscations from disloyal allies) to keep them happy for the time being.[12] So the Roman people ratified the *senatus consultum* and instructed Galba to issue a formal declaration of war on his arrival with the army in Illyris.

THE GRAND TOUR

Sending Laevinus to Illyris was not the Senate's only action in response to the Rhodian–Pergamene embassy, before the Roman people had voted for war; they also dispatched a second three-man commission to test Greek waters. The members were Gaius Claudius Nero, conqueror of Hasdrubal at the Metaurus; Publius Sempronius Tuditanus, the Roman commander at the end of the First Macedonian War; and Marcus Aemilius Lepidus, later the most respected man of his generation, but then just beginning his career with this early acknowledgment of his brilliance. Their mission had many facets, or perhaps it grew as they traveled around and gathered more information. It must have been a truly amazing journey, a seven-month round trip of some 6,000 kilometers (3,600 miles) by land and sea. They would have been put up by local dignitaries wherever they went, an arrangement that would begin the process of dividing local elites into pro- and anti-Roman factions, which was to play such a vital role in securing Roman dominance of Greece.

After landing in Illyris, they journeyed south, stopping first for successive discussions with the Epirotes, Amynander of Athamania, and the Aetolian and Achaean leagues. Just about then, Philip was breaking out of Bargylia. The Romans' message was everywhere the same: the Greeks should be aware that, if Philip refrained from making war on Greeks and indemnified Attalus for the invasion of his territory (the amount to be fixed by an independent tribunal), there would be peace; otherwise, war.

This, again, was an extension of an old policy: Roman protection was being offered not just to those who had already entrusted themselves to Rome—the southern Illyrians and the co-signatories of the Peace of Phoenice—but to the Greek states and leagues at large. If Philip acted aggressively towards *any* of them, he would face war from Rome. The Romans were now openly laying claim to hegemony of all Greece, not just selected areas; they were positioning themselves as the Greeks' common benefactors and Philip as the villain. The unpopularity of Philip's raids over the preceding few years guaranteed the envoys a warm reception, and if anyone remembered how Rome had treated Greek states in Sicily and southern Italy, or in Greece itself during the First Macedonian War, they were too polite to mention it.

The meaning of the envoys' message depended on its recipient. To those who were, usually, Philip's friends (the Epirotes, Amynander, the Achaeans) it was a threat, or an invitation to change sides or at least stay neutral; the Romans were attempting to undermine Philip's Common Alliance. The Aetolians and other presumed Roman friends were offered profit and advancement if they sided with Rome. Everywhere the envoys went, they collected charges against Philip, encouraged anti-Macedonian factions, and generally tried to raise trouble for Philip and allies for themselves. The effect of all this was to put the Greek states in a terrible quandary, because the price of choosing the wrong side could be total destruction. It was not just that political leaders would be killed or exiled and replaced with more amenable men; military occupation might well ensue, leading to economic ruin for the community, and personal degradation and disaster for individuals, with houses and public buildings burnt and robbed, women, girls, and boys raped, and enslavement or mutilation for the men. That was the implied threat of the Roman envoys, and the Greeks already knew from experience that both the Romans and Philip had the will to carry it out.

The envoys' meeting with the Achaean League was particularly delicate. Philopoemen had the most influence in the league, and he had for some time been an advocate of gradual independence from Macedon. A scrappy little war against Sparta, resurgent under Nabis (ruled 207–192), was being competently managed, and Philopoemen had turned the Achaean army into the kind of force that could back up such a stab at independence. For twenty years, the league had been Macedon's mainstay in Greece, and it was bound to be vital to Philip that it continue in this role. Could the Romans bring about the shift from an attitude of neutrality towards Macedon to one that positively favored Rome? That must have been the purpose of their visit to Achaea. They had to wait a year or two to find out if their efforts had borne fruit.

From Achaea, the envoys made their way to Athens, arriving just as the crisis there came to a head, late in April 200. They found Attalus and the Rhodians already there, having just driven the Acarnanians back home. The Roman delegates were able to listen and offer their potent, but silent, support as Attalus and the Rhodians persuaded the Athenians to join them in their war against Macedon. The Athenians were incapable of tackling Philip on their own, but they could see that they would be part of a powerful team, and they duly declared war on Macedon. After thirty years of neutrality (ever since expelling their Macedonian garrisons in 229), Athens was once again committed. So, within the space of two years, war had been declared twice against Philip, resulting in a coalition of Athens, Rhodes, Pergamum, and Byzantium (which had lost its satellite, Perinthus). Now that a satisfactory result had been obtained, the Rhodians sailed for home, driving some of Philip's garrisons from the Cyclades on the way.

While all this was going on, a Macedonian army arrived outside Athens' walls, under Philip's general Nicanor, to continue the plundering and pillaging that the Acarnanians had begun a few weeks earlier. Nicanor started well, but was halted by the request of the Roman envoys for a meeting. They were improvising—this meeting was not part of their original brief—but all they did was pass on the same strongly worded message that they had been carrying around Greece: they told Nicanor to tell Philip that if he stopped attacking Greek cities, all would be well between them, but if he continued, there would be war. It was a Popillius Laenas moment, with the Roman envoys challenging Nicanor to face the consequences if he did what he had come to do and punished the Athenians. He disengaged, and returned to Macedon with the message for his king.

Philip's response was unequivocally defiant: he sent a small force under a general called Philocles to continue raiding Athenian land from nearby Macedonian bases on Euboea and at Corinth, while he set off on the campaign that would lead to the siege of Abydus. Clearly, he had no intention of giving in to Roman pressure.

Leaving the Athenians in the safe hands of Attalus, the Roman envoys continued on their journey, to Rhodes. The Rhodians were actually less united than their declaration of war might suggest; at any rate, the Achaeans thought it worthwhile to appeal to the pro-Macedonian or at least antiwar faction there to come to terms with Philip. But the Romans stiffened Rhodian resolve, and the Achaean delegation was sent packing. The island was also a good stepping-stone for the envoys to complete their grand tour by meeting both Ptolemy V of Egypt and Antiochus III of Syria. They were to try to arrange an end to the Fifth Syrian War, and to encourage Ptolemy to maintain the good terms he currently enjoyed with Rome (that is, not to side with Philip); and Antiochus must have received the same request for neutrality. The negotiations seem to have been successful, because Antiochus did indeed soon break off his assault

on Egypt itself, and campaigned instead first against Ptolemaic possessions in Cilicia, and then in Asia Minor. This was the first occasion when
the Romans mediated between major Greek states, their first formal contact with Antiochus, and the first time they had actively extended their
reach further east than the Greek mainland.

While the envoys were on Rhodes, they heard about the siege of Abydus,
and Lepidus went on alone to Philip there. This was probably when the
others went to the Egyptian and Syrian courts. Once Philip granted
Lepidus an audience, the Roman delivered a slightly expanded version of
the same forceful message: Philip was to keep his hands off not just Greek
states, but Egyptian possessions as well—such as, most immediately,
Abydus—and was to compensate Rhodes as well as Pergamum. In effect,
he was insisting that Roman policy in Greece should take precedence
over Philip's; there was, of course, no way that Philip could accede to such
an idea. Why would he let a barbarian occupy the position Macedon had
held in Greece for well over a hundred years?

The meeting was stormy: a Hellenistic king was not accustomed to be
addressed so peremptorily by a young foreigner, or bullied in this way by
anyone, but Lepidus was there to deliver an ultimatum, not to enter into a
debate. Philip ended by reminding Lepidus that, technically, both he and
the Romans were still bound by the treaty they had signed at Phoenice
in 205. The Romans should therefore not go to war against him, but "If
they do, we will defend ourselves bravely, with the help of the gods!"[13] Not
bothering even to feign humility was a huge gamble by Philip: with the
Romans more or less free of other military commitments, he must have
known that they would come against him in full force. This is a measure
of how determined he was.

It was to be war, then, and Lepidus returned to Rhodes to join his colleagues and return to Rome. They could report a successful mission. The
pact between Antiochus and Philip had broken down, and Antiochus
would not intervene when the Romans went to war with Macedon. The
Fifth Syrian War had been ended, without Ptolemy asking for Roman
help. It looked as though the Romans would gain the active or passive
support of a number of Greek states and leagues—as though Pergamum,
Rhodes, Byzantium, and Athens were just the first dominoes in the row.

They were free to concentrate on Philip, who had received the ultimatum and had understood it. In actual fact, however, the Romans had already declared war by the time the envoys returned. And so the Second Macedonian War began.

THE SACK OF ANTIPATREA

Galba set off for Illyris just as the siege of Abydus was coming to a horrendous end, with the mass suicide of those inhabitants who could not face the prospect of Macedonian rule. When Philip returned to Macedon in November 200, he was greeted by the news that the Romans had already arrived: an army of more than twenty thousand was at Apollonia and a fleet of fifty warships at Corcyra.[14] In response to an Athenian embassy, twenty ships from the fleet sailed under Gaius Claudius Centho to Athens, to combat Philocles' raids from Corinth and Chalcis.

Claudius proved very effective, and these were risky campaigns, by sea in the winter in the hazardous waters of the Euripus Strait between Euboea and the mainland. He ravaged Chalcis and came close to starting the war with a dramatic coup, but he did not have the manpower both to garrison Chalcis and defend Athens. He withdrew, then, but this was a great symbolic victory, as well as inflicting actual harm on Philip by annihilating his garrison, burning a major granary, and destroying an important arsenal, stocked with expensive siege equipment. Chalcis was one of three Greek cities that Philip considered so important that he called them the "Fetters of Greece," the other two being Corinth and Demetrias. Generally speaking, whoever held the Fetters could control most of the traffic in Greece. All three were strongly defended—so strongly that in Chalcis the Macedonian garrison had grown careless, and that is how Claudius got in.

Philip retaliated immediately by re-garrisoning Chalcis and launching an attack on Athens which was barely repulsed. Philip then left Athens to Philocles, and carried on to the Peloponnese, where he attended one of the regular meetings of the Achaean League. He knew that they were wavering, and he knew how badly he needed them. He offered to take over their war against Nabis if they would garrison Corinth, Chalcis, and Oreus, and so protect his rear while he advanced on Sparta. But the Achaeans rejected his offer and carried on the Spartan war themselves. Philip now knew that he could no longer rely on the Achaeans (though he made one last attempt the next year to win them to his side by bribing them with the gift of some of his Peloponnesian possessions), and he took his forces back to Macedon for what must have been a busy and anxious winter.

Meanwhile, in Illyris, Galba had established his camp and was conducting raids inland in preparation for the next year's campaign. His lieutenant, Lucius Apustius, captured a number of fortresses and raided in Dassaretis, more or less with impunity, since Philip was only now on his way back from Abydus. Then Apustius came to Antipatrea. After failing to take the town by negotiation, he entered it by force. All men of military age were put to death, and the town was thoroughly plundered before being burnt to the ground. The town did not recover until its resurrection in the fifth century CE as a border town of the Byzantine empire. It looks as though Galba was clearing the way for operations in the coming season deeper in Macedonian territory; otherwise, he would have held Antipatrea and garrisoned it. But, on top of their reputation from the First Macedonian War, the savagery of the Roman forces continued to be a gift to Macedonian propagandists.

At the news of these initial Roman successes, several fence-sitters visited Galba in his camp over the winter. Pleuratus of Scodra came to pledge his support, as did Bato, the ruler of a Dardanian confederacy. Galba told them to be ready when he advanced on Macedon in the spring. Amynander of Athamania also appeared; following the Roman embassy of 200, he had decided to throw in his lot with the Romans. Amynander had long been on good terms with the Aetolians, and Galba gave him the job of trying to bring them in too. But the Aetolians, still angry at being rebuffed by the Romans in 202, were not yet ready to commit themselves. It looks as though Galba might have been planning a triple invasion of Macedon for the next year, with the Aetolians coming up from the southwest, through Thessaly, as a third force in addition to his own troops and the Illyrians. If so, the Aetolians' hesitation was costly.

PLUNDER

Nowadays, soldiers are expected to refrain from looting (though no doubt a little "souvenir-hunting" goes on), but this is a relatively recent development. Battlefield looting disfigured the aftermath of Waterloo, and Moscow was terribly sacked by Napoleon's troops in 1812, as Washington was by British troops in 1814. These practices have only gradually died out since (in Europe, at any rate), especially as soldiers gained a better basic rate of pay. We have to try to cast our minds back to an era when looting was not considered immoral, but was expected, on the principle of "winner takes all," and was indeed one of the primary motivating factors of soldiering. Official plundering, however, is more familiar to us. In the ancient world, booty was glory made visible. Victory monuments boasted of the plunder taken in the war, and booty was displayed in triumph as evidence that the mission had been accomplished. The theft of artwork in the Second World War reminds us that we are not so far removed from the same mindset.

Everyone in a Roman army profited. In the field, all booty was pooled, and then redistributed in a hierarchical fashion, so that officers and cavalrymen got proportionately more than footsoldiers. A soldier could also expect to receive a cash bonus at the end of a successful war, which might even be enough to set him up with a smallholding. The state gained too: Rome expected its returning generals to restock its treasury with the profits of ransoming or selling captives, selling captured livestock, reselling captured slaves, and so on.

Back home, booty was either sold or recycled. Property looted from private homes tended to end up in Roman homes. Paintings and statuettes might be bought by collectors. Although containing mostly copies of Greek originals, the Villa of the Papyri in Herculaneum, destroyed in the eruption of Vesuvius in 79 CE (and imitated as the Getty Villa in California), gives some idea of how wealthy Roman collectors filled their homes with Greek sculptures, over eighty pieces in this instance (see Fig. 4.1). After the final overthrow of the Macedonian monarchy Aemilius Paullus, who famously avoided profiting himself, gave the royal Macedonian library to his sons, a fabulous gift.[15]

FIGURE 4.1

Resting Hermes. This bronze sculpture from the Villa of the Papyri at Herculaneum (a Roman copy of a Greek original from the late fourth century BCE) gives some idea of the quality of the pieces that were beginning to find their way into the collections of wealthy Romans.

Public monuments, however, tended to be rededicated in the temples and public spaces of Rome, and there is the rub. A good number of these public monuments were sacred and had long served as focuses of worship for the Greek communities from which they were stolen. To remove them was bad enough, in the sense that it undermined the cohesion of the community, but to rededicate them in Rome, for all that it was an act of reverence, was also an act of imperialism. The Macedonians, for instance, had a famous statue of Zeus, and after Cynoscephalae Titus Quinctius Flamininus had it carried off to Rome, to grace the Capitoline Hill in Rome, the center of the worship of Jupiter, the Roman equivalent of Zeus.[16] The symbolism is unmistakable: the protection of the king of the gods has passed from Macedon to Rome. Similar tales could be told of the sack of many towns and cities in Sicily, southern Italy, Greece, and Asia Minor. Looting was a tool of imperialist suppression.

The value of the official booty—the booty we know about—taken from the Greek east between 229 and 167 has been estimated at 70,000,000 *denarii* (perhaps $7 billion).[17] Much more, of course, escaped notice. But it is not just the overall value that is astounding; certain individual items stand out. By the first century CE, the list of forty-six masterpieces of Greek painting and sculpture that we know had been removed to Rome reads like a list of Old Masters in the National Galleries of London or Washington.[18] Many of these will have reached Rome from the sack of Athens in 86 BCE by Sulla's troops, but some of them certainly arrived earlier. We know that Lysippus's statue "The Labors of Heracles" was removed from Tarentum in 209, as was a famous painting by Zeuxis from Ambracia in 189.[19] Either of these pieces alone would be beyond price. We know that a single painting of Parrhasius was valued in the first century CE at 150,000 *denarii*, and that at much the same time Marcus Vipsanius Agrippa spent twice that much on two paintings.[20]

Many works of art were stolen during the sack of Greek cities by Flamininus in the 190s, during the sack of Ambracia by Fulvius Nobilior in 189, and during the sack of Achaea by Lucius Mummius in 146. We can be sure, even without evidence, that the same happened in the course of all other sackings, great and small. We rarely hear details because it just became taken for granted: triumphs from wars fought in the east included the display of numerous stolen works of art. Fulvius Nobilior, who considered himself an intellectual and a connoisseur, displayed over a thousand statues in bronze and marble in his triumph; after the Achaean War, Mummius "filled Rome with statues." In short, in the years between Marcellus's sack of Syracuse in 211 and the destruction of Corinth in 146, Rome and other Italian towns became veritable museums of Greek statues and paintings, and Polybius was surely right to argue that this aroused particular resentment. Rome took the best from Greece.[21] The degradation of a plundered town or city was moral as well as economic: its pride and sense of identity were often closely tied up with its public monuments.

GALBA'S LAST GASP

Philip's main weakness was at sea, and in 199 the Romans exploited his shaky control of the Aegean. Philip's fleet was pinned in the Gulf of Demetrias by the Rhodians, and he could do nothing as the Romans and their allies pillaged at will, until their ships were so weighed down with booty that they could take no more.[22] But, apart from the island of Andros, they made no substantial gains until they were on their way back to winter on Corcyra, when they took Oreus, a very important gain. The town was entrusted to Attalus, but the Romans profited by selling the inhabitants into slavery.

The Romans had similarly limited success on land. With the Aetolians still out of the picture, Galba attempted a two-pronged invasion of Macedon. While Pleuratus and the Dardanians came from the northwest, he marched down the Apsus valley (past the ruins of Antipatrea), and then struck east through the mountains, south of the Prespa Lakes—a long and difficult route. Philip sent a force north (under the nominal command of his 13-year-old son Perseus, but really under his general Athenagoras) to contain the Dardanians and Illyrians, and marched to confront Galba. The Romans struggled to fight their way through to Orestis and Eordaea, within striking distance of the heartland of Macedon. The mountainous terrain precluded anything but skirmishing and the occasional cavalry engagement, but the Romans performed better than Philip had expected, and he summoned Perseus and some of the northern army to help him. And so Galba was turned back, but he had at least cleared the ground for a further attempt the following year.

But Galba was ill and tired, and his command was not further extended. He was replaced in the autumn of 199 by one of the consuls, Publius Villius Tappulus, who first had to quell a near mutiny that Galba had left unresolved. Some of the veterans in the army had been fighting abroad for years, without respite or a chance to see their families. Villius listened to their grievances and promised to put their case to the authorities in Rome. This seems to have quietened things down—and it was just as well, for the Romans could ill afford to lose them. Given their length of service and experience, these disgruntled men were the backbone of the army. Villius then sailed to winter quarters on Corcyra, and nothing happened until the spring.

The chief consequence of Galba's push towards Macedon was that it galvanized the Aetolians. The news of the Dardanian invasion of Macedon and the fall of Oreus made them think that it was all over for Philip, and they revealed their decision to come in on the Roman side by launching an ill-disciplined plundering raid into Thessaly, in conjunction with Amynander. But they failed to link up with Galba and were badly mauled by Philip. At the same time, Athenagoras finally chased the Dardanians out of northern Macedon. It was an inconclusive year, but Philip had done well to keep it inconclusive.

5.

THE FREEDOM OF THE GREEKS

AROUND THE TIME OF the first Roman expedition to Illyris in 229, a boy was born in Rome who would translate the Roman desire for dominion in the Greek world into a coherent, if ultimately impractical, policy. The consummate diplomat, he would perfect the instrument that would allow Rome to maintain control from a distance, committing little in the way of resources. Titus Quinctius Flamininus was born into a somewhat faded patrician family (a cousin was a consul in 208, but before that the family had been undistinguished for half a century), but he and his brother Lucius revived the family name as they rose rapidly through the traditional ranks of Roman public service. Lucius turned out to be a disreputable character, however. In 184 he was expelled from the Senate for abuse of power in his province—the first high-ranking officer to be expelled for twenty-five years. He was said to have murdered a Celtic prisoner to gratify the whim of a catamite.[1]

Be that as it may, in 205 Titus was appointed to the governorship of Tarentum, and did a good enough job for the post to be extended for two further years. We do not know what his responsibilities were, but they must have required both tact and firmness, because Tarentum was recovering from its terrible sack by the Romans in 209, in the course of the Hannibalic War. During his time there, he became proficient in Greek—but no more than proficient: a letter he wrote in Greek has survived as an inscription, and reveals certain weaknesses.[2]

The minimum ages at which a man might hold the various offices in Rome were not all set in stone until 180 BCE, and regularization of the process by which a man gradually ascended to high office was also undertaken in the 190s and 180s. Even before this, however, it was expected that a man would ascend in an orderly fashion through the ranks: starting in his late twenties, he would leave a decent gap between holding one office and standing for the next (a 10-year interval was stipulated between holding the same office), and would be in his late thirties or, more likely, early forties when he held a first consulship, a senior and responsible citizen. But Flamininus's career was on a roll: governorship of Tarentum was followed by two commissions for the delicate task of settling veterans and colonists on southern Italian land. He had held praetorian rank for the governorship of Tarentum; he now decided to aim for the very top, and he gained one of the consulships of 198 despite the protests of two tribunes of the people.[3] He was not quite thirty years old when he first came to Greece.

THE AOUS CONFERENCE

Philip joined up with Athenagoras and they encamped in Illyris at the entrance to the Aous narrows, where they could command both of the two most likely routes toward Macedon that the Romans would take from Apollonia in 198: the difficult mountainous route that Galba had attempted the year before (the best bet because Galba had left garrisons and depots on the route), and the more southerly route past Antigonea and into Epirus. The consul Villius Tappulus, drawn from Corcyra by the news of Philip's arrival, made his camp a few miles west of the Macedonians, but that was his final act as commander because Flamininus arrived to relieve him. He was assigned Greece as his province by lot, and his brother Lucius, who had served as a praetor the previous year, was sent out with him and put in charge of the fleet.

The Epirotes made one last attempt to see if the two sides could come to terms. The meeting took place with king and consul, and their respective entourages, glaring at one another from opposite banks of the swift-flowing Aous where it was at its narrowest. Flamininus made it clear that, as far as he was concerned, Philip had to remove all his garrisons from Greek communities, and recompense those he had plundered.

Philip argued that it made no sense to lump together all the Greek cities under his control: he had come by them in different ways, and so they would require different treatment, to be decided by an independent tribunal. Flamininus was not prepared to compromise, however, and named the Thessalians as the first people who should be freed, no doubt in an attempt to stir hopes in the breasts of the anti-Macedonians there. But Thessaly had been a satellite of Macedon for 125 years; Philip stormed away from the meeting.

Flamininus must have expected this result. If Philip had accepted Flamininus's demands, he would be acknowledging the right of the Romans to dictate the future of Greece. In his eyes, this would be an abdication of responsibility and an irreparable blow to his dignity. And Flamininus's demands represented a considerable escalation. The envoys' conditions in 200 were that Philip should refrain from making further war in Greece; now Flamininus was looking not just to the future, but to the past as well. Philip was to "free" all the Greek states that had ever come under his control; he was to evacuate Greece altogether. If Flamininus had been prepared to compromise, and repeat the envoys' demands, the war could have been over right then. But that was not enough for an ambitious young man in search of glory. The Senate had sent him out with no more than a vague commission, to bring Philip to heel. Flamininus was free to interpret this as he desired, knowing that the Senate would be happy with any solution that allowed them to concentrate for the time being on the Po valley.

THE BATTLE AT THE AOUS NARROWS

With the breakdown of negotiations, battle became unavoidable. Flamininus outnumbered Philip. He could either attempt to advance towards Macedon, being harried all the way, or he could try to drive Philip from his position. He chose the latter course, but the prospect cannot have looked hopeful. Philip was well entrenched, and had placed men and artillery on the flanks of the magnificent, steep slopes that rise to either side of the gorge up to 2,000 meters or more.

At first, the fighting was indecisive. But then—in an echo of the famous battle at Thermopylae in 480 BCE—Flamininus was informed about a back route, up and over the mountains. He sent a strong force off and waited, resting his men. Once the others were in place, behind and above the enemy, Flamininus advanced—it was about June 25, 198[4] —and the Macedonians fled to avoid being trapped front and rear when the Roman troops on the top of the mountain came down behind them.

Twice the gorge narrows even further, until it is pretty much filled by the river bed alone (see Fig. 5.1). The fighting must have been terrible. But at least the terrain worked in Philip's favor, in the sense that Flamininus could not easily chase the Macedonians as they fled, and so the slaughter was not too severe, limited to about 2,000 men. Philip rallied his men at the eastern end of the gorge and returned to Macedon via northern Thessaly, while Flamininus's troops plundered his camp. Philip left strong garrisons on the route, in case Flamininus should

FIGURE 5.1
The Aous Narrows, showing one of the narrowest spots through which Flamininus's legions drove Philip V's troops. The milky-blue water must have been running red.

follow immediately, and also destroyed towns, villages, and farmland as he went, preferring to risk the anger of his subjects rather than leave Flamininus provisions.

But Flamininus did not follow immediately. He had only just arrived in Greece, and there was still preliminary work to do. He wanted to make sure of the Epirote League, not just because he did not want to leave it as an enemy in his rear when he advanced east, but because he wanted to secure the final route from the west coast toward Macedon. In the north, his Dardanian friends controlled the northern end of the Axius valley approach to Macedon, via Bylazora. In Illyris, the Romans already commanded the future Via Egnatia to the north of the Prespa Lakes, and the long mountainous route to their south (Galba's route in 199), but there was also a fourth route, short but difficult, from Ambracia across the Pindus mountains to Gomphi, where the two main passes through the mountains of Athamania reached the Thessalian plain. The campaign was coordinated with Amynander and the Aetolians, who ravaged western Thessaly and secured Gomphi for him.

Once Flamininus was assured of the neutrality of the Epirotes, he retraced his steps and took the same route Philip had taken to retreat to Macedon, mopping up the Macedonian garrisons on the way, and linking up with Amynander in western Thessaly. Philip's scorched-earth policy no longer bothered him. Thanks to the cooperation of the Epirotes, his supply vessels moved from Illyris to Ambracia, and Gomphi became a major depot for the Romans and their allies. Philip restricted himself to sorties to relieve fortresses, but avoided pitched battle.

After employing the usual terrorist tactics to cow the local Thessalian population into submission, Flamininus was humiliatingly held up by the siege of a single fortress, Atrax, and in September 198 he decided to put an end to his Macedonian campaign for the year. There was still an important line of communication to secure before the year was out: he wanted Anticyra. He stormed into Phocis and forced the surrender of town after town, including Anticyra and Elatea, until he had gained most of Phocis and eastern Locris. Elatea became Flamininus's headquarters in central Greece. His brother Lucius had already made the area safer by driving Macedonian garrisons from Eretria and Carystus in Euboea (Eretria was also looted of its "statues and paintings of ancient workmanship"), though Philip still held Chalcis.[5]

From Elatea, and later from Corinth, Flamininus acted almost as a Hellenistic king. Most remarkably, shortly after 197 he issued, or allowed to be issued, a series of gold coins (very few remain), bearing his image in the place where one would expect to find a king or a god (see Fig. 5.2); it would be 150 years before another living Roman—Julius Caesar—dared to be so presumptuous. Hellenistic kings had been doing so for about 100 years, however, and Flamininus, clearly aware of Greek practices, was taking a leaf from their book, displaying his power, wherever these coins circulated, in a fashion Greeks would understand.

Moreover, he constantly dealt with Greek leaders in a regal manner. In 191, for instance, he gently chided the current general of the Achaean League for failing to consult him before undertaking a campaign, and a short while later told the Aetolians that he had been divinely appointed to take care of Greece.[6] As the years rolled by and his commission in Greece was extended, this expectation of obedience became more pronounced. But this was not unusual: Roman consuls acted like kings out in the field because they almost were. The *imperium* they were granted in their provinces was nearly absolute, given that they could not consult the distant Senate; they relied on their staff officers and legates to deliberate and

FIGURE 5.2

An extremely rare gold stater in the name of T. Quinctius Flamininus, for use in Greece. Note, then, the Latin legend, an assertion of cultural dominance. It was unknown at this period for a Roman to put his head in the place on a coin reserved for gods or kings.

ratify their decisions. The Senate's knowledge of geographical and political factors abroad was often sketchy, and it could take several weeks for a question to reach them, and several more weeks for their reply. They often relied on the ad hoc decisions made by their commanders in the field.

With or without the Senate's immediate approval consuls and proconsuls founded colonies; made kings; had enormous armies at their plenipotentiary disposal; could demand further troops from their friends and allies; sent and received embassies; dealt as equals with kings; destroyed cities and enslaved populations; set the terms of peace treaties; issued edicts, and had the right to reward obedience or punish disobedience. When Polybius came to describe the Roman constitution, he likened consuls to monarchs. An envoy of Pyrrhus compared the Senate to kings meeting in council. The Greek word for consul, *hypatos*, means "highest."[7] Sometimes, the easiest way for Flamininus and others to slot into Greek categories was to present themselves as kings, even though they could not of course achieve the longevity of a king's reign since they would soon be recalled to Rome. Again, Flamininus's coinage is remarkable: he was expecting, and he received, a prolonged stay in Greece.

TWO COUPS FOR FLAMININUS

Not long before Flamininus overran Phocis and Locris toward the end of 198, the Achaeans held a fateful meeting at Sicyon. One by one the delegates got up and spoke; Lucius Flamininus was there, supported by Pergamene and Athenian delegations, and Philip's men too were allowed their say. The speeches and deliberations took the entire three days allowed by the Achaean constitution for such a meeting, and it was a very close call. Three member states even walked out of the meeting, refusing to have anything to do with breaking ties with Macedon; but in the end the Achaeans voted to become allies immediately of Rhodes and Pergamum, and to send envoys to the Senate to begin negotiating an alliance with Rome as well.

The Romans had done it: Philip lost the Achaeans, who for twenty-five years had been the spine of the Common Alliance. Certainly, fear of the consequences of making enemies of the Romans was the stick, but there was also a carrot: we will help you drive the Macedonians from Corinth and the Peloponnese. Alliance with Rome, rather than Macedon, now seemed a better way to achieve their constant goal of unifying the Peloponnese. But if the prospect of recovering Corinth was what had tipped the scales, they were to be disappointed in the short term: an attempt on Corinth followed the meeting, but failed. Acrocorinth is a very formidable target (see Fig. 5.3).

But the town of Argos, one of those that had walked out of the meeting, immediately seceded from the Achaean League and entrusted itself to Philip (whose first wife was the daughter of a noble Argive house). Philip decided to give the town and its considerable territory to Nabis of Sparta, hoping to strengthen the hand of the man who was now his main ally in the Peloponnese. But before long Nabis used his position of strength—his control over much of the eastern Peloponnese—to convince the Romans to take him as a friend, not an enemy. This was a canny move by Nabis, since it simultaneously ended his war with the Achaeans, now his allies, and protected him against retaliation by Philip, who had already received numerous complaints from his friends in Argos about the constitutional changes Nabis was imposing upon

FIGURE 5.3
The Acrocorinth dominates the Isthmus joining the Peloponnese to mainland Greece and was a formidable obstacle for all pre-modern armies. Its possession made Corinth one of the "Fetters" of Greece.

them, and even before this treachery had been regretting giving Nabis the city. Partly because he needed troops elsewhere, and partly because they were now in danger, Philip removed the last of his Peloponnesian garrisons, except for the one at Corinth, which was reinforced.

In the meantime, Philip contacted Flamininus for a meeting; it was perhaps his last chance to negotiate peace on halfway favorable terms: this was in the interval between the Achaeans' joining the Romans and Nabis's following their lead. The place chosen for the meeting in November 198 was Nicaea, on the south coast of the Maliac Gulf. In a time-honored practice, Philip remained offshore, seated at the stern of his ship, while Flamininus and the representatives of the allies arrayed themselves on the strand. Philip invited Flamininus to speak first, and the Roman consul listed his demands, which again represent an escalation even over what he had said at the Aous conference, let alone over the envoys' original message. Now Flamininus was demanding not only that Philip completely evacuate Greece, but also return to Pleuratus those parts of Illyris that he had captured subsequent to the Peace of Phoenice in 205, and return to Ptolemy V all the Egyptian possessions he had taken since the death of Ptolemy IV in 204. Then Flamininus's allies spoke one by one, listing their own grievances and the reparations that would assuage them, such as the return of their Peraea to the Rhodians and the removal of all Philip's Aegean and Hellespontine garrisons, the return of Perinthus to Byzantium, and so on. Evacuation—that is, the dismantlement of the new Macedonian empire—was now the common demand of all the allies.

Philip showed himself prepared to make concessions, but continued to argue, as he had on the bank of the Aous, that his possessions fell into different categories and so should be treated differently. The first day ended with no resolution. On the second day, Philip increased his concessions, but still balked at the insistence on a general evacuation. On the third day, the full convention met at nearby Thronium. It was agreed that all should send representatives to Rome to state their various cases, and Philip was granted an armistice of two months for this to take place, on condition that he immediately evacuate Phocis and Locris (not that much of them was left to him by now).

The speeches the allies delivered to the Senate early in 197 were so similar that they must have been scripted by Flamininus. The delegates not only complained bitterly of their losses (as they had at Nicaea), but this time they all focused specifically on the three Fetters of Greece, insisting that Greece could never be free as long as Corinth, Chalcis, and Demetrias were in Philip's hands. They argued that even all the rest of his concessions amounted to nothing if he still held the Fetters. Philip's representatives were accordingly asked, no doubt by senatorial friends of Flamininus, whether the king would evacuate the Fetters, but the king had given them no definite instructions on that score.

Negotiations foundered, then, and the Senate could only continue the war. The speeches of the Greek envoys had convinced the Senate that Flamininus was the man for the job, so, rather than send out one of the consuls for 197 to replace him, his command was extended. Philip's evacuation of Greece had become identified with the slogan of freeing the Greeks from the fetters that bound them. The vague general protection that the envoys of 200 offered the Greeks had evolved into a call for their freedom from Macedonian rule.

THE BATTLE OF CYNOSCEPHALAE

Philip had a strong defensive position in Macedon, but the Acarnanians and Boeotians were his last remaining allies in Greece. Flamininus's first task in 197 was to separate them from Philip. He assigned his brother Lucius the Acarnanians, and took the Boeotians for himself.

The Boeotian League had become seriously divided over the issue of whether to side with Macedon or Rome. Flamininus needed to make sure they saw things his way. He approached Thebes, the main city of the league, with Attalus of Pergamum and only a few retainers, but with 2,000 armed men following out of sight a little way behind. He and Attalus were formally greeted, as was the custom, by the local dignitaries. No doubt flowery speeches were delivered and even Brachylles, the leader of the anti-Roman faction, played his diplomatic part in this ritual occasion alongside his rival Zeuxippus and others. Then Flamininus walked with them toward the city gate, engaging them in conversation and gradually decreasing his speed to allow his troops to catch up, while the city gates were still open.

The Roman armed presence in the city guaranteed an outcome to the Boeotians' deliberations that would be favorable to Rome—not that they had much choice, anyway, since they were completely isolated—and not surprisingly, one after another, the cities of the league voted for friendship with Rome. The drama of the occasion was considerably enhanced by the fact that, in the course of his speech to the Boeotians, encouraging them to come over to Rome, Attalus suffered a stroke and had to be stretchered out of the meeting. He was taken back to Pergamum, where he soon died, and was succeeded by his son Eumenes II, then in his mid-twenties. Eumenes inherited his father's friendship with Rome, on which Pergamene prosperity was now predicated.

Roman diplomacy was continuing to be highly effective. With the expulsion of the anti-Romans from Boeotia—Brachylles and his friends found refuge in Macedon, of course—almost all Greece was in Roman or neutral hands, all the way up to Thessaly. In Caria and the Rhodian Peraea, the Rhodians, with Achaean help, were recovering some of the places Philip had taken in 202–200. But the Rhodians had a different task in this last year of the war. Antiochus, having settled his new gains in Coele Syria, was advancing along the southern coastline of Asia Minor with a huge army and navy, seizing Ptolemaic possessions as he went. The Rhodians ordered him not to proceed past the Chelidoniae Islands of Lycia—something they would never had dared to do without the implied backing of the Romans, whose support over this issue suggests that they were already wary of the Syrian king, thinking perhaps that he might be intending to link up again with Philip. Antiochus protested, but the affair was overtaken by the end of the war, at which point Rhodes withdrew its demand and the king continued on his conquering way.

Over the winter, Philip enlarged his army by recruiting and training youths and old men—never a good sign—and in the spring of 197 he advanced south, but halted near Pherae at the appearance of Roman scouts. After concluding his business in Boeotia, Flamininus had marched rapidly north with his full army (two legions, supplemented by Aetolians, Athamanians, and others) of over thirty thousand, outnumbering Philip by several thousands. No doubt at the instigation of the Aetolians, he tried to bully Phthiotic Thebes into surrender, but to no avail. He advanced past Demetrias—a critical advance, denying Philip the resources of Thebes and Demetrias—and made camp on the plain near Pherae. It was scouts from this camp that Philip's men encountered. Until then, neither commander had known the other was so close.

Philip tried but failed to force his way through to Demetrias, where he had granaries. The unsuitability of the terrain near Pherae for a phalanx operation, and his need for provisions, forced him to turn west. Flamininus trailed him, at least partly to make sure that this was not a feint—that Philip was not going to turn back to Demetrias—and set up camp on a low hill, where there was a shrine to the sea deity Thetis, the mother of Achilles, and where there were (and still are) springs (see Fig. 5.4). The night passed. Philip's camp lay to the north of Flamininus's. Each knew that the other was close—but no more than that, because

FIGURE 5.4

A spring with a Turkish inscription at Zoodokhos Pigi, Thessaly. The spring was within Flamininus's camp before the battle of Cynoscephalae in 197 BCE

torrential rain, followed by a thick mist, severely reduced visibility. At dawn, Philip sent a squadron of cavalry forward to a ridge, to wait for the mist to clear.

The name of the ridge was Cynoscephalae, "Dog-heads."[8] As Philip's men were waiting there in the slowly dispersing mist, a squadron of Flamininus's cavalry, out on patrol, stumbled upon them. This small engagement rapidly developed into a general battle, as more and more men emerged from their camps to join in. Philip had the advantage of the higher ground, and his troops pushed the Romans down on to more level ground; but there, thanks largely to the courage of the Aetolian contingent, they were able to make a stand. The Aetolians fought hard because this was the battle that was supposed to deliver their long-desired prize, hegemony in Greece.

Flamininus now had his whole army deployed, while a good number of Philip's men were still on their way. While the cavalry divisions of both armies were engaged with one another, Flamininus sent his left legion forward, but Philip's phalangites pushed them back again down the slope, and it looked as though they were going to crumble. Abandoning hope there, Flamininus led his right legion around and up to the top of the hill where Philip's troops were still arriving and too disorganized to put up much resistance. At the same time, about 2,000 men from this right legion peeled off to take the victorious Macedonian phalangites further down the hill in the rear. Before long, it was all over: 8,000 of Philip's men lay dead, with another 5,000 taken prisoner. Roman losses came to 800. It was a decisive defeat.

A few years later, with the Macedonian dead at Cynoscephalae still unburied, Philip's poetic enemy, Alcaeus of Messene, impugned the courage of the Macedonian king in the form of a fake epitaph for the fallen troops (whose number he greatly exaggerated):

> Unwept and unburied, traveller, on this ridge
> Of Thessaly we lie, thirty thousand of us,
> Brought low by Ares of the Aetolians,
> And by the Latins led by Titus from the plains of Italy
> To bring great woe to Macedon. Philip's boldness has fled,
> Passing quicker than a shy-footed deer.

To his credit, Philip responded with his own mocking couplet:

> Unbarked and unleaved, traveller, planted on this ridge
> A cross of crucifixion looms, awaiting Alcaeus.[9]

THE TEMPE CONFERENCE

So the Second Macedonian War was over, and the bargaining began. At more or less the same time as Cynoscephalae, the Achaeans defeated Philip's Corinthian garrison in battle, and the Acarnanians surrendered to Lucius Flamininus. With what was happening in Caria, it really was all over for Philip, and he contacted Flamininus for a meeting. Flamininus agreed, and so brought an end to the fighting. But that displeased the Aetolians, who spread the rumor that Flamininus must have been bribed, otherwise he would have continued and crushed Philip completely. They were doing their best to aggravate Flamininus: in what he could only see as a personal attack on his glory, they were claiming responsibility for the victory, and they had pillaged Philip's camp at Cynoscephalae for their own profit, even while their allies were still mopping up the enemy. The Aetolians thought they would now take over the reins of Greece; Flamininus saw that as a Roman job. As Polybius says, the quarrel "contained the seeds of great evil for Greece."[10]

The day before the start of the conference, which was to take place at Gonni, at the entrance of the beautiful Vale of Tempe, Flamininus called a meeting of the allies to find out their expectations. Much of the meeting was taken up by acrimonious argument between the Aetolians and Flamininus. The Aetolians insisted that the only way to secure peace for Greece in the future was to depose Philip, to end the Macedonian monarchy. Flamininus disagreed, arguing that Philip should be left in place because, as was well known, Macedon served as a bulwark for Greece against marauding tribes from the north. It was therefore in the Greeks' best interests for Philip to be left in place.

When Phaeneas, the Aetolian representative, pushed on, Flamininus bluntly told him to shut up. The decision would be up to Flamininus (and the Senate), not the Aetolians, or any other Greek. But he promised to leave Philip with so little power that he would never again be able to harm the Greeks. The illogic of his position was glaring: if Philip was strong enough to resist barbarian incursions from the north, would he not be strong enough to harm Greeks as well? Why not demolish the monarchy and find some other way to guard the northern borders? What Flamininus did not say, though no doubt everyone present understood it well enough, was that a prime reason for leaving Philip in place was to prevent the Aetolians growing too strong. A balance of powers in Greece was Flamininus's goal.

The next day, when Philip arrived, he immediately showed himself willing to accept in full the demands the allies had made at Nicaea the previous November—the full evacuation of Greece and Illyris, restoring to Egypt everything he had gained from it since 204, and reparations to the allies—and to submit all other issues to the Roman Senate. Sensing weakness, Phaeneas added four cities in Achaea Phthiotis, picking these places because they had been lost to Aetolia relatively recently and had been held by them for a relatively long time. Philip, totally crushed, said they could have them—but Flamininus intervened. They could have Phthiotic Thebes, he said, but the other three places had surrendered to Rome. Phaeneas angrily slammed down his trump card: by the terms of the alliance of 211, the Romans were supposed to get only movable property, not actual towns. Flamininus replied that, when the Aetolians had made a separate peace with Philip in 206, they had dissolved the 211 alliance.

At bottom, Flamininus's argument was moral: by making a separate treaty in 206, the Aetolians had shown themselves to be no true friends of Rome, and therefore Flamininus did not feel obliged to treat them as friends. A fragment of the actual treaty of 211 seems to suggest that he was wrong to distinguish between towns that had surrendered to Rome and others: they were all due to be given to the Aetolians.[11] But the fundamental question was whether or not the 211 treaty was still in force— whether it was intended to be a permanent treaty, or specific only to the First Macedonian War. If it was context-specific, Flamininus was on solid ground—but if it was context-specific, why did he not say just that, which would have been a knock-down argument? But the terms of the 211 treaty do seem very specific, and on balance Flamininus was probably right, in strict legal terms. It is also perfectly clear, however, that he was doing nothing to heal the rift between himself and the Aetolians.

Flamininus's authority as Roman commander outgunned the Aetolians, and the terms of the peace that were subsequently ratified in Rome were fundamentally dictated by him. They were as harsh as he had promised the allies. Macedon was reduced to the level of 150 years earlier. All its possessions south of Mount Olympus, west of the Prespa Lakes, and east of the Nestus river were given up—including, then, the three Fetters of Greece, Thessaly, Lissus, and all Philip's gains in the Aegean, Hellespont, and Caria. The Greeks were to live "free and according to their own laws." Philip had to pay 200 talents immediately, out of a total indemnity of 1,000 talents,[12] and send hostages to Rome. The hostages included his 11-year-old son Demetrius. Both money and hostages were to be returned if the Roman people did not ratify the terms—which they did, early in 196, adding that Flamininus was to write to Prusias about liberating Cius, and that Philip's garrisons were to be removed and prisoners repatriated by the time of the Isthmian Games at Corinth in the spring. Flamininus would use the games to announce his provisions for Greece's future.[13]

THE ISTHMIAN DECLARATION

The Dardanians, naturally, took advantage of Philip's discomfiture to invade northern Macedon, and repelling them was the king's first order of business after the peace talks. Flamininus, meanwhile, found himself unexpectedly further embroiled in Boeotian affairs. As a gesture of good-will, he had allowed Brachylles and the other Boeotian exiles to return, even though they had fought on Philip's side in the war—but contrary to his expectations the Boeotians immediately reinstated Brachylles as one of their leaders and re-opened lines of communication with Philip. Zeuxippus and the other leaders of the pro-Roman party persuaded Flamininus that Boeotia would never be secure, from a Roman point of view, as long as Brachylles remained alive. Flamininus said, like Pontius Pilate, that he could not be directly involved, and told Zeuxippus to get in touch with the Aetolians, experts at arranging such things. Brachylles was assassinated by an Aetolian hit squad, and Boeotia descended into chaos. In the course of the disturbances, a number of off-duty Roman soldiers were killed, and Flamininus restored order by force.

The Senate sent out ten distinguished legates, including Galba and Villius, to Elatea to confirm the peace terms and help Flamininus with his settlement of Greece; there were literally dozens of outstanding petitions along the lines of whether the Achaeans or the Messenians should be awarded Pylos, adding to the turmoil of the times, and hundreds or thousands of private suits for reclaiming land or something.[14] They could handle only the major cases themselves, but they needed to set up structures and systems for the rest; they did well to get it all done within two years. No doubt they received local help along the way, but the Romans' assumption was that they had the right to dictate the future.

One of the main things they had to think about was Antiochus, who was continuing to storm through virtually defenseless Asia Minor, and had by now reached the Hellespont, where he had taken Abydus, for instance. Two Asiatic Greek cities, Lampsacus and Smyrna, had opportunistically appealed to Flamininus and the Senate to be specifically included in the treaty with Philip, in an attempt to force the Romans to commit themselves to their protection. Nothing came of this in the short term, but the appeal, on top of a complaint by Attalus in 198, served to keep Asia Minor and Antiochus in senatorial minds, and they promised, vaguely, to help in the future.[15] Lampsacus sweetened its appeal by claiming kinship, via Trojan ancestry, with Rome (putatively founded by Aeneas of Troy), and the people of Smyrna, even while under siege, instituted the worship of the goddess Roma, the first to do so: she was not a Roman deity but a personification of Rome for non-Romans. The cult then spread fairly rapidly through Asia Minor and beyond, as communities saw the advantages of deference to Rome.[16]

Although Antiochus remained officially a friend of Rome,[17] the Romans had been wary of him ever since his secret pact with Philip, and their influence now extended into Asia Minor. Indeed, at the Nicaea conference and in the final settlement, they had made sure of that extension, so that when the ten legates arrived in Greece, one of their stipulations was that all Greeks in Asia as well as Europe were to be free. But Antiochus considered Asia Minor his own domain by right of inheritance, and he was determined to exclude others. No sooner had the Romans defused one tense situation than another loomed. But this would never have happened if they had not committed themselves to involvement in Greece; without that involvement Antiochus's doings were more or less irrelevant. The Romans felt that they could not consistently champion the freedom of one set of Greek communities without the other.

As news spread around Greece of the contents of the settlement, the Aetolians continued their attack. They argued, by letter and at meetings, that it looked as though the Romans were planning to take over the garrisoning of cities in Greece, and especially the Fetters, themselves. This was not freedom for the Greeks, but the replacement of one master with another. And the Aetolians had pinpointed an ambiguity: the purpose of the war had been to humiliate and contain Philip, and so the first meaning of "Greek freedom" was just freedom from Macedonian hegemony. Did Flamininus's announcement also mean freedom from Roman hegemony? The subtext of the Aetolians' complaint was: leave Greece to the Greeks—that is, to us.

The Aetolians were right to push this issue, because, while the Senate had given the legates clear instructions on how to proceed in other cases, it had left it up to them to decide on the spot what to do about the Fetters. If they felt that Antiochus was or soon would be enough of a threat to Roman interests in Greece, then perhaps the Roman garrisons should be retained in the Fetters, and Oreus and Eretria, also currently garrisoned by the Romans, should be given to their loyal ally Eumenes—securing Euboea and the east coast of Greece, where Antiochus would come, if he came.

In response to the Aetolians' accusations, Flamininus made the final escalation. His instructions so far were to free Greece from Macedonian dominion; he would go one step further, proving the envoys of 200 right in portraying Rome as the common benefactor of Greece. The only way, he argued, to convince the Greeks that the Romans were truly their benefactors, and to check the Aetolians, was to follow the evacuation of

Macedonian garrisons with the withdrawal of Roman garrisons from the Fetters and everywhere else. The legates, his advisory council, agreed. Flamininus may have been making it all up as he went along, riding the waves of Greek responses to his ideas, but the legates recognized that he had found a powerful tool.

Flamininus picked the Isthmian Games of spring 196 for his proclamation. Like all the major games of Greece (such as, most famously, those at Olympia), the festival was attended by people from all over the Greek world. It was a holiday, a time of celebration, entertainment, and worship. It also made a suitable venue for major public announcements, and anticipation was running high this year. This was not an occasion that any notable from any Greek city could afford to miss.

The Isthmian Declaration was short and to the point: "The Roman Senate and Titus Quinctius, general and consul, having conquered King Philip and the Macedonians, leave free, ungarrisoned, untaxed, and autonomous the Corinthians, Phocians, Locrians, Euboeans, Phthiotic Achaeans, Magnesians, Thessalians, and Perrhaebians"—that is, everywhere that had formerly been under Macedonian hegemony, and/or had been members of the Macedonian Common Alliance.[18]

For all its patronizing assumption that Greek freedom was Rome's to give or withhold, the assembled Greeks greeted this announcement with rapture: at a stroke, they had gained their freedom, lost to them since the Macedonian conquest almost 150 years earlier. If the declaration meant what it said, even the Fetters would be ungarrisoned. The Greeks had been expecting the Romans, as the victors, more or less to step into the masterful shoes of Macedon.[19] Instead, they were promising to leave the country as soon as they could, and let the Greeks get on with their lives. Flamininus's political philhellenism (to distinguish it from his doubtful personal philhellenism) had now become official senatorial doctrine.[20] Flamininus was mobbed at the festival, and over the next few weeks and months was showered with honors from grateful cities.[21] And in Rome the Senate decreed five days of thanksgiving for the victory at Cynoscephalae. Flamininus's stock had never been higher.[22]

Flamininus and the legates next began to implement the details. So thorough was their re-organization of Greece—the substitution of structures amenable to Rome for those the Macedonians had put in place—that it was as though they were making up for their relative lack of intervention before. The basic tactic was simply to ensure that local elites and pro-Roman factions were in power, but more radical changes were imposed too. Thessaly, so badly ravaged in the war, was now broken up: Dolopia was given to the Aetolians; Perrhaebia and Magnesia became independent leagues, and the rest of Thessaly, including Achaea Phthiotis, was formed into a third confederacy. This would make it less easy for either the Macedonians or the Aetolians to effect a takeover of Thessaly in the future.

The independence of Orestis, which had risen in revolt against Macedon shortly after Cynoscephalae, was recognized. The entity called "Macedon," like modern India, was a land empire forged by annexation, and was always therefore potentially unstable if the center became too weak to support the interests of the outlying cantons. Orestis, on the border of Epirus, was merely the canton that was currently least satisfied with being part of Macedon. Further south, Phocis and eastern Locris were given to the Aetolians (prompting Flamininus to move his headquarters from Elatea to the Acrocorinth). Achaea gained Corinth and Triphylia, edging closer to total domination of the Peloponnese. The cities of Euboea were formed into a league. Finally, though his contribution had been slight, Pleuratus's loyalty was rewarded: he gained the Parthini and, more importantly, Lychnitis, a canton of Macedon for almost two hundred years.

Naturally, the new power-possessors of Greece felt properly grateful to Rome for their elevation, and that was the point of the legates' work: Greece was now in the hands of a number of states, none of which greatly outweighed any of the others, and they were, mostly, indebted to Rome and would therefore maintain contact with the Senate. For by now the habit of sending emissaries to Rome to consult over every major policy decision that might affect it was well engrained in the Greek states. Greece could therefore be controlled from a distance, with no further commitment of armed forces. The promised withdrawal could safely take place. This was a triumph for Flamininus and for Roman aggression.

GREEK FREEDOM?

The legates then went their separate ways in Greece and Asia Minor, supervising the fulfillment of their orders—advising, chastising, and fixing Roman authority deeper into Greek soil. The overall goal of their work, as it emerged, was to preserve the coalition of states they had developed in Greece without letting any one state outweigh the others. The Achaeans' gains, for instance, re-established them as the most potent force in the Peloponnese, while with their gains in Phocis and Locris the Aetolians were left strong, but not overbearingly so, in central Greece. The freedom of the Greeks from Macedon was reinforced by making it harder for any Greek state to gain dominion over others; dominance was a Roman prerogative now.

The point of the Second Macedonian War had been to break Philip's power. The Romans came and succeeded in doing just that. Flamininus's proclamation at the Isthmian festival was in the first place a shout of victory: job done! But it is hard to resist the idea that it was also a cynical maneuver. A glimpse only a few years ahead shows him working alongside men who were opposed to a policy of evacuation, suggesting either that he had come to see that the policy had failed, or that he was not sincere in the first place. Another glance ahead shows that, after the defeat of Antiochus, talk of Greek freedom died away, suggesting not only (again) that the policy had failed, but also that one of its original purposes had just been to strengthen Greece against Antiochus. Moreover, the final escalation of the slogan into absolute freedom for the Greeks appears to have been a response to the Aetolians' damaging rehearsal of the propaganda of the First Macedonian War, that the Romans had come to enslave the Greeks. It was not the case that Flamininus, as a philhellene, arrived in Greece wanting to see the Greeks free and determined to find a way to do it; he developed the slogan as a way to shut the Aetolians up and keep the Greeks happy.[23]

A moment's reflection shows the hypocrisy of the Roman position. It is not just that there were Greek cities in Sicily and southern Italy whose freedom was being trampled on daily by the Romans, but also that Flamininus and the legates applied the freedom policy erratically in Greece itself. The cities were to be free, autonomous, and ungarrisoned—except for Aegina, for instance, and Andros. Why did the Senate make a fuss about Cius and not about them? Clearly, other factors could easily take precedence over Greek freedom, in these cases the need to keep Eumenes happy, their chief informant against Antiochus. Or, if the Greeks were to direct their own affairs, why did Flamininus connive at the assassination of Brachylles? People at the time were aware that the Romans were being hypocritical; at any rate, Livy has one of Antiochus's agents talk of their using "the specious pretext of liberating Greek states."[24] The freedom doctrine was followed not as being in the Greeks' best interests, but because it suited the Romans best.

Furthermore, given an impending struggle with Antiochus and the rift with the Aetolians, Greece was almost bound to become a battleground again, and then the freedom policy would be overtaken by the necessity to garrison cities and bend them once again to Roman aims. Most importantly, however, and most subtly, the freedom of the Greeks was a sham because of Roman authority there. Flamininus had no intention of abandoning Greece, and would not make himself popular at home if he did so. He meant that there would be no Roman military presence in Greece, and no formal or institutional power. Roman authority was another matter, and Greek connivance at the Roman reorganization of their states, and the stream of embassies that made their way from Greece to Rome over the succeeding years, proved its strength. They removed their troops, but they did not cut back their interventions in the Greek world, and every such intervention increased their future obligations until disengagement was out of the question. The success of this hands-off approach in Illyris had encouraged the Romans to extend it to all Greece. The whole point of the war had been to make Rome the dominant power in European Greece.

The Romans wanted to be major players in the Greek world without being drawn into colonialism; they wanted political control without administrative control, just as over recent decades the USA has avoided the structures of empire while ensuring a widespread hegemony. Flamininus had discovered a powerful diplomatic instrument, and he lost no opportunity to boast of his achievement. When, after Cynoscephalae, he made a dedicatory offering of some silver bucklers and his own war shield, he had the following words inscribed:[25]

O sons of Zeus, who delight in feats of swift horsemanship,
O Tyndaridae, lords of Sparta, Titus, descended from Aeneas,
Has made the best of all possible gifts to you,
By fashioning freedom for the sons of Greece.

The dedication to the Tyndaridae (perhaps better known as Castor and Polydeuces/Pollux, the Heavenly Twins) was made at Delphi, one of the most important religious centers of the Greek world. As the home of Apollo's famous oracle, Flamininus's dedication, boasting of the good he had done the Greeks, would be seen by countless dignitaries on their visits to Delphi as representatives of their cities for official consultation of the oracle or attendance at some festival. But it was cynical, because his first concerns had always been his own good and that of Rome. He showed the Romans how to pursue their traditional policy of imperialist expansion while seeming to be the benefactors of those they came to control.

Even the withdrawal of Roman troops was little more than an exercise in public relations. In the first place, the Romans had forcefully demonstrated their ability and will to return if they felt it necessary, and the determination with which they prosecuted the Second Macedonian War proved that what had looked before like indifference was actually prioritizing their engagement with the Carthaginians. In the second place, seasonal warfare was still the norm. Armies would appear in spring, fight, and disappear back home or to winter quarters in the autumn. Given the Romans' proven ability to bring large armies to Greece, the withdrawal of their troops would be felt as part of this normal military rhythm, so that departure would be understood as a temporary measure, a comma not a full stop. It did not carry the emotional baggage that "evacuation" does nowadays.

The future of all Greece lay more or less entirely in Roman hands for the first time. It had taken thirty-three years from when they had first set a military foot on Illyrian soil in 229. The legates left Greece a more stable entity, but only in the short term. Since one of their basic strategies had generally been to support local elites and pro-Roman factions, the settlement was bound in at least some cases to set up resentment and an unstable dynamic for the future. Social harmony for the Romans depended on the subservience of the masses to the elite; despite all their talk of freedom, they had little use for democracy. In reality, Greek freedom meant that the Greeks were free to serve Rome's interests.

6.

THE ROAD TO THERMOPYLAE

IF ANYONE EXPECTED CYNOSCEPHALAE and the Isthmian Declaration to settle the eastern Mediterranean, they were wrong. In fact, over the next few years the crisis grew until, having reduced one Hellenistic king, Rome did the same, far more effectively, to another, and at the same time subdued one of the great Greek leagues. By the early 180s, Rome was the sole remaining superpower not just in Greece, but in the Hellenistic Mediterranean. Gone were the glories that were Carthage, Macedon, Syria, and Egypt. The last was moribund from internal causes, but the other three were reduced by Rome.

POSTURING FOR POSITION

Antiochus sent senior and trusted men to represent him at the Isthmian Declaration in 196; they went to Corinth to congratulate Flamininus on his victory over Philip and to assure him of the king's peaceful intentions. But the Roman legates gave them a stern message to take back to their master, an implied threat, sanctioned by the Senate: Antiochus was to keep his hands off Greek cities, withdraw his garrisons from those he had just taken from Ptolemy and Philip, and not attempt a crossing to Greece, since he had no reason for doing so. There was no state in Greece that needed to be protected or freed by him; the Romans had it all in hand. Energized into aggression by the rapturous reception of the proclamation, the Romans were posing as the common benefactors of all Greeks everywhere, and preempting the possibility that, with Philip crushed,

Antiochus would take on the role of Greek champion. And they clearly felt they now had the right, and the firepower, not just to intervene in Asia Minor, but to curb the king of Syria, the greatest king in the known world. After all, they had just crushed the second greatest.

Later in the year, three of the Roman legates found Antiochus at Lysimachea, whose former glory he was restoring; it had been abandoned by Philip during the Second Macedonian War, when he needed to consolidate his forces, and then looted and burned by Thracians, but Antiochus had already designated it as the future residence of his second son, Seleucus, about twenty years old at the time. The significance of this was that Lysimachea, on the Thracian Chersonese (the modern Gallipoli peninsula), was in Europe, not Asia, so that Antiochus was planting one of the major cities of his empire beyond his traditional boundaries; he was also in the process of forcing the other communities of the Chersonese to accept his garrisons, to further strengthen his European bridgehead.

At the same time, he was making no secret of his intention to take over all southern and western Asia Minor, traditional Seleucid territory; he must have seen even his arrangements with Rhodes and Pergamum as temporary measures (and, knowing this, they became his unremitting enemies). He already had a larger empire than any Seleucid ruler since Seleucus I himself, and was clearly hoping to present it to Rome as something they would have to live with. But the legates had just spent the past few weeks "freeing" (that is, removing Philip's garrisons from) places like Bargylia and Thasos, which Antiochus certainly intended to add to his empire—Bargylia had been the last place in Asia Minor with a Macedonian garrison—and he still had Lampsacus and Smyrna under siege, which, even if vaguely, had been promised Roman support.

At Lysimachea, the Romans repeated their earlier demands, but also raised the question of his intentions. Why had he established this bridgehead in Europe? It looked very much as though he wanted to provoke the Romans. Antiochus's response was brilliant. First, they had as little right to interfere in his affairs as he had to interfere in Italy—where, he was implying, the Romans also had Greek cities under their imperialist thumb. Second, the places he had taken in Asia and Europe were his by ancestral right; they had been stolen from him or his predecessors by Egypt and Macedon, and he was just taking them back.[1] Third, they had no need to tell him to reconcile with Ptolemy, because he was about to enter into a marriage alliance with him. Then, when envoys from Lampsacus and Smyrna were introduced by the Romans, he preempted them by suggesting that their business should be submitted to the arbitration of the Rhodians, rather than handled by the Romans.[2]

The Romans had come to accuse Antiochus of stirring up war; at a stroke, Antiochus turned things around so that the Romans appeared the aggressors. Following the conference, the Roman envoys returned to Rome to report to the Senate, and Antiochus returned to Antioch. His first business over the winter of 196–195 was to finalize the arrangements for the betrothal of his daughter to Ptolemy V.

In 195 and 194, while the Romans more or less completed crushing the Celts of the Po valley and attempted to pacify Spanish tribes, Antiochus expanded further into Thrace. After his election as one of the consuls for 194, no less a person than Scipio Africanus argued that "Macedon" should be retained as a province for the year, in view of the fact that Antiochus had ignored the Romans' warning. The Senate disagreed; both consuls were needed in northern Italy.

The difference between Africanus (see Fig. 6.1) and Flamininus was slight—just a matter of how obvious the threat of force was to be in Greece. On Flamininus's policy, it was well in the background, muffled by diplomacy and propaganda; if Africanus had won the argument, the Romans would have continued to negotiate, but with an army immediately at their backs. But a majority of the senators preferred, for the time being, to stick with Flamininus's approach. Whenever the conflict with Antiochus came, the gratitude and goodwill of the Greeks would stand them in good stead.

The Senate's commitment to Flamininus's policy is particularly impressive because, at the time of this debate, the end of 195, they had recently gained a further reason to be concerned about Antiochus: Hannibal had arrived in his court. In Carthage he had been trying to undermine the aristocratic faction that was friendly to Rome, but came to fear assassination by Roman agents and fled. Antiochus welcomed him and made him one of his advisers for the coming war against Rome. Hannibal held out

FIGURE 6.1

Scipio Africanus the Elder (a bust of the first century BCE, from the Villa of the Papyri at Herculaneum). Scipio's military genius made him one of the most beloved leaders of the middle Republic, but also a potential threat to the constitution.

some hope of fomenting a rebellion in Carthage and bringing his people in as Antiochus's allies, but the plot was discovered and aborted.

Hannibal was just over fifty years old, and his name could still strike fear into the hearts of all Romans. The weird prophecy with which I ended chapter 3, about a king who would come from Asia to avenge Greek suffering at Roman hands, was read by many Romans as referring to Hannibal, now resident in Asia. Under these circumstances, we should certainly imagine a sharply divided Senate, with Flamininus's friends a narrow majority. In all likelihood, it was the news of Hannibal's arrival in Antiochus's court that got Scipio Africanus, Hannibal's old nemesis, elected to one of the consulships of 194.

EVACUATION POSTPONED

The Romans were indeed conflicted. On the one hand, consistency with their posture as champions of freedom required their swift withdrawal from Greece. On the other hand, there was unrest here and there in Greece, and the threat of Antiochus. The conflict was especially pressing for Flamininus himself at the end of 196. He was unlikely to receive a further extension of his command, beyond the three years he had already enjoyed, unless there was a very good reason for it. If there was further glory to be won in Greece, it had to be found now. But the implication of the Isthmian Declaration was that the Roman evacuation of Greece was imminent.

Nabis of Sparta resolved Flamininus's dilemma. Since the Isthmian Declaration, Flamininus had been putting pressure on Nabis to "free" Argos—to return it to the Achaeans. This is another example of cynical use of the freedom slogan: the real issue was the possibility that Nabis might become a useful ally of Antiochus. Nabis kept refusing to bow to Flamininus's pressure, and the report the ten legates delivered back in Rome had warned the Senate not just about Antiochus, but also about the Spartan king—a huge tumor in the entrails of Greece, they called him, as they exaggerated the importance of Argos.[3] But why was Argos's membership of a league any more liberating for it than being owned by a king? We will find the Romans within a few years (starting in 182) counting membership of the Achaean League also as a restriction of freedom, further exposing the cynical pragmatism of Flamininus's posture to Nabis.

Since Antiochus had returned to Antioch, he was not felt as an immediate danger; instead, after some debate, Flamininus's command was further extended, and he was given *carte blanche* to deal with Nabis in 195, despite the fact that Nabis's presence among the Roman co-signatories of the Peace of Phoenice proves that he had been taken at least as a friend of Rome, and may even have had a treaty with them.[4] This extension was just what Flamininus wanted, and not merely for personal reasons: it was certainly also on his mind that, when it came to war with Antiochus, he would need the Achaeans to look after the Peloponnese. The recovery of Argos would be a sop to them.

Flamininus invited all the Greeks to a conference at Corinth to consider war with Nabis, to make it seem that they were making the decision, not Rome. The Aetolians argued that the Romans should keep their promise, withdraw their troops from Greece, and leave Nabis to them. But the vast majority of the allies agreed with Flamininus and voted for war. They put together a massive invading army of 50,000, the largest army ever seen in Laconia. Nabis resisted better than might have been expected, but it did not take the allies much of the summer of 195 to defeat him and recover Argos for the Achaean League. At the Nemean Games that year, held at Argos, Flamininus hailed the city's liberation as a luminous example of Roman policy in Greece.

Nabis's wings were clipped—a heavy indemnity, his fleet reduced to two warships, and his territory to a rump of Laconia—but the Romans, in pursuit as usual of a balance of powers, overrode the wishes of the allies and left him in place. Flamininus then withdrew all his forces from the Peloponnese, except for the strong garrison at Corinth, and delegated the job of policing the new disposition there to the Achaeans. But this was asking for trouble, given that Achaean policy was to get rid of Nabis altogether and incorporate Sparta into the league. They wanted Elis and Messene too. The invasion of Laconia had certainly not settled the Peloponnese, but it shows that the Romans were not unwilling to get involved in a local Greek dispute to assist their friends. This one stood out from other such disputes mainly because it could be portrayed as a freedom issue.

EVACUATION AND TRIUMPH

Once Nabis had been put in his place, there was really no further excuse for not withdrawing the troops. Of course, there was still the imminent threat of Antiochus, but Flamininus had won the argument with the legates, and his policy of withdrawal, trusting in the balance of powers and relying on a network of friends in Greece, had been adopted in Rome as well. So, in the spring of 194, Flamininus called another conference at Corinth. He ran through all that he and the Romans had done for the Greeks, admonished them to behave themselves in future, and promised the evacuation of Demetrias and Chalcis within ten days, and the return of the Acrocorinth to the Achaeans. With a nice sense of theater, Flamininus arranged things so that the representatives could actually witness, from their meeting-place, the Roman troops filing off the Acrocorinth.

The combined Roman army, once withdrawn from the three Fetters and elsewhere, marched through Thessaly and Epirus to Oricum, its point of departure, while Lucius Flamininus took the fleet around the coast to rendezvous there with his brother. It was a significant moment for all concerned. The Romans had been a prominent presence in Greece for four years, and now there they were, thousands upon thousands of them, in all their glittering glory, marching over the dusty roads of Greece and bound for Italy. I imagine that the crowds lining the roads watched mutely, many expecting them back before long. In Italy, however, they marched toward Rome for all the world like a triumphal procession, with cheering crowds acclaiming their victory.

In their train, they carried enormous amounts of booty (see Fig. 6.2). When he got back to Rome Flamininus was, not surprisingly, awarded a triumph, and for the first time a Roman triumph burst the bounds of a single day and was allotted three:

> On the first day, Flamininus displayed on floats the armor, weaponry, and statues of bronze and marble....On the second, it was the turn of the gold and silver, worked, unworked, and coined. There were 18,270 pounds of unworked silver, and in worked silver many vessels in every style, most of them with carvings in relief, and some masterpieces. There were many artifacts of bronze, and ten silver shields as well. In coined silver, there were 84,000 Attic tetradrachms,...3,714 pounds of gold, a shield made of solid gold, and 14,514 gold Philippics. On the third day, 114 golden crowns which had been gifts from the city-states were carried in the procession; and sacrificial animals were paraded, and before the triumphal chariot went many prisoners and hostages of high birth, including Demetrius, son of Philip, and Armenas of Sparta, the son of the tyrant Nabis.[5]

FIGURE 6.2

The Derveni krater. Made in Thessaly or Macedon in the last quarter of the fourth century BCE, and weighing in at 40 kg., it gives an idea of the kind of booty Roman generals were plundering from Greece.

Where did all this booty come from? A ton and a half just of silver coinage? The Second Macedonian War saw less plundering than usual, since Flamininus was trying to win the hearts and minds of the Greeks. The staggering amounts remind us of what ancient historians often omit to mention. Every time they simply say that a town was captured or taken, they assume their readers knew what followed—that the town was systematically robbed by the victorious troops. After Macedon fell, the soldiers would have been free, for a while, to gather whatever they could from private and public buildings alike. This explains the statues and artifacts, and some of the bullion and coinage; but the bulk of the money came from selling captured soldiers and civilians into slavery, or from reselling captured slaves. Whenever we read an account of a Roman triumph, it is salutary to think of the bloodshed and misery by which such treasure was gained.

So the Romans kept their promise and withdrew their forces from Greece. In military terms, the error of this would soon become clear, and the Aetolians would seem like prophets, until in 172 the Romans found they had to set about removing the Macedonian monarchy, exactly as the Aetolians had urged in 197. For the time being, however, Flamininus's policy seemed best. But the theatricality of the evacuation is telling: it was a cosmetic display. In actual fact, Roman influence in Greece had never been stronger, and they could return at short notice.

FLAMININUS AND PHILOPOEMEN

In 193, envoys of Antiochus stopped off in Delphi on their way back home from Rome, where they had tried, and failed, to negotiate an alliance between Antiochus and the Romans as a way of staving off the war that now seemed inevitable.[6] So far from accepting Antiochus's deal—effectively, joint rule of the Mediterranean, with the borders at Thrace and the Aegean—the Romans, led by Flamininus and the ten legates (then back in Rome), had made it clear that they intended to free the Greeks from Antiochus, as they had from Philip. In response to Antiochus's offer, Flamininus insisted that the king either withdraw altogether from Europe or allow the Romans to intervene in the affairs of their friends in Asia (that is, Lampsacus and Smyrna, in the first instance). This was the same old bluster—but it is also noticeable that Flamininus was prepared to sacrifice the freedom of Greek cities if a simple solution could be found. For, if he had got his way, either the Greeks of Thrace or the Greeks of Asia Minor would still be under Antiochus's rule.

Since war was now certain, the purpose of the envoys' visit to Delphi was to hold discussions with the Aetolians, the only fully committed enemies of Rome in Greece. As a result of this meeting, the Aetolians sent emissaries to Philip, Antiochus, and Nabis, to try to put together an anti-Roman coalition. Philip, however, was in no position to contemplate another war against Rome, and, although Antiochus must have responded positively, he could do nothing for a few months since he was campaigning in Pisidia. Nabis, however, was enthusiastic. A powerful ally was just what he needed, and so, taking advantage of the withdrawal of the Roman troops from the Peloponnese, he began to try immediately, by assassination and military force, to recover some of the possessions he had lost in 195, especially the port of Gytheum, which had been strongly garrisoned by the Achaeans.

Flamininus, back in Greece in 192 as the head of a delegation tasked with counteracting Aetolian influence and rallying the Greek states against Antiochus, told the Achaeans that a fleet would soon be on its way to protect Rome's friends in the Peloponnese, but Philopoemen declared war on Sparta straight away. Philopoemen's spring campaign at sea was decidedly inconclusive—Gytheum was retaken by Nabis and Philopoemen's ancient flagship more or less fell to pieces, to his embarrassment—but he did successfully ravage Laconia. Hostilities ceased at Flamininus's instigation, and during the armistice Nabis got in touch with the Aetolians for help. Since they had originally approached him just a few months earlier, he presumably felt confident that his request would be well received—but instead the Aetolians had him assassinated (by the same man who had arranged the sudden demise of Brachylles of Boeotia in 196). They were finding him unreliable and had decided to incorporate Sparta into their league, but the Spartans drove them out before they succeeded in this wider aim. Philopoemen seized the moment, marched on Sparta, and, with the help of the pro-Achaean faction in the city, took

Sparta and Laconia into the Achaean League instead. This had been the Achaean dream for decades—but Philopoemen was laying up a store of difficulties for himself and the league.

Any slight tension between Flamininus and Philopoemen was patched up at the autumn 192 meeting of the Achaean League. The Achaeans hoped to continue their policy of expansion within the Peloponnese— Elis and Messene beckoned—under the screen of their powerful friends. Emissaries from Aetolia and Antiochus, there to see if they could gain the league for their coalition, were told in no uncertain terms of the Achaeans' friendship with Rome, and to prove it they voted to finalize their alliance with Rome, the alliance that had first been mooted in 198.

The Peloponnese remained troubled. A coup in Sparta, just a few months after its incorporation into the league, brought the anti-Achaean group there back into power. The Achaean general for 191, Diophanes, raised an army, along with Flamininus, to deal with the situation, but was strongly opposed by Philopoemen, the architect of the new Sparta the previous year, who wanted to negotiate, not fight. Philopoemen took the extraordinary step of occupying Sparta *against* the army of Flamininus and Diophanes. And since he succeeded in quietening things down and bringing Sparta back into the league by peaceful means (for the time being, at any rate), Flamininus was hardly in a position to complain, though this episode marked the beginning of open antagonism between him and Philopoemen, and a widening of the rift between the pro-Roman and anti-Roman (or at least pro-independence) factions within the league. The antagonism, though personal, was politically based: Flamininus wanted to limit Achaean power, Philopoemen wanted it to grow.

Flamininus got his way in 191 by dictating the terms of the re-incorporation of Messene into the league, but when it was the turn of the Eleans a few months later, they refused his help. Seeing his influence declining in Achaea, Flamininus flexed his muscles when the Achaeans bought the island of Zacynthos from Amynander, and forbade the incorporation of the island into the league. "You should behave like the tortoise," he said, "and keep your head within your home, which is the Peloponnese."[7] The pleasantry did little to alleviate his authoritarian insistence that the Achaeans give the island to Rome.

All this jockeying was resolved in Achaea's favor when Philopoemen insisted, in the face of Roman prevarication, on the Achaeans' right to sort out Sparta's troubles on their own (the city had again seceded from the league in 189). This they did, in 188, with considerably more bloodshed and less tact than Philopoemen's earlier settlement there. In an attempt to make sure that Sparta stayed quiescent from then on, the ancient, unique Spartan way of life was swept away (or what little was left of it), and the city's constitution was redrafted along lines familiar to other members of the league. The Senate let the Achaeans know that it disapproved of what Philopoemen had done, but took no further action. That, really, was how it should have been, for the alliance Rome and the Achaeans had entered into in 192 in theory treated both parties as equals.[8] And so Philopoemen was known as "the last of the Greeks," for his doomed, last-ditch insistence upon Greek action free of Rome.[9]

THE AETOLIAN POWER PLAY

Of the three Fetters, the most troubled was Thessalian Demetrias, where honors were almost even between the pro-Roman and anti-Roman factions. Flamininus had to take steps to ensure the stability and loyalty of the city, even at the risk of exposing the hollowness of his withdrawal of the Roman troops in 194, and the rumor began to spread in 192 that he was going to restore it to Philip. This rumor would soon be confirmed, and even at the time Flamininus made no attempt to deny it. It was an economical way of gaining Philip's loyalty for the coming war—but, of course, it trampled on the supposed freedom of the citizens of Demetrias. This not only infuriated the Aetolians, but Flamininus very nearly lost control of the assembly he attended in Demetrias, before finally succeeding in making it prudent for Eurylochus, the head of the anti-Roman faction, to flee to Aetolia.

Everything came to a head at the spring 192 assembly of the Aetolian League. Eurylochus was there, complaining loudly that the Romans were still pulling the strings and had arranged his illegal banishment. Representatives were there from all the interested Greek states; Flamininus attended in person, to warn the Aetolians off war. But the Aetolians were already committed, and there and then, in front of Flamininus, they drafted a formal invitation to Antiochus to come and free Greece, and arbitrate between themselves and the Romans—or, in other words, renegotiate the Roman settlement of Greece, in which the Aetolians felt cheated of their due.

The phrasing of the invitation was a further insult to Flamininus, who felt he had already "freed Greece," and the insult was compounded when he asked for a copy of the assembly's resolution. The Aetolian general replied that he would deliver it in person—on the banks of Rome's river, the Tiber. As things stood, of course, this was an extravagant fantasy; the Aetolians were not even close to putting together a coalition capable of invading Italy. But it reveals the Aetolians' determination; they could see that it might be their last chance to push for hegemony in Greece.

Following this meeting, the Aetolians took steps to strengthen their position in Greece. The attempted incorporation of Sparta into their league, already narrated above, was part of a package that included coups in Demetrias and Chalcis as well. In Demetrias, Eurylochus was successfully restored to power, but Chalcis stayed loyal to Rome. The instability of the Roman settlement of Greece was further exposed, and the Aetolian League gained one of the Fetters.

At much the same time, in the autumn of 192, the Senate ordered Marcus Baebius Tamphilus to take the army of 3,000 he had gathered at Brundisium earlier in the year over to Apollonia. They then waited for Antiochus to make his move, so that they could attribute the outbreak of the war to him. The Aetolian invitation to come and free Greece reached Antiochus while he was campaigning in Thrace, and as soon as he was free, perhaps in October, he sailed over to Demetrias with a force of 10,000 foot, 500 horse, and six war elephants.

The relatively small size of this army does not indicate pusillanimity on Antiochus's part. He was confident, and the Aetolians had repeatedly assured him, that many Greek states would flock to his banner. Moreover, he assured them on his arrival that more troops—the main force, in fact—would be coming in the spring when the weather improved. But it *was* a relatively small force, and it might also have been meant to send a message to Rome: that his only intention was to oversee the freedom of the Greeks, now that the Roman settlement was plainly in tatters, and that therefore the Romans need not overreact by declaring war. After all, he was there simply as an ally of Aetolia and, since the Aetolians had no formal relations with Rome, the whole affair was really none of the Romans' business. Perhaps the small size of this initial force was even a bargaining counter, implying that he would withdraw peaceably once his rights in Thrace and Asia Minor had been properly acknowledged by Rome. Neither the Romans nor Antiochus were in a hurry to go to war, but they were both subject to pressures from others—Antiochus especially from the Aetolians, and the Romans from Eumenes of Pergamum, who was terrified of being eclipsed by Antiochus.

THE OUTBREAK OF THE SYRIAN-AETOLIAN WAR

Any or all of these reasons may have passed through Antiochus's mind, but he must also have known that the Romans would never tolerate his armed presence in Greece. On landing, he made his way to the Aetolian council at Lamia. The first thing the Aetolians did was appoint him their general for the year, thus, as it were, legitimizing his presence on Greek soil and his mission of liberation. They advised him to start his campaign by trying, where they had failed, to win Chalcis, as a second Fetter.

At Chalcis, Antiochus first offered a peaceful solution. He was still, it seems, seeking the diplomatic advantage of being able to claim that he had done nothing to provoke the Romans. The overriding political concern for every city and state in Greece was where it stood, and where it was perceived to stand, in relation to Rome, on the spectrum running from hostility to friendliness. So Antiochus's first tactic for taking the city was to encourage his partisans to rise up and take control on the basis of his offer of peace. But the pro-Roman party became alarmed and called for armed help from Flamininus.

The news that Chalcis was about to be reinforced prompted more decisive action from Antiochus, and he sent his fleet to block the reinforcements' approach. His ships arrived too late to prevent an Achaean contingent entering the city, but the Romans were turned back and made camp at Delium. They were not expecting any trouble, but Antiochus's admiral attacked the camp and about 250 Roman troops lost their lives. The admiral was surely acting of his own accord, and Antiochus must have regretted what happened since he had so far been careful to avoid direct provocation, but now war was inevitable. He brought up a substantial army, and the city of Chalcis opened its gates rather than suffer a siege. The rest of the cities of Euboea followed suit, proving the importance of this single Fetter. Antiochus made Chalcis his headquarters, leaving a garrison in Demetrias. He now had control of much of the east coast of Greece.

By arriving in Greece late in the year, Antiochus had bought himself several months, before the Romans could arrive in force in the spring, for diplomatic initiatives. At the end of January 191, he married the daughter of a local Chalcidian dignitary. Antiochus was no longer young, and he already had a wife, but neither of these factors was an impediment to royal romance in Hellenistic times. Misunderstanding this move by Antiochus, our sources paint him as an oriental potentate, lusting after young girls and occupying his time in Chalcis with debauchery.[10] But the true meaning of the incident is revealed by Antiochus's renaming his bride "Euboea." The message to the Greeks was that he was here as a friend and ally.

Antiochus looked for further allies all over Greece, with approaches to Philip, Boeotia, Athens, the Achaeans, Amynander, Acarnania, and Epirus. Of these, the most important were the Achaeans and Philip. The Achaeans, as we have seen, responded to the approach by voting overwhelmingly to side with Rome. Philip, however, remained for the time being uncommitted.

It was a patchy diplomatic offensive for Antiochus. The Aetolians had promised him enthusiastic Greek support, but none of those he first approached leapt at the chance; they preferred to wait and see if one set of masters was any better than the other. The Romans' freedom policy survived its first big test, but perhaps chiefly because the Greeks were frightened of reprisals. Only Elis, a longtime Aetolian ally, and Amynander of Athamania joined Antiochus. Amynander, lately a staunch friend of Rome, was persuaded to change sides by the crazy suggestion that he would be able to replace Philip on the throne of Macedon with his own brother-in-law, Philip of Megalopolis, formerly Amynander's governor of Zacynthos; with him went not just Athamania, but Gomphi and western Thessaly, which he had been awarded for his part in the Second Macedonian War. Before long, some, but far from all, of the Acarnanian states joined, but a fragmented league was never going to be very useful; and after the massacre at Delium, the Boeotian League half-heartedly professed its favor for the Aetolian cause. The Epirotes tried to remain neutral in this war, as they had in the last.[11]

War had only been awaiting an excuse, and the Roman deaths at Delium provided it. "Flamininus," we are informed by Diodorus of Sicily, "called on both men and gods to bear witness to the fact that it was Antiochus who had started the war."[12] The Romans formally declared war on Antiochus early in 191, immediately after the consuls' entry into office.[13]

THE BATTLE OF THERMOPYLAE

Antiochus and his allies held a council of war, and then began to prepare for a muster of the joint army near Pherae and for a winter campaign in Thessaly. But they failed to gain Philip. In the end, it was a personal affront that tipped the scales. The affront came about as a result of the strange affair of Philip of Megalopolis, whom Antiochus and the Aetolians were touting as a candidate for the Macedonian throne. The elevation of this pretender in itself could have been enough to drive Philip into Roman arms, but then early in 191, in order to ingratiate Philip of Megalopolis with his putative future subjects, Antiochus sent him to Cynoscephalae to gather up and bury the bones of the Macedonian dead that still littered the battlefield after six years. It was the duty of a Macedonian king to see to the proper burial of his fallen men, but circumstances had so far prevented Philip from doing so.[14] Philip naturally took this reminder of his failure personally, and he got in touch with Baebius in Apollonia to discuss joint action against the enemy, in return for substantial territorial gains.

Antiochus failed with Philip—but he was very successful in Thessaly, where a combination of force and diplomacy quickly netted him most of the important towns, so that he now controlled the entire east coast of Greece from the borders of Athens to the borders of Macedon, and his allies controlled much of central Greece. When he retired to late winter quarters, he could feel satisfied with a decent, if not outstanding, few weeks' work.

In spring of 191, the consul Manius Acilius Glabrio arrived in Apollonia with 36,000 troops. While establishing himself there, he sent one of his staff officers to travel around the southern Greek cities, and to link up with Flamininus and the Roman commissioners at Corinth. This officer was Marcus Porcius Cato, famous as the rather stern ideologue of Rome's traditional values and already of consular rank; in 184 he would crown his remarkable political career with the censorship, but he is known as Cato "the Censor" as much for his conservatism as for his rank. A fragment of a speech Cato delivered at Athens survives, in which he argued that Antiochus was weak—that he was making war only with pen and paper[15]—so no doubt the overall purpose of his mission was to encourage Rome's allies or potential allies. But it was true that Antiochus was weak. Things were moving too fast for him, and there was no sign yet of the reinforcements from Asia that he had promised the Aetolians.

Meanwhile, Baebius had advanced from Illyris for a joint campaign with Philip, which secured them northern Thessaly, before being joined by Glabrio and the main Roman army, which had advanced through Epirus. Further towns in Thessaly fell until they had more than undone Antiochus's successes of the previous winter. They also captured Philip of Megalopolis during this campaign; he was interned in Italy, no doubt after featuring in chains in Glabrio's triumph, and we hear no more about him. Glabrio made no attempt on Demetrias, however: he did not want to get tied up with a long siege.

The successes of the Roman and Macedonian forces in Thessaly drew Antiochus from Acarnania, where he had been trying to secure west-coast ports for himself and deny them to the Romans. But he was too late to save Athamania, most of which fell to Philip; Amynander fled to Ambracia, which was in Aetolian hands.[16] Glabrio and Philip were poised on the borders of Aetolia, which was effectively surrounded now by enemies. Antiochus called on the Aetolians to send as many troops as possible for a muster at Lamia, but under the circumstances they could spare only 4,000, well short of Antiochus's requirements and expectations.

With a nice sense of history, Antiochus chose to make his stand at the site of the most famous battle in defense of Greek freedom from barbarian hordes. He posted his own men at the east end of the Thermopylae narrows and used the Aetolians to garrison the nearby towns of Heraclea and Hypata; Heraclea guarded the route south that Glabrio would take to attack Boeotia. So, in April 191, Glabrio advanced to confront Antiochus by the sea at Thermopylae.

Everyone was familiar with Herodotus's account of the original battle in 480, when Leonidas of Sparta held up the massive Persian army of invasion;[17] everyone knew that there was a route through the hills that rose up steeply from the coastline. In fact, in the centuries between the first battle of Thermopylae and this one, fortresses had been built along the route of that upper pass. At Antiochus's orders, the Aetolians moved their garrison from Hypata to man these fortresses (see Fig. 6.3).

FIGURE 6.3

The high pass at Thermopylae, secured by Cato before the battle in 191 BCE. The photograph is taken from Mendenitsa castle, built in the thirteenth century CE on the site of earlier castles with the same function of defending the pass.

Glabrio sent Cato and another officer, each with two thousand men, to clear the upper pass. This was essential because it was very unlikely that he would be able to force the lower pass; after all, Leonidas had held it with only a few thousand men, and Antiochus had many times more than that and was well entrenched. Cato's men had a tough climb up the tree-clad Callidromon mountain, but they drove the Aetolians off the heights, and then the Romans were able to come at the Seleucid army from front and rear. Antiochus's men broke and fled. The fleet gathered at Demetrias after some action in the Aegean, and the remnants of the land army, along with Antiochus himself, reassembled at Chalcis. Glabrio sent Cato home to deliver news of the victory to the Senate. Relations between the men soured when Cato claimed, then and on future occasions, that the victory was due almost entirely to his own efforts.[18]

7.

THE PERIPHERY EXPANDS

D EFEAT AT THERMOPYLAE IN 191 spelled the end of Antiochus's war in Greece, and he decided to return at once to Asia Minor. His troops were dead or distributed among various garrisons, and he was unsure that he could hold Chalcis. Glabrio allowed his soldiers to plunder in Boeotia, as a way of getting the league to change sides once again, before arriving at Chalcis more or less as Antiochus left for Ephesus, with his new family, the remains of his army, and his war chest. Chalcis opened its gates to Glabrio, and the rest of the cities of Euboea again followed suit. Glabrio decided not to follow Antiochus across the Aegean—strictly, his province for the year was Greece—and turned back to deal with the Aetolians. While Philip put Lamia under siege, Glabrio did the same to nearby Heraclea, and by the early summer Heraclea had fallen without the Aetolians doing anything beyond sending a desperate appeal after Antiochus as he disappeared over the horizon.

Antiochus's response to the plea, once he was back in Asia Minor, was positive, and the Aetolian agents returned with his promise of cash now and troops later. It was in Antiochus's interest to prolong the war in Greece as long as possible, while he prepared for war in Asia Minor. But, in the meantime, before their agents had returned with Antiochus's glimmer of hope, Aetolian morale plummeted and they approached Glabrio to make peace. A darkly amusing case of international confusion followed.[1]

Glabrio offered the Aetolians peace if they made an unconditional surrender to Rome, a *deditio in fidem*, but the Aetolians did not understand that this entailed the complete surrender of "all things, human and divine," so that the entire future of the surrenderer was in the hands of the enemy commander.[2] The Aetolians, however, saw "surrender," not unnaturally, as a way to bring the fighting to an end, to create space for the negotiation of terms, and that is why they agreed to the *deditio*. To their astonishment, Glabrio began making haughty demands, as he was now entitled to do— and then, to their further astonishment, threatened to have them clapped in irons when they protested. They were ambassadors, and the bodies of ambassadors were sacrosanct; they did not know that a *deditio in fidem* wiped every slate clean.

Eventually, the misunderstanding was cleared up and Glabrio decently released the Aetolians from their *deditio*, but made it clear that his demand for unconditional surrender was not negotiable. At an emergency general meeting, the Aetolians therefore decided to continue the war. Glabrio responded by putting Naupactus under siege, while Philip recovered a great deal of Achaea Phthiotis, including Thebes, before negotiating the departure of Antiochus's garrison from Demetrias and recovering the city for himself. Eurylochus, the head of the anti-Roman party, killed himself. Soon after, Philip also regained some places in Perrhaebia that had been lost when his kingdom was reduced at the end of the Second Macedonian War; and he had already taken over Athamania and regained its south Thessalian neighbor, the no less mountainous region of Dolopia. Meanwhile, in the south the Achaeans forced Antiochus's garrison in Elis to surrender and re-incorporated Messene into the league.

By July fresh Roman ships, under the praetor Gaius Livius Salinator, had arrived in the Aegean, bringing Roman naval strength up to a hundred ships, with which they could confront anything Antiochus could send against them, especially since they had the support of Pergamum and Rhodes. Livius's job was to pursue Antiochus into Asia, while Glabrio mopped up the Aetolians in Greece.

THE BATTLE OF MYONESSUS

Polyxenidas, in charge of Antiochus's Hellespontine fleet, based at Lysimachea, chose to await Livius's arrival at the Erythrae peninsula, with the intention of dividing the Romans and Pergamenes to the north from the Rhodians to the south. But the joint Roman and Pergamene fleet drove him back to Ephesus, linked up with the Rhodians, and cheekily paraded their ships before the mouth of Ephesus harbor. A later historian, reflecting Roman propaganda of the time, crowed over the victory, orientalizing Macedonian Antiochus by counting it the equivalent of the Greek defeat of Persia in 480–479.[3] Then everyone withdrew to winter quarters.

Over the winter of 191–190, Seleucid and Pergamene forces clashed, to no great effect, and Antiochus was rebuilding his fleet and strengthening his army (chiefly from his own resources, but aided by King Ariarathes IV of Cappadocia and by the Galatians).[4] He also sent Hannibal east to see to the construction of another fleet in the Phoenician and Cilician shipyards, and contacted local dynasts and pirate chiefs, even if they owned only one or two ships. He got in touch with Prusias of Bithynia, but after some prevarication Prusias decided to remain neutral, which was more of a help to the Romans than to Antiochus. Moreover, Antiochus's supposed ally Ptolemy was doing his best to gain the favor of the Romans, presumably as a preliminary to retaking Coele Syria in the event of Antiochus's distraction or defeat. The Romans kept Ptolemy at a distance, however, waiting in the wings should they need him. In the meantime, they repatriated Philip's son Demetrius, in gratitude for his help; and a few months later they remitted the remainder of his war indemnity.

In Rome, Lucius Cornelius Scipio, one of the consuls for 190, gained Greece as his province, with permission to carry the war into Asia, and took his famous brother with him on his staff. By coincidence, Africanus had just completed the construction and dedication of a triumphal arch in Rome, commemorating his victory over Hannibal. And now Hannibal was in Antiochus's court. Lucius Aemilius Regillus was put in command of the fleet, currently based at Samos, and both fleet and land army were reinforced. A stalemate developed in the Aegean, since both fleets were of approximately the same size—Regillus at Samos, and Polyxenidas in Ephesus.

Anticipating the arrival of Hannibal's fleet from Syria, the Romans tried, but failed, to take ports in Lycia and Caria which might serve as havens. Naval sieges were technically demanding and invariably protracted. It was now up to the Rhodians to do what they could to halt him. The two fleets engaged off Side in July 190, but the battle was indecisive;

although Hannibal's small fleet was halved, he was able to regroup and continue west along the Pamphylian coast while the Rhodians pulled back and prepared to meet him again. But the delay was frustrating for Antiochus, since without Hannibal's ships he could not end the stalemate in the Aegean. And before long the Egyptians took advantage of the absence of an effective fleet on the Phoenician and Cilician coastlines to raid and plunder the rich island of Aradus (taken by Antiochus in the Fifth Syrian War), forcing Hannibal to return with his fleet.[5]

On land, Antiochus had launched an invasion of Pergamum in May, and a simultaneous attack on the Pergamene naval base at Elaea. Neither attack was successful, but they did force Eumenes to abandon the war in Greece. The Pergamene fleet was given the job of safeguarding the Hellespont in anticipation of the crossing of Scipio's land army, which was even now marching through Macedon and Thrace, with Philip's permission and logistical support. Then Antiochus marched west to the coast and put the town of Notium under siege, while Polyxenidas moved the fleet there from Ephesus. Notium was unimportant in itself, and the move was designed to try to break the deadlock by tempting Regillus out from Samos and into battle. It worked. The two fleets met off Myonessus. But the battle so eagerly anticipated by Antiochus proved disastrous for him and, as it turned out, his defeat brought to an end Greek or Macedonian control of the eastern Mediterranean. From then on the whole sea was for centuries more or less a Roman pond.

THE BATTLE OF MAGNESIA

Antiochus still had substantial numbers of ships here and there, but he had lost control of the sea, and that meant there was nothing to stop the Roman land army crossing the Hellespont. Regillus prepared the way by taking and sacking Phocaea, while Antiochus raised the siege of Notium, effectively abandoning the northwest coast of Asia Minor. He needed to consolidate his forces quickly to meet Scipio. Evacuating Lysimachea helped—though it is a mystery how he was able to withdraw from Europe unopposed, under the nose of Eumenes' patrols.

In 229, the Romans had first set military foot on Greek soil; now, thirty years later, in July 190, they invaded Asia Minor. At the arrival of the Romans, Prusias climbed off his fence (which was leaning well over to the Roman side anyway) and indicated his willingness to assist them. After some skirmishing Antiochus chose to open negotiations, and he approached the consul, Lucius Scipio, through the intercession of his brother Africanus; for, under unknown circumstances, Africanus's son Lucius, who had evidently accompanied his father to Asia, had already fallen into Antiochus's hands.[6]

Antiochus offered to recognize Roman protection of Lampsacus and Smyrna, and even to abandon Thrace, as well as to accept half the costs of the war. But the Romans were negotiating from a position of strength, and Africanus, knowing that Antiochus was treating his son well and would likely return him unharmed, bluntly pointed out the weakness of Antiochus's position: offering to cede European Thrace would have been more effective *before* the Romans occupied it. And for the first time he faced Antiochus with the Romans' uncompromising demand: he must surrender Asia Minor in its entirety and pay the full costs of the war. Antiochus had done nothing commensurate with such a crippling pun-ishment, and it was plain that the Romans wanted nothing less than to extend their authority into his territory. Antiochus accordingly brought diplomacy to an end and prepared to fight. Roman aggression left him no choice.

Despite his having to leave a substantial force in Syria, Antiochus's army numbered in the region of 50,000, about the same size as Scipio's. The Romans moved down the west coast, pausing at Elaea for Africanus to recover from an illness. Antiochus returned his son to him there, and then marched to Magnesia (modern Manisa), a wealthy town lying under the mass of Mount Sipylus, to block their further advance south. Lucius Scipio, soon to earn his honorific *agnomen* "Asiagenes" ("of Asian stock"), set out after him and camped nearby, confidently offering battle on Antiochus's chosen field. In fact, he wanted to fight sooner rather than later since he was deep in enemy territory now, and provisioning his men would be problematic. In any case, it was already December, and fresh generals would soon be on their way east to relieve him and deny him the glory of victory. Antiochus's defeat was assured when on both wings Eumenes' Pergamene cavalry drove his cavalry off the field, and when his war elephants, driven mad by their wounds, ran amok and broke up his phalanx, leaving it vulnerable to the Roman legionaries. It was a total Roman victory.

PHALANX VERSUS LEGION

It goes without saying that, in war, luck or morale or even the stand made by one brave man can be more decisive factors than strategic or tactical superiority.[7] Nevertheless, even allowing for such imponderable factors, tactical differences between the Macedonian phalanx and the Roman legion do seem to have helped to tip the battlefield scales in the Romans' favor. The Macedonian phalanx had been more or less invincible for 160 years, and yet it was consistently beaten by the Roman legion.[8]

The main weapon of a phalangite since the innovations of Philip II in the middle of the fourth century was a long, sturdy pike, called a *sarissa*. This could be as long as five meters (16 feet or more), and it needed strength to manage it. Phalangites took up a tight formation, and the length of the pikes meant that those of the first five rows projected out beyond the front rank. The pikes had butt-spikes, so that they could be planted firmly in the ground. In defense, then, a solid phalanx was more or less impregnable since no sword could reach past the fence of pikes and cause damage, and horses refuse to charge such a formation. In attack, the phalanx lumbered forward, often packed eight rows or more deep; at Magnesia, Antiochus deployed his phalanx in thirty-two rows. Again, provided the phalanx stayed solid, it was very hard to defeat; its sheer weight and solidity were often the decisive factors, if the enemy had not broken and fled in terror just at its fearsome advance. Phalangites were also equipped with a small shield and a short sword or dagger for hand-to-hand fighting.

The heavy infantry of a Roman legion, by contrast, were equipped with two short but sturdy throwing or thrusting spears, of differing weights, with an effective range of about fifty feet when thrown. Each spear ended in a long iron shank, tipped with a pyramid-shaped point; the length of the shank meant that it could penetrate both shield and body armor at once, and the barbed point meant that an enemy soldier would often have to jettison his shield, now made useless by having a spear stuck in it. But a legionary's main weapon was his Spanish-style sword, made out of high-quality steel to preserve its edge. Legionaries also carried a long shield; as with phalangites, the rest of their armor—helmets, greaves, and so on—depended on personal preference and wealth. Armor was designed to overawe or terrify the enemy, as well as to protect. There was no uniform.

Legionaries took up a looser formation than phalangites, in only three rows. The youngest, fittest men, the *hastati*, occupied the front row; the second row consisted of experienced men in their prime, the *principes*; the third row of the oldest and most experienced veterans, the *triarii*. A regular legion contained 1,200 *hastati*, the same number of *principes*, and 600 *triarii*. Every row was divided into ten tactical units, called "maniples," each consisting of 120 men in the first two rows, and 60 at the back. For battle, the rows took up a checkerboard formation, with a *principes* maniple positioned in the gap between two *hastati* maniples in front, and a *triarii* maniple doing the same for the *principes*. A phalanx was more unwieldy, but a well-trained phalanx also consisted of smaller tactical units, each with its own officer, which were capable of independent action and of rapid response.

The cores of the armies that clashed in the period covered in this book were the phalanx and the heavy infantry of a legion, but a regular legion also contained 1,200 light-armed troops (archers, javelineers, slingers) and 300 cavalry, and would be supported by a hoplite phalanx and cavalry supplied by Greek allies. A Macedonian phalanx too was supported by cavalry, light-armed troops, and very likely a corps of allied or mercenary hoplites—heavy infantry using an older style of Greek weaponry. A consul's army generally consisted of two legions—about 9,000 Roman citizens, but up to 12,000 in emergencies—and then however many allies he had brought with him or could call up on the spot.

Typically, in a pitched battle on good ground, the heavy infantry would occupy the center of the formation, flanked on both sides by cavalry, and with light infantry skirmishing in front and to the sides. The job of the light infantry was to screen the deployment of the main army, and do as much damage as possible before slipping back through their lines to take up a position in the rear. If they still had some missiles left, they could act as a reserve in case of an encircling or outflanking movement by the enemy; more usually, their work was done. They were also useful as marauders, or to run down fugitives. If the battle involved war elephants, it was the light troops' job in the opening stages to try to cripple them, while protecting their own. Elephants acted as a screen against cavalry, since horses are repulsed by their sight and scent, and they could also break up a heavy-infantry formation; but there was a danger that, when wounded, they might trample their own troops, as Antiochus's did at Magnesia. They were as important, terrifying, and unreliable as the new armored tanks of World War I.

Light cavalry, archers and javelineers, were used mainly as scouts, skirmishers, and scavengers. A heavy cavalryman was typically armored from head to foot, and wielded a long lance. As in all eras (think of the *hippeis* of classical Athens, the *equites* of Rome, the *chevaliers* of medieval Europe), the cavalry tended to be the social elite, because by tradition a cavalryman was expected to provide and look after his own horse, and horse-rearing was expensive. Only the wealthy had spare pasturage and the time to acquire equestrian skills. The cavalry usually went into battle in waves of squadrons consisting of perhaps fifty or a hundred horse, operating as semi-independent units. Usually, the cavalry's work was divided between attempting to outflank the enemy and defending against the enemy cavalry's attempts to outflank their own infantry.

The formulaic layout of the troops meant that, provided numbers were more or less equal, each unit was most likely to clash first with its counterpart: cavalry against cavalry, heavy infantry against heavy infantry. Normally, it was only in the event of success or failure, or of ambush, that they would find themselves fighting dissimilar troop types. After the light infantry had expended their missiles, one side or both would make a general advance, either in a straight line, or obliquely, favoring one wing or the other. Typically, it would be the right wing that was weighted with more shock troops than the other and would lead the attack. For Greeks and Macedonians, the right wing was the place of honor, and this was where the king or commander tended to take up his position. In the Greek world, generals still often fought from the front, but Roman commanders stayed behind and kept a broader eye on events.

While the cavalry were engaged, trying not to race too far from the field, the phalanx and the legion met with a massive crunch, literally shoving at their opponents with shields and weapons, trying to fell enough men to create gaps, to sow panic (thought to be induced by the god Pan), and to force the enemy to break and flee. The first two Roman ranks, the *hastati* and the *principes*, will have thrown their two spears (first the lighter one, then the heavier) from close quarters while advancing—a terrifying barrage—and turned to sword and shield. Their spears might have thinned the enemy ranks enough to open the enemy up to close-quarters fighting; otherwise, the Romans tended to stop and await the oncoming phalangites, since it was very hard for them to hack their way into a solid phalanx.

The phalanx was superb for both defence and attack, as long as it held solid. This strength was also its weakness, for there is very little ground that is so even that a phalanx could be sure of retaining formation. In most battles, the phalanx would begin to break up, either as it advanced or, in defense, as men fell to javelins or slingshot. Moreover, even if the phalanx managed to retain formation during the charge, it was bound to break up when it came to hand-to-hand fighting. Any opening potentially allowed enemy troops to infiltrate the formation. Once they were inside, the Roman sword and shield were far superior to a phalangite's equivalents, and the slaughter could begin. But the more ranks a phalanx adopted, the greater its staying power and the harder and more exhausting it was for the enemy to hack their way inside.

So one weakness of the phalanx was its dependency on retaining a solid formation. Another problem was that it was a single, massive unit, relying as much as anything on terrifying the enemy as it bore down on them, eight, sixteen, or even thirty-two ranks stretched over an enormous front, yelling and clashing their weapons, plumes waving fiercely, blinding sunlight glittering on newly polished armor. By contrast, a Roman general would usually send only his first row, the *hastati*, into battle at first, supported by allied infantry. Their hideously dangerous job was to halt the enemy, and begin to prise open some gaps in their formation. Meanwhile, the second row, the *principes*, would have come up behind them, with further allied support, to fill gaps, release another storm of missiles, and provide extra forward impetus.

The *triarii* might not be needed at all ("It's down to the *triarii*" was a proverbial way of describing a desperate situation), and could therefore act as a reserve, if the general felt it necessary—another feature that a phalanx generally lacked. Since the commanding officer of a phalanx usually led from the front, reserves were useless: he had no way of knowing when to deploy them. At both Cynoscephalae and Magnesia, the Roman line was broken—but the *triarii* were there to remedy the situation. They were equipped with longer, defensive spears, to form a fence behind which their colleagues could rally and regroup.

The two main weaknesses of the Greek phalanx, then, relative to the Roman legion, were its lack of flexibility and its lack of reserves (in so far as that is a different factor). But there were other secrets to the Romans' success. One of the imponderables I mentioned above was morale and, in most of their wars in the east, the Romans' confidence was high, chiefly because many of the men who fought the Greeks and Macedonians in the east already had considerable experience of warfare as a result of the Punic wars. These were the best armies the Republic had so far produced, and they knew that their experience and discipline gave them the edge. The Romans generally formed their armies entirely from citizens and allies, whereas Greeks and Macedonians had for a long time relied heavily on mercenaries, for all that they were not entirely reliable.

Something else that was daunting to the enemy was a Roman army's sheer efficiency. Although they preferred to advance quite slowly, sacrificing speed to security, at the end of a day's march, they quickly constructed an easily defended camp, and packed it up just as quickly the next day. Over the course of their earliest wars abroad, they developed a brilliant supply system, so that one very rarely hears of Roman armies being in difficulties in this respect. They were constantly learning from their enemies and improving their equipment; the legionaries' deadly sword, for instance, was a recent acquisition, modeled on what they had met in Spain and in the hands of Hannibal's Spanish mercenaries.

But there was another factor that raised Roman morale and lowered the enemy's confidence. This was what came to be known as Roman savagery. Warfare, as it had developed among the Greek states, was quite ritualized in nature. The point was to humiliate your enemy, to rise above him in the pecking order of states, as much as it was to destroy his soldiery. When facing mercenaries, the main idea was to demoralize or bribe them enough to get them to change sides. Battlefield massacres were rare, and the worst casualties always occurred after an army had turned to flight, when men became vulnerable and their victorious opponents were driven by a lust to kill and despoil corpses of their valuable arms and armor.

The Romans knew nothing of this etiquette. There was a regulation, although it was not consistently applied, that a Roman general had to have killed 5,000 of the enemy to earn a triumph—a deliberate encouragement to massacre. At Cynoscephalae, the Macedonian phalangites held their pikes upright to indicate their surrender, but the Roman legionaries continued to kill them until the gesture was explained to them. Roman troops did not surrender. There were terrible punishments for those who did, such as decimation (the execution of every tenth man in a unit) and running an often deadly gauntlet. Roman soldiers fought to the death. Even their sword gave them a reputation for ferocity. It was very sharp, and its blade was smooth, ungrooved. Thrust into a man's body, it tended to get stuck, as the flesh closed back over it. A Roman legionary therefore gave his sword a sharp twist as he pulled it out, inflicting a horrendous gaping wound. Even worse, the sword was good for both slashing and thrusting, whereas Greek and Macedonian daggers were for thrusting only:[9]

> In fighting Greeks and Illyrians, the Macedonians had seen wounds caused by spears, arrows, and (though more rarely) lances, but now they saw bodies dismembered by the Spanish sword, arms taken off shoulder and all, heads detached from bodies with the neck sliced all the way through, innards exposed, and other disgusting wounds.

The purpose of warfare, as far as the Romans were concerned, was to damage the enemy so badly that he never again took up arms against Rome. Besieged towns were generally sacked and plundered, with all the rape and violence that implies, and entire populations might be sold into slavery. Terror tactics—massacre, enslavement, deportation—were supposed to break the enemy's spirit. Based on the certainty of their superior manpower and abilities, the Romans fought brutal wars, with no compromises given or expected.

THE PEACE OF APAMEA

Following the victory of the Roman legions at Magnesia, Antiochus, Seleucus, and the royal family fled east to Apamea in Phrygia, one of the royal courts. Africanus, recovered from his illness, joined his brother at Sardis, and that was where they received Antiochus's emissaries for the peace conference. The Romans' terms had not changed. Antiochus was to withdraw his forces beyond the Taurus Mountains—abandoning Thrace and all Asia Minor—and pay the full cost of the war, which now had a figure attached to it: 15,000 talents (perhaps $9 billion, in today's money), of which 500 was to be paid immediately. Reparations were to be made to Eumenes, Antiochus was required to hand over a few individuals, including Hannibal (who fled to the court of Prusias of Bithynia), and he had to give twenty hostages, including one of his sons. Wherever possible, the Roman demands were couched in the terminology developed by Flamininus: Antiochus was to "free" the cities of Asia Minor from his rule. The Scipios could recognize a useful slogan when they saw one.

Antiochus accepted these terms—he had little choice—and a truce was arranged for all interested parties to send delegations to Rome to negotiate the final treaty. Antiochus returned to Syria, leaving Asia Minor in the hands of Seleucus, who, since the death in 193 of his elder brother, had become the heir to the Seleucid throne. During the truce, early in 189, Gnaeus Manlius Vulso, the new consul, arrived with fresh troops, to replace the Scipios and replenish the army. Lucius Scipio returned and celebrated the most fabulous triumph yet.[10] In making Asia one of the provinces for the year (the other being Greece, of course, where the end of the war against the Aetolians was drawing close), the Senate was showing that it did not consider Asia Minor pacified. It was not just that Antiochus still had considerable troops available, and the Senate wanted to crush any thoughts of resurgence before they even started. It was also that they had a vision of the future of Asia Minor, and military force was needed to realize it.

So Vulso immediately launched a savage campaign against the Galatians. They had provided troops for Antiochus, and might have assumed that, as his allies, they were included in the armistice, but Vulso saw it otherwise. It was an economical plan, because it would simultaneously give a vivid demonstration to Antiochus of Roman determination, and take one of his main allies out of the picture. Vulso took a roundabout route from the coast to Galatia in order to receive the surrender of Seleucid towns and fortresses along the way, and Seleucus was further humiliated by having to supply the Roman army. The truce meant that he was incapable of helping his allies, and could only watch as two of the three Galatian tribes were massacred. By the time it was all over, in the autumn, Seleucus had been left isolated in Apamea. Everyone else had, by force or diplomacy, come to an accommodation with Rome.

Toward the end of 187, Vulso celebrated a triumph. Despite the fact that he had lost some of his loot on the way home to Thracian brigands, it was still remembered as a fantastically profitable campaign. The Senate was delighted, because it was at last able to repay its wealthy citizens the money they had loaned for the Second Punic War. Vulso paraded "212 golden crowns; 220,000 pounds of silver; 2,103 pounds of gold; 127,000 Attic tetradrachms; 250,000 *cista* coins; 16,320 gold Philippics."[11] No fewer than fifty-two enemy chieftains and commanders were displayed in bonds. Every soldier in the army received 168 *sestertii*, and every officer and cavalryman proportionately more. It was so fabulous that, in moralizing mode, Livy marked the significance of the occasion in terms of the introduction into Rome of decadent fashions:[12]

These were the men who first brought into Rome bronze couches, expensive bedclothes, tapestries....This was when girls playing harps and lutes began to appear at dinner parties...and when a cook began to be a valued possession.

There was opposition to Vulso's triumph, political in nature. The Scipios accused him of triumph-hunting, arguing that his war against the Galatians was unauthorized by the Senate, that Vulso had tried to provoke Seleucus into renewed war, and that he had conducted himself with undue savagery. These were feeble attempts:[13] undue savagery was a respectable way to win a triumph, and Vulso's campaign was not illegal. Every Roman field commander had the right to make on-the-spot decisions about where and how to campaign within his province, and Vulso's work had certainly been in line with Roman aims in Asia Minor. After all, as a result of Vulso's campaign Antiochus would be more inclined to see Asia Minor as a lost cause, and therefore to accede to Roman conditions without making further trouble. As usual, the Senate set the political parameters of war, and it was up to the general on the spot to decide how best to carry out his commission. The Scipios were reacting at least partly because they knew that Vulso's triumph would outshine even that of Lucius Scipio two years earlier.

Meanwhile, in 189 the negotiations in Rome were quickly over, as the Senate ratified the conditions Scipio had made in the field, adding only a few details, such as that Antiochus was to surrender all his war elephants, and all but ten of his warships. Two and a half thousand talents were to be paid immediately, on the ratification of the treaty, with the balance of 12,000 talents paid at the rate of 1,000 talents a year. This was the moment when Rome's public finances changed forever, and the city became accustomed to a higher degree of wealth. The final details were sorted out with Seleucus at a conference in Apamea in 188, the peace treaty was duly accepted on oath by Vulso and Antiochus, the Seleucid fleet was put to the torch, and that was that. The greatest king in the known world had been crushed by Rome, for the crime of having challenged it for supremacy in Greece. Over a century of somewhat patchy Seleucid rule of Asia Minor was brought to an end.

A NEW DISPOSITION FOR ASIA MINOR

At the same time as it finalized the terms of the treaty, the Senate took thought for the future settlement of Asia Minor, now that it was theirs to dispose of, by appointing a ten-man commission to go there and help Vulso. Just as the Romans had reorganized Greece after Cynoscephalae, so they now made sweeping changes in Asia Minor, altering its political landscape forever. There was little to stop them doing exactly what they wanted, and what they wanted was an Asia Minor which was so thoroughly in the hands of their friends that they could continue to dominate by remote control and save the expense of maintaining armies there.

Their friends in Asia Minor were Eumenes and the Rhodians, both of whom had been consistently helpful in the war. Seleucid Asia Minor was basically divided at the Meander river, with the northern half going to Eumenes and the southern half to Rhodes. All of Antiochus's former tributaries would now pay Pergamum or Rhodes—another sign of the weakening of Flamininus's freedom doctrine—while cities that had long been tributaries of Pergamum or Rhodes would keep that status, except that all cities which could claim friendship with Rome (the commissioners decided each case on the spot) were to be free, subject to neither Rhodes nor Pergamum. In Bithynia, Prusias was allowed to remain because of his last-minute support for Rome. Pergamum and Rhodes had been enemies as often as they had been friends. Ironically, the arrival of the balance of power that both had long desired for commercial reasons made unwilling allies out of these rivals.

THE END OF THE AETOLIAN WAR

Assuming the role of senior Greek expert, Flamininus was displeased with Glabrio's siege of Naupactus in 191—not just for his stated reason, that it was a waste of time,[14] but because Glabrio seemed determined to reduce the Aetolians, and that would undermine Flamininus's attempt to create a balance of powers in Greece. So, late in 191, Flamininus brokered another request from the Aetolians for a truce, so that the possibility of peace could be explored in Rome. Glabrio agreed, and broke off the siege. The Aetolians arrived in Rome early in 190, but negotiations quickly broke down and they were sent packing. All was not quite lost, however, as back in Greece Lucius Scipio, the newly arrived consul, soon granted them a six-month truce, which the Aetolians accepted even though they knew that the reason for such a long truce was to give their enemy time to deal with their ally in Asia Minor.

The truce came into effect in the spring of 190, and Aetolian ambassadors traveled to Rome. They were then kept waiting for months, without gaining an audience with the Senate. While they were stuck in Rome, they had to suffer the humiliation of being present for Glabrio's triumph, with the usual display of enormous quantities of valuables and numerous prisoners, including Aetolians.[15]

It was not until November that the Aetolian ambassadors were eventually granted an audience—and the reason for the delay was obvious: the Senate wanted to hear the result of the Scipios' campaign against Antiochus before dealing with the Aetolians. But the news still had not arrived when they needed to act, because the six-month truce was close to expiring. The Aetolians were expected to approach the Senate in abject humility, to ask for peace, but by now they were fed up. They were heads of state, and they felt insulted. So, instead of humility, the senators were treated to a rant on how the Aetolians did not deserve such treatment for their past services to Rome, and it soon became clear that they had set their faces against any possibility of peace on Roman terms. They simply remained silent whenever the issue came up. The meeting broke down so completely that in the end the Aetolian emissaries were given fifteen days to leave Italy.

So the war in Greece, in abeyance in 190 (while Antiochus was being finished off in Asia Minor), would resume in 189. The result of the provincial lottery was that Vulso got Asia, as we have seen, and Marcus Fulvius Nobilior got Greece. A fresh army had already been taken across to Apollonia in the previous year, and, with those Fulvius took with him, he would have a force of about 35,000, the same size as the one Glabrio had fielded against the Aetolians. Fulvius also received further warships for the fleet, with which he was instructed to clear Cephallenia of pirates. The island just happened to be a member of the Aetolian League.

The Aetolians, however, had already gone on the offensive. As soon as their ambassadors returned with the bad news from Rome, they launched a stunning winter campaign in which they recovered much of Athamania for Amynander, and drove Philip's reduced army out of Dolopia and all the Thessalian cities he had recently recovered. For these cities, changing hands twice in one year, the truce was all too short. Thinking that they could now negotiate with Rome from a position of greater strength, the Aetolians sent a fresh batch of ambassadors for talks in Rome—but they were captured by Epirote pirates, and by the time the Romans heard about it and ordered their release, Fulvius was marching on Ambracia and there was clearly no longer any point in negotiating for peace.

The siege of Ambracia by Fulvius became the stuff of legend.[16] The Romans employed massive force, with no fewer than five siege towers deployed at various parts of the city wall, but the Aetolians found ingenious ways to combat them, by constructing cranes on the wall to drop rocks onto the towers, and by sallying out of the city at night to sabotage the machines. Every time the Romans succeeded in breaching a section of wall, the Aetolians built counter-walls and fought on in the breaches. Finally, the Romans tried to undermine the walls, but the Aetolians dug counter-tunnels and found a way to fan the acrid smoke of burning feathers down the tunnels to drive the enemy out. (See Fig. 7.1.)

The fame of the siege was due in large part to the Roman poet Quintus Ennius. He accompanied his patron Fulvius on this campaign and celebrated the siege twice—once in the climactic final book of his *Annales*, his epic account of Rome's history (though toward the end of his life he added three more books), and once as a play, simply called *Ambracia*. No significant lines survive, unfortunately, from either work. The defenders eventually surrendered only when Amynander, who had been resident there until recently, got the consul's permission (he was an enemy, after all) to enter the city and persuade them to spare themselves further suffering.

While the siege was going on, Philip's son Perseus recovered Dolopia from the Aetolians, who were now fighting on three fronts—not just at Ambracia and in Dolopia, but in defense of their coastline against Pleuratus and the Achaeans. When they next approached Fulvius about peace, he stated his terms, which the Aetolians accepted. According to the conditions that were subsequently worked out in Rome, they were to pay an indemnity of 500 talents over six years, they were to "acknowledge the

FIGURE 7.1

This panel from Trajan's column in Rome (113 CE) shows Roman soldiers in "tortoise" formation (shields interlocked over heads) attacking a besieged town, whose defenders are visible on the wall.

rule and dominion of Rome,"[17] and their territory was reduced to the pre-war status quo, so that they lost, most importantly, Ambracia, Delphi, and Oeniadae. Cephallenia was taken from them separately, simply by Roman fiat, but Fulvius's takeover of the island was far from smooth, and he had to sack the main town after a long and bloody siege over the winter of

189–188. Oeniadae was at last returned to the Acarnanians, and, in poor compensation for the catastrophe it had suffered, Ambracia was made a free and autonomous city. And so one of the great leagues of Greece reverted to a minor role in Greek history; their capitulation stressed the league to breaking point and before long we find them further reduced by civil strife.[18]

Again, as with Vulso, there was political opposition to Fulvius's triumph when he returned home—typical of senatorial competitiveness—with Marcus Aemilius Lepidus, holding his first consulship in 187, claiming that, since Ambracia had not been taken by force, Fulvius did not deserve a triumph. Lepidus was supported by Marcus Porcius Cato, who had been on Fulvius's staff and primed the Ambraciotes to give a heart-rending account of their suffering. In the end, Fulvius got his triumph, but the senators agonized over the loot, the quantity and value of which embarrassed them, especially since it arrived in Rome at much the same time as Vulso's Asian plunder. And well it might have embarrassed them: Ambracia, for instance, was bankrupted and, after a long decline, disappeared as an independent entity about 150 years later.[19]

ENNIUS AND EARLY LATIN LITERATURE

Quintus Ennius, in the train of his patron Fulvius at Ambracia, was one of the stars of early Roman literature—all of whom were Italian "half-Greeks," whose first language was Greek or Oscan, or at any rate not Latin. Ennius, originally from Calabria, drew extensively on Greek models for all forms of verse, even in *Annales* and *Ambracia*, where his themes were centrally Roman. He placed himself squarely in the Greek tradition, claiming to be a reincarnation of Homer, disdaining native Roman meters as rustic, and insisting that his adaptations of Greek forms opened up a whole new world for Rome. He was well repaid for celebrating Fulvius's achievements: not only did Fulvius arrange for him to become a Roman citizen, but among the booty he brought back from Ambracia was a statue group of the Muses, which became the centrepiece of a new temple in Rome (in the Field of Mars), dedicated to "Hercules of the Muses." It was the first literary temple in Rome, and became the haunt of poets and other men of letters.

Ennius and his fellow "half-Greeks" were well placed to act as brokers between one culture and the other. The playwright Gnaeus Naevius (last half of the third century) came from Campania and wrote comedies and tragedies, most of which were based on Greek originals, both in meter and in plot. His contemporary, Lucius Livius Andronicus, came from Tarentum and wrote all kinds of verse, adapted to a Roman audience, but drawing often on Greek tradition for his meters as well as his storylines and methods. It is a significant irony that the first major work of Latin literature was the translation into Latin by a Greek of a Greek master-piece—Livius's translation of Homer's *Odyssey*.

Plays feature predominantly in early Latin literature, and new oppor-tunities for theatrical performances mushroomed towards the end of the third century, until by the middle of the second century almost twenty days a year were given over in Rome to theatrical performances, not counting private productions. Terence's comic masterpiece *The Brothers*, for instance, was first performed at the funeral of Lucius Aemilius Paullus in 160. Comedies were especially popular, with Titus Maccius Plautus the star of the first generation, on the cusp of the third and second centuries, followed by Terence (Publius Terentius Afer). Both of them adapted exist-ing Greek plays, light situation comedies, for their Latin productions.

Plautus and Terence are the first two Latin writers any of whose work survives complete; even for Ennius, we have only about six hundred lines of *Annales*, mostly disconnected fragments, but we have twenty-one more-or-less complete plays by Plautus and six by Terence—enough to see that Terence's work occupied a slightly higher linguistic register, and involved more sophisticated plots, than Plautus's frequent slapstick. To generalize, Plautus still stood within the rustic tradition of Italian popu-lar comedy, while Terence appealed to a more refined audience. But both of them straddled the Greek and Roman worlds: Latin puns abound in Greek cities; Roman morals are grafted onto Greek institutions. The plays were known as *fabulae palliatae*, "tales in Greek dress," but both play-wrights, particularly Plautus, naturally used their productions to com-ment on the contemporary Roman scene.[20]

A similar tale of Greek influence could be told for early Roman prose works as well. When Quintus Fabius Pictor and Lucius Cincius Alimentus wrote the first histories of Rome towards the end of the third century BCE (sadly lost), they chose Greek because there was no tradition of such writing in Latin—and, interestingly, they already expected their peers to be able to read their work. The first prose works written in Latin were composed by Cato the Censor in the first half of the second century. It was only in the first century BCE that Latin literature became distinctively Roman, with its own genres, meters, and conventions. But, as its roots in the third and second centuries show, the foundation of Latin literature was Greek. Virgil, writing toward the end of the first century, represents the end of this first phase of Latin literature: his poetry is utterly Roman in sentiment and language—but quite impossible without Greek precedents. Cicero's jingoistic claim at the start of his *Tusculan Disputations*, that the Romans had improved on what they had learned from the Greeks, seems arguable, but by Virgil's time they had, at any rate, absorbed Greek culture so thoroughly that the new Roman literature was an organic unity formed by both cultures.

ROME ALONE

Philip's position at the end of the war was somewhat better than at the beginning, and he might have hoped for generous treatment by the Romans in return for his considerable military and logistical assistance. But he was also an old enemy. The terms in which Flamininus criticized Glabrio's siege of Naupactus were telling: it has gained you nothing and Philip a great deal.[21] Also telling was the way Philip was treated over Lamia in 191: Glabrio was simultaneously besieging Heraclea, and when that fell first he quickly granted the Aetolians an ad hoc truce, which prevented Philip from taking Lamia.[22] On the other hand, Philip had got Demetrius and Demetrias back, and had his indemnity canceled.

What would the Romans do with Philip now that the war with Antiochus was over? They continued to snub him: Athamania was allowed to remain independent;[23] the independence of Orestis was reconfirmed; the Aetolians had Heraclea restored to them, and the rest of Philip's new possessions were passed over in ominous silence, awaiting the Romans' decision.[24] Philip was the victim of the balance-of-powers policy, of leaving no state in Greece in a position to dominate the rest, so that Rome could dominate them all. He must have been particularly aggrieved by the Roman decision to award parts of Thrace to Eumenes. Why should an Asiatic king gain territory in Europe, territory adjacent to Macedon? The way the Romans saw it, however, Philip's assistance had merely been repayment for their leaving him in place after Cynoscephalae, instead of removing him as the Aetolians wanted; they did not feel they owed him anything more. He was retained now as one of the four powers with which Rome had replaced all the many minor powers they had first found in Greece and Asia Minor: the Achaean League and Macedon in Greece, and Pergamum and Rhodes in Asia Minor.

But the snub festered in Philip's heart, and his resentment was known, or guessed at. There is a story that, every day for the rest of his life, he had the terms of the peace treaty of 196 read out to him, to taste his bitterness.[25] When in autumn 188, just a few months after the end of the war, Vulso withdrew the Roman forces from Asia Minor, his route back to the west coast of Greece took him through Thrace and Macedon. He was attacked by a coalition of Thracian tribes and lost many men, and (as mentioned earlier) some of his booty. The rumor arose that it was Philip who had put the Thracians up to it and, in general, that he was already committed to the renewal of war.

THE IRON FIST

The Roman defeat of Antiochus was their third victory over a Mediterranean superpower in less than twenty years: Carthage, Macedon, and now the Seleucid kingdom. None of them would ever fully recover, and the Romans were left in control. The dynamics of the Mediterranean were altered for ever and, in acknowledgment of that fact, the flavor of Roman dominance changed. The settlements that were imposed on Asia

Minor and Greece made little attempt to pretend that the freedom of the Greeks had the slightest relevance. The new Roman policy, perhaps developed by the Scipios, was an extension of the same basic idea—to create a balance of powers such that all the main powers involved would depend on Rome—but Flamininus had at least pretended that he trusted the Greeks to look after their own affairs, and had maintained the pretense as a way of getting the Greeks on his side.

But now the Romans were dictating the norms and standards of Mediterranean international affairs, and no longer felt the need for Flamininian camouflage. On the blunter, Scipionic policy, there was no need to keep the Greeks happy, just compliant; they transformed Flamininus's reliance on Rome's authority into a more immediate reliance on the threat of force. The ebb and flow of Roman withdrawal and return had already made the Greeks aware that the velvet glove could very quickly be stripped off. And the four powers that had been set up in balance were made aware that their local power was dependent on the goodwill of Rome, and that Rome's goodwill was dependent upon their behaving themselves. Prophecies assured those Romans who were inclined to believe them that the defeat of Antiochus was the last important step toward world dominion—that the four empires of the Assyrians, the Medes, the Persians, and the Macedonians, would be followed by a more glorious fifth and final world-straddling empire[26] —and the Romans acted accordingly.

In 1997 an inscription was published that had been found in a village in central Turkey; it preserved three (or two and a bit) letters written by Eumenes to the town of Tyriaeum, one of the many places he inherited after the defeat of Antiochus from the Seleucid empire. The details of the letters do not concern us, but a sentence occurs in the first one that confirms what we might have guessed anyway. Eumenes assures the citizens of Tyriaeum that any benefaction of his to the city will be secure because his authority is guaranteed by the Romans.[27] He was perfectly aware, as no doubt the Rhodians were too, that he owed his position to Rome, and therefore that Rome could take it away at will. And he impressed upon his subjects that his power was really just Rome's power at one remove. He apparently enjoyed being a puppet; Pergamum certainly prospered at this time.

A few years earlier, a Roman praetor had written to the people of the Asiatic Greek city of Teos, in response to their request that, as a sacred site, their city should be inviolate.[28] Again, the details need not concern us (Teos was granted inviolability, and proudly preserved the letter as an inscription), because what is significant is the last sentence in which the praetor tells the Teans that the Romans would continue to do them good "as long as in the future you maintain your goodwill toward us." The Greeks were to be free provided that they did not forget who their benefactors were and behaved appropriately.

So also, leaving inscriptions aside, we find Eumenes consistently behaving in an obsequious manner towards the Senate. In one speech there, for instance,[29] he professed himself their greatest and most loyal friend, and reminded them how he had always bent over backwards to do Rome good. In another, he echoed the Tyriaeum inscription by acknowledging to the Senate that his kingdom "owes its greatness and prominence to you," and ended by saying that he, like all Rome's allies, was entirely dependent on Rome.[30] Of course, in both cases he was trying to manipulate the Senate for his own advantage, but he knew the key that unlocked their favors.

From now on, this was the way to get into the Senate's good books. In 189 the Aetolians were told off for not approaching the Senate with sufficient humility; in 172 some Carthaginian emissaries to the Senate got their way by prostrating themselves on the ground before the senators; in 167 Prusias II of Bithynia, though a king, did the same, while addressing the senators as Savior Gods. Deference, or obsequiousness, was the natural counterpart of the arrogant Roman assumption that they could act as they liked. The Romans were determined to have no equals in the Mediterranean, and it pleased them to be reminded once in a while of their success at this.[31] Eumenes so successfully proved himself a Roman puppy that he was remembered for it: the historian Sallust, writing in the middle of the first century BCE, said that the Romans "made him the custodian of territory they had captured, and used taxes and insults to change him from a king to the most abject of slaves."[32]

There was a recognition at the time that, withdrawal or no withdrawal, the Romans were now dominant in the Mediterranean. In a speech before the Senate in 189, a Rhodian claimed (according to our sources) that the gods had already given Rome dominion over the entire known world and spoke of Rome maintaining control in the east not by standing armies, but by "jurisdiction": all the land you have conquered by force of arms, he said, should now be subject to your jurisdiction, and the former subjects of Antiochus's empire will be happy to have their freedom protected by your weaponry.[33] This speech shows awareness, then, of the nature of the new version of remote control: first force, then authority backed up by the threat of re-invasion. Other speakers in Livy show the same awareness: a spokesman for Antiochus in 192 described the whole world as "subject to the will and sway of Rome."[34] The presence or absence of a standing army was relatively unimportant. Acquiescence in Rome's superior status was an acceptable alternative to direct rule.

8.

REMOTE CONTROL

IN THE COURSE OF the Syrian–Aetolian War, the Romans had deliberately extended their influence into Asia Minor as well as fixing it
deeper in Greece. Asia Minor now occupied the more remote periphery,
while Greece was closer to the center, easier to control. By the end of
the war in 188, the process that Polybius identified as beginning in 217,
the fusion of the two halves of the Mediterranean into an organic whole
under Rome, was irreversible. Everyone in the eastern Mediterranean
looked to Rome for everything from advice to assistance, and in so doing
positioned themselves on the periphery of its center. Of course, Greek
states still interacted with one another as well; they were neighbors, old
friends or rivals, and they met at the conference table and occasionally
(though far more rarely than before) on the battlefield. But Rome was
now the recipient and umpire of all important business, everything that
might have wider implications in the Mediterranean, and at the same time
it continued (as in the case of Nabis in 195) to intervene from time to time
at a local level as well. The tactic of occasional local intervention worked
well: it kept even that kind of dependent petition coming in because the
petitioners never knew when they might be successful.

Rome occupied a canonical imperialist position, that of a dominant center with subordinate peripheries, but it did so in an unusual
way. The Romans were a long way from making Greece a permanent,
exploitable province, with an army, colonial administrative structures,
and tribute-payment. Instead, thanks above all to Flamininus, they had
developed instruments that allowed them to maintain their budding
eastern empire by remote control. But Flamininus was only building on

diplomatic concepts that had long governed Rome's relationships with other states. The most important of these was friendship.

DIPLOMATIC FRIENDSHIP

We still think of relations between states in terms of friendship: the original articles of confederation of the thirteen colonies of the United States committed them to friendship with one another; we talk of the "special relationship" between Britain and the USA. This manner of thinking was even more natural in the ancient world. Much Mediterranean diplomacy had for centuries been carried on by aristocrats who had a special relationship (called by the Greeks *xenia*, "ritualized friendship") with their peers in other states, Greek or non-Greek. Then, even in Roman times, it was not so much "Rome" that entered into a relationship with "Athens," as "the Romans" with "the Athenians." States were considered less as geographical entities with borders than as peoples. This too made it easier to think in terms of friendship.

States or peoples or kings became "friends of Rome" in a number of ways. Full alliance by treaty was one, but was rarely used by Rome at first in their dealings with Greeks. They had a treaty of alliance in place with the Achaeans (192), and peace treaties with Philip (196), the Aetolians (189), and Antiochus (188), but all their other relationships were informal. There was a record (the *formula amicorum*) of all those who had been accepted into friendship with Rome, and there was certainly a sense in the Senate of how their friends ought to behave, because this drove many of their foreign-policy responses. But there were no written stipulations. The situation differed from the Roman administration of Spain, where the inhabitants were regarded as barbarians with no true political structures, in need of more direct forms of control by Rome. The Greeks, however, were cultured and civilized, and already had structures such that the Romans could hope to leave them to administer themselves (or to be administered by their proxies, such as Eumenes and the Rhodians), while they remained a more remote presence.

There were other ways in which a state became a friend of Rome. Military or even just diplomatic cooperation made one a friend; surrender to Rome, either voluntary or involuntary, sometimes resulted in friendship, because it was understood that the now-dominant Romans would not make demands that were too outrageous. On one model of personal friendship familiar to the Romans, the junior partners in the relationship were expected to provide a range of services to the senior partner: financing, legal advice, accommodation, insurance, and so on—services which, in Rome of the middle Republic, were all but nonexistent. Something similar obtained in international friendship as well. Rome's friends were not just expected to be courteous, serviceable, and loyal, but they were also expected not to threaten Roman security, and to help Roman wars, by providing men, matériel, supplies, intelligence, and advice. Failure in these respects might be taken to constitute a breach of the friendship.

Rome might ask for this kind of help, but it was even better if it was unsolicited. Rome's friends were also expected to help the Romans keep the peace, for instance by mediating between two states which were threatening to disrupt it. They were expected to consult with Rome before undertaking any extreme action. Friends of Rome had the right to travel to Rome at any time to present their case; others had to get permission from the local Roman commander, and in a time of war a truce was arranged to give them time for the journey. Hence a good tactic for a non-friend was to get a third party, a friend of Rome, to travel there and present the case. Only official friends were allowed to cross the *pomerium*, the boundary just outside the original city walls that distinguished "Rome" from "the outside world," and embassies from non-friends might be kept hanging around for ages, as a form of insult.

The Romans too had obligations, as friends. Their side of the bargain was that, in a crisis, they would act to preserve their friends' liberty— by diplomacy or, if there were no choice, by military intervention. At a local level, they would help those factions or political groupings within particular cities whose petitions seemed to further Roman interests. But none of this was cast in iron; friendship is more flexible than that. There was no automatic equation such that "event A gets response B." It is clear that Greek petitioners to Rome often hoped for armed intervention,[1] but as far as the Romans were concerned a range of responses was possible, from inaction to invasion; international friendship was as flexible as interpersonal friendship. A friend was expected to act like a friend, that was all. Buffered by obligations, international friends were not even required to like each other.

The system had advantages and disadvantages, but most of the disadvantages were on the side of the subordinate partner. Just as in unequal personal friendships, it was generally up to the dominant partner to decide whether or not the subject partner had behaved appropriately, and how leniently or severely to respond. Hence, just before evacuating Greece, Flamininus warned the Greeks to use their freedom responsibly.[2] Underscoring the Roman legates' insistence that Antiochus withdraw from Thrace was the suggestion that his Thracian ventures were not the behavior of someone who had entered into friendship with the Roman people.

The Romans could not act too outrageously, or they would jeopardize the whole house of cards built on the vague concept, the whole network of friends. But, generally, the subject partner had far less room for maneuver than Rome itself, and was frequently forced into a kind of paranoia, where it had to try to guess in advance what it could get away with, and what Rome's reaction would be. Of course, there were situations that were beyond the pale, such as if one of Rome's friends made war on another of its friends, but generally there was a lot of flexibility. Fear is an economical way of ruling, a useful tool of remote control.[3] From this perspective, the efforts of Greeks to be independent look pretty futile, but the Romans still had no military presence, and so even behavior of which they might disapprove could be got away with, as long as it was not too extreme and did not impinge on other factors that the Senate might take seriously. The very inconsistency of Roman responses was itself a tool of subordination, since it kept both friends and enemies uncertain and fearful.

One of the great advantages, for the Romans, of Flamininus's diplomacy in Greece was that it enhanced the asymmetry of their relations with the Greek states. By conferring the gift of "freedom," at a stroke Flamininus made them all subordinate friends of Rome. "The hand that gives is above the hand that receives," as Napoleon is supposed to have said. Even though the weaknesses of Flamininus's policy soon became clear, the rhetoric of "freedom" was still used, precisely because it enhanced the asymmetry.

Nor was it just Rome's friends who were made to recognize their subordinate position, but even its supposed equals. Though we do not have the text of the 192 treaty with the Achaeans, it is clear from references to it that it was a treaty between equals.[4] Nevertheless, Rome's relations with the Achaeans throughout the 180s were marked by repeated attempts to bully them into doing what the Romans wanted, until the Achaean general of 184 cried out in exasperation to a Roman legate: "So you're saying that our treaty only appears equal! That in fact Achaean freedom is fragile and all power is vested in Rome!"[5]

Rome's relationships with its subordinate partners were sustained and developed largely by diplomacy. Immediately after the defeat of Antiochus, "almost all the peoples and communities" of Asia Minor made their representations to Rome,[6] and so it continued, from both Asia Minor and Greece. This must have generated an enormous amount of tedious business in the Senate, but the senators seem to have accepted it as the unavoidable consequence of remote control, and to have expected to be consulted even on minor matters.[7] It is an obvious, instinctive way of maintaining control, familiar to everyone from his or her experiences of office or family dynamics.

It also slotted right into Greek modes of thought: the Greek states had always seen their relations with other states in terms of a pecking order; every time they appealed to Rome, then, they maintained Rome's position higher up the order than theirs. It makes no difference that probably none of the Greeks' petitions to Rome was free of self-interest. And it makes no difference that the initiative for most of these diplomatic missions came from the Greeks themselves, not the Romans. The diplomacy still maintained the pecking order. The military theorist of the early nineteenth century, Carl von Clausewitz, famously quipped that war was the continuation of diplomatic goals by other means. For the Romans of the middle Republic, diplomacy was no less a tool of subjection than war. They arranged things so that the Greek states had to turn to them, and were bound to be divided among themselves, and internally into pro- and anti-Roman factions.

The Greek states came as petitioners, but they also often came with news that they thought might alarm the Senate, especially when they stood to profit if Rome's reaction was to quell or reprimand a trouble-some neighbor. They phrased this information so that it seemed threaten-ing to the balance of power. Since balances of power are often fragile, at least once a year the Romans felt they had to respond to these petitions with investigatory senatorial missions. The regularity of these missions was another tool of remote control. All the important Greek states, and many minor ones too, were frequently reminded of their position with regard to Rome, and of the threat of military intervention that these leg-ates explicitly or implicitly wielded. They remembered the brutality of Roman warfare—brutality whose purpose was to create the conditions for deference—and were reminded of their obligations as Roman friends. Naturally, the only way that these diplomatic relationships could develop was to further subordinate Rome's friends to its authority and might. The balance of powers was important to Rome not least because it was a way of ensuring that Rome stood out as the only true wielder of power.

At the very beginning of their expansion in Italy, the Romans found that local elites were often prepared to accept them as overlords as long as the Romans were prepared to help them retain power. The tactic is famil-iar from imperialists of all times and places, especially as "indirect rule" in British India; enrichment of the power-possessors breeds loyalty.[8] Just as it had in Italy, so in Greece and Asia Minor Rome had a tendency to raise local elites to power and leave them to look after their communities. In Thessaly, for instance, Flamininus "chose both a council and judges essentially on the basis of property."[9]

But Roman support of elites was not a revolutionary move: other fac-tors were tending to make the cities increasingly dependent on local plu-tocrats anyway. Civic impoverishment, for instance, made it imperative for the local rich to shoulder the expenses as well as the duties of gov-ernment, with the result that many Greek cities were now oligarchies or covert oligarchies. All the Romans did was accelerate the process. It would be a Marxist exaggeration, however, to claim that any of Rome's wars in the east were class wars. The common people, in so far as they could have their views heard, would probably have found it hard to distinguish, in terms of the quality of their lives, between Roman rule and Macedonian rule. It was largely the elites themselves, the power-possessors, who were divided into pro- and anti-Roman factions, and they used their powers of persuasion to win the common people to their respective causes.

CENTRAL GREECE

The establishment of Roman dominion after the Syrian–Aetolian War did at least have the positive effect of suppressing major warfare in Greece, its first taste of *pax Romana*. Asia Minor was another matter, but, apart from Philip's campaigns in Thrace and the Achaeans' ongoing conflict with Messene, the Greeks of the Balkan peninsula could resume normal life and activities in the 180s and 170s, and try to recover from the devastations of previous decades. Nevertheless, the air was thick with potential, and there was a gradual escalation of tension. The reason was that a great many of the complaints that reached Rome concerned Macedonian activity, and it was clear that the Senate welcomed such petitions, that it was still inclined to think the worst of Macedonian rulers.[10]

Over the years of peace, there were plenty of signs that the balance of powers was unstable. Even before the evacuation was complete, the Senate was receiving complaints about Aetolian activity in and around Delphi. The denial of Aetolian control of the sacred center, and of the prestigious Amphictyonic Council that was based there, was a major element in the Roman curtailment of the league. Delphi was declared free, and even land owned privately by individual Aetolians was summarily confiscated.[11] But Aetolia had been bankrupted by the peace terms, and individuals as well as the state found themselves in financial difficulties; a few years later, the league had to institute a general cancellation of debts to relieve individual suffering.[12] Not unnaturally, some Aetolians attempted to recover some of the property—especially slaves and flocks—that had been abandoned on their estates. Delphian emissaries complained to the Senate about these raids and asked for a restatement of their freedom from Aetolia, which they obtained. But these emissaries were murdered on their way back from Rome, presumably by Aetolians. Fulvius was ordered to go to Delphi as soon as he had completed the subjugation of Cephallenia, and he oversaw the eviction of the Aetolians and the return of all stolen property to the Delphians.[13]

Then, also in 188, there was further trouble in ever-troubled Boeotia. At the instigation of Flamininus, the Senate wrote to the Boeotian authorities, ordering them to restore from exile Zeuxippus and other members of the pro-Roman faction who had been banished after the murder of Brachylles. The pro-Macedonian Boeotians responded by condemning Zeuxippus *in absentia* for the murder (and, for good measure, for robbing a temple) and then politely explained that they could not countenance the return of such a dreadful criminal to their land. Zeuxippus appeared in person before the Senate, and the Senate asked the Achaeans and Aetolians to see to his restoration. The Aetolians did nothing, and Philopoemen seized the opportunity to push for the settlement of a number of Achaean property claims in Boeotia. The situation became very tense indeed, and the Senate wisely refrained from making things worse by insisting on the fulfillment of its order about Zeuxippus. Eventually, the situation died down of its own accord.

The first of these two cases, the turmoil in Delphi, went unreported by Polybius (and, therefore, by Livy), and we know about it only from inscriptions. It can hardly be doubted that, if more inscriptions had survived, we would know about more such cases. There must have been dozens, or even hundreds, given the sweeping arrangements the Romans had been making for Greece since 196. But these two examples will do to show that Greece was still unstable, and that, with or without an army, the Romans expected to have a say in local Greek affairs. In the years following the Syrian–Aetolian War they maintained their involvement in Greek affairs, and so, inevitably, came to see Greece more and more as a dependent satellite.

THE PELOPONNESE

The worst turbulence in the decade following the Roman withdrawal of 188 arose within the Peloponnese. The annexation of Sparta by the Achaean League proved troublesome: Sparta had been in turmoil for so long that dozens of its leading citizens had ended up in exile. Once Sparta became a member of the league, these men pushed for their restoration and the return of their family properties, so the Achaeans were faced with complex and time-consuming claims dating back thirty years or more, as well as by hostile political factions that wanted Spartan independence and Rome as its guarantor. And then there was also, as always, Messene. In 183, Messene seceded from the league, having rejoined it only in 191. The terms of its re-incorporation had involved the loss of some of its outlying villages and towns, and it was probably resentment over this that led to the new rebellion.

The Romans did their best by means of successive visits by senior legates—Quintus Caecilius Metellus in 185, Appius Claudius Pulcher in 184, Quintus Marcius Philippus in 183—to retain control of the situation themselves, and to defuse the increasing potential for violence. But Philopoemen and his group were still strong within the league, and they resented Roman interference. Their insistence on sorting out the Peloponnese by themselves irritated the legates, and all of them returned to Rome with unfavorable reports about the league's intransigence. Not only was the rift between the league and Rome widening, but awareness of Roman hostility also strengthened those Achaeans, especially Callicrates, who were more prepared to find some accommodation with Rome, and who saw that now the very survival of the league depended on obedience to Rome.

In the winter of 183–182, when everything was ready for the war against Messene (except that Philopoemen was ill), the Achaeans first asked the Senate for military help, since the treaty between them stipulated, in the traditional phrase, that they should have the same friends and enemies. The request coincided with the meeting at which Marcius gave his unfavorable report about the league, and the Senate gave an extraordinary reply: not only would they not help them in this venture, but they would not lift a finger even if other members of the Achaean League wanted to secede. As an attempt to argue that the affairs of the league did not concern them, this response was utterly hypocritical, since they involved themselves in its affairs whenever they felt like it. As an attempt to undermine the league by encouraging the secession first of Sparta, and then of any other member of the Achaean League, it was bound to set rival Achaean politicians against one another, the pro-Romans arguing that without Rome their league would be dissolved, and the anti-Romans confirmed in their determination to go it alone.

Throwing aside his illness and his seventy years, Philopoemen leapt from his sick-bed to lead the attempt to regain Messene, but he was taken prisoner and executed by his enemies within the city. The murder was futile, because Lycortas (the father of Polybius), now head of the Philopoemenist faction, very soon re-incorporated the city into the league. More territory was removed from it and, as in Sparta in 188, the anti-Achaeans were violently and crudely eliminated. Further land disputes followed, but Lycortas's settlement endured for a while. In the meantime, Sparta had taken the Romans' hint and had again seceded from the league, but Lycortas followed up his success at Messene by re-incorporating Sparta as well.

But the many divisions within Spartan society remained, and there was a real risk now that the Romans, who were becoming increasingly impatient with the Philopoemenists' recalcitrance, would take action of some kind against the league. Under these circumstances, it was perhaps fortunate that Philopoemen's death allowed his political opponents to gain greater power, and that there was an Achaean statesman who was looked upon favorably by Rome. During his generalship in 180, and on a subsequent mission to Rome in 179, Callicrates gained Roman approval of the settlement of Messene, and brought the Spartan problem to an end, not so much by measures that had not been tried before, but just because everyone knew that he had the backing of Rome.

According to Polybius, in fact, when in Rome Callicrates lectured the senators and told them they needed to be more assertive in Greece—that the only way to resolve local issues such as Sparta was to let it be known, in every case, which side they were on and what they wanted to see done. They should not make suggestions, but give orders. With the implied threat of force behind these words, Greek statesmen would soon see that they had no choice but to do Rome's bidding, and pretty soon all Greek states would be Roman puppets.

What Polybius was doing here was personalizing, by means of his loathing for Callicrates, something that he rightly saw as an outcome of the Spartan problem: a considerable strengthening not just of the pro-Roman party in Achaea, but also of their counterparts all over Greece. The senators' backing of Callicrates made it clear to the leaders of Greece that they wanted to see more quislings in power, and they also wrote to a number of Greek states, asking them to make sure that the provisions they had put in place for Sparta were this time carried out by the Achaeans. This was a canny move: all the states involved (Epirus, Aetolia, Acarnania, Boeotia, Athens) would immediately learn what kind of behavior was expected of them in the future. And in the longer term, it was clear that equality was no longer an option, for the Achaeans or anyone else; the problems had been generated precisely by the treaty of equality that Rome had entered into with the Achaeans, which had given the Philopoemenists the mistaken idea that they could pursue their own policies. Legally, they were right; but their shaky grasp of the new Mediterranean reality gave Callicrates the lever with which to topple them. And so for the next twenty years it was Callicrates' group that held most power in the league.

MACEDON

As we have seen, Philip emerged from the war with Antiochus somewhat better off than before, in the sense that he was one of the powers the Romans left in place to achieve an overall balance—the Achaeans and Macedon in Greece, Rhodes and Pergamum in Asia Minor. But he still felt himself to have been snubbed. He had rendered good service to the Romans—suffering a defeat by the Aetolians in the winter of 190/189, for instance, or supplying troops under his eldest son Perseus for the siege of Ambracia in 189. But the defeat of Antiochus canceled the Roman need to keep Philip sweet; they made peace with the Aetolians without consulting him or any of their allies, and failed to reward him. In pursuit of a balance of the Greek powers, they even allowed Aetolia some gains, and gave Eumenes, an Asiatic king, territories in Europe that Philip might have expected.

As a Hellenistic king, Philip's choices were circumscribed. If he did nothing, he would lose face and even risk being deposed from within Macedon; there were plenty of precedents for that in Macedonian history, and at some point in the closing years of his reign he did in fact feel obliged to put a number of Macedonian nobles to death. We do not know for certain that the purpose of their conspiracy was to replace him on the throne, but it is hard to see what else it might have been. So Philip prepared to resist by military means. It was clear now that the Romans had treated him as a friend only as long as Antiochus was a threat, and that they intended to keep him down as well.

Philip began, in 187 or 186, by occupying Aenus and Maronea, from which Antiochus's garrisons had been cleared at the end of the war. Eumenes complained most bitterly at this, since these places had been two of his prizes in the settlement. When Caecilius Metellus was in Greece in 185, he arranged two meetings to hear all the complaints against Philip and give him a chance to defend himself. The upshot was that Philip was ordered to withdraw immediately from all the territories he had gained during or after the war. As in 196, Macedon was to be reduced to its "ancient borders."[14] This was devastating for Philip, but perhaps not unexpected: many of these possessions were precisely the ones that had been passed over in ominous silence in the treaty with the Aetolians. He had no choice but to comply, but he warned the meeting: "The sun has not yet set on Macedon."[15]

During the turmoil of the evacuation in 184, a band of Thracians burst into Maronea and massacred all the main opponents of Macedonian rule. This happened just before Claudius Pulcher's ambassadorial visit, the primary purpose of which was to respond to Thessalian and Pergamene complaints from the previous year that Philip was being slow to evacuate his garrisons. Claudius reprimanded Philip for the massacre, but he denied responsibility and blamed it on factional feuding among the Maroneans themselves. Claudius was unimpressed, and insisted on sending the man who was widely known to have instigated the affair at Philip's behest for interrogation to Rome. Philip agreed—but had the man murdered before he reached Rome.

In order to answer these charges, and perhaps in order to buy some time, Philip sent a senior delegation to Rome, consisting of some close advisers and his son Demetrius, now aged twenty-four. Demetrius was Philip's best bet as a front man in Rome, since his earlier sojourn there as a teenage hostage had earned him influential friends. And, indeed, the senators did take pity on Demetrius's being placed in such a stressful situation. They sent him back to Macedon with a message for his father: it is only thanks to Demetrius that we are not pressing these charges, but you can expect another commission shortly to make sure that from now on you obey the stipulations of the settlement.

This next commission was the one headed by Marcius Philippus in 183. The report he brought back to Rome about Philip was extremely negative. He told the Senate that Philip was conforming only to the letter of the treaty, and doing the bare minimum to comply. More importantly, he told them of his conviction that Philip was gearing up for war. For instance, he had resettled central areas of Macedon with the populations of outlying areas and moved Thracians into the abandoned outlying areas. This was one of a number of measures Philip took to replenish the Macedonian population—and hence restock his army. For the Macedonian system was that, in return for being granted land by the king, a settler was obliged to serve in the army. His garrisons from Aenus, Maronea, and elsewhere would also be returning, of course, and he could always surreptitiously hire mercenaries. At the same time, he did his best to bring Macedonian farmland, forests, and mines back to full production, to maximize his income, and, looking to the future, he encouraged his subjects to take advantage of these years of peace to produce children. The Senate's response to Marcius's report, therefore, was to thank Philip for his compliance, and warn him that not even the appearance of disobedience would be tolerated. This was not, of course, any indication of indifference, and Philip did not take it as such; he knew that the Romans were only awaiting an opportunity.

A Hellenistic king must campaign, but Philip could not afford to antagonize the Romans. So throughout the late 180s he launched successive expeditions against the non-Greek Thracians and other tribes to the north, until he had established a greater Macedonian presence there than perhaps any king before him. This is one of the things that made Aenus and Maronea important to him: the interior was less useful without these places on the coast. Since he could not have Aenus and Maronea, he got on good terms with Byzantium instead by sending them troops for some affair the details of which are lost to us.

Philip's first aim was recruitment: by subjugating the northern tribes, or even entering into alliances with them (as Perseus was offered a Bastarnian princess, and Philip gave one of his daughters to a Thracian dynast), they would be obliged to serve in his armies. Eumenes would later claim that Thrace had the potential to act as a never-failing source of troops for Macedon.[16] Philip's second aim was security: he wanted the Bastarnae (a Germanic tribe that had recently moved into territory just north of the Danube) to help him against the Dardanians. There was an element of risk in this, since at least some of the Dardanian tribes, those controlled by Bato, had helped the Romans during the war. But it had long been a Macedonian dream to eliminate the perennial Dardanian threat.

Since everyone knew that the Romans were glad to hear complaints about Philip, this Thracian activity of his generated an enormous number of emissaries to Rome. In the winter of 184–183 alone, three whole days of senatorial time had to be allotted just to complaints about Philip.[17] The petitioners did their best to portray his campaigns as threatening to the balance of power or even to Rome: knowing Roman fears, Philip's dealings with the Bastarnae were made out, against all likelihood, to be attempts to persuade them to invade Italy. In actual fact, what Philip was doing was strengthening his kingdom, and his position on the throne, in the only way he could. Ironically, by coming to terms with the tribes on his northern borders, he was making Macedon precisely the kind of bulwark against them that Flamininus had envisaged.[18] But everyone knew that the Romans were carefully monitoring his activities.

A DIVIDED COURT

There is no doubt that, of Philip's two sons, the Romans favored Demetrius. After the young prince's visit there in 184, Flamininus, acting not ex officio but in his capacity as senior Greek expert, even wrote to Philip, saying that Demetrius would be welcome in Rome any time. But, apart from this solid fact, the story of an intriguing episode in Macedonian history has been badly tainted by rumor, gossip, melodrama, and propaganda—as coups or attempted coups over the Macedonian succession always tended to be. Philip was ill, approaching sixty, and unlikely to live for much longer. It makes sense in this context to think that the Romans might have tried to groom Demetrius for rulership in his father's place. Nothing could be more in keeping with the policy of remote control, and in their later imperial history they made considerable use of friendly kings, especially on the borders of the empire. Demetrius would be the Macedonian equivalent of Callicrates in Achaea, the kind of compliant leader that the Romans wanted to see in power.

That is exactly the story we get in Polybius. He claims that, during Demetrius's visit to Rome, Flamininus and others took the prince aside and began to tempt him with the idea that they could secure the Macedonian throne for him, in place of his elder brother Perseus.[19] In the Hellenistic courts, the eldest son was usually the prime candidate—but not always. Perseus, however, had clearly been marked out as the heir apparent, in traditional Macedonian ways: Philip had used him from an early age to lead significant military campaigns, and in 183 he gave the name Perseis to a new fortress town in Paeonia, the sensitive district between Macedon and the Dardanians.[20]

Any such conversations that took place between Flamininus and Demetrius were of course private; nevertheless, it came to be believed in Pella that they had taken place, because Philip later sent trusted men to try to worm the truth out of their contacts in Rome. This does not prove that the conversations did take place; the rumor could have been started as part of a plot to discredit Demetrius and sow dissension within the Macedonian court. A letter was later forged to do just that. But we should not dismiss the story out of hand; it seems exactly the kind of thing Flamininus would do, and some trigger is needed to explain the fact that there is no record of bad feeling between the brothers before this visit to Rome by Demetrius, and there is plenty of evidence for it afterwards.

The most likely scenario is perhaps this. Demetrius returned from Rome in 184 high in the Romans' favor, and with his ego considerably inflated by that—but by no more than that. However, he also came back with a markedly different attitude towards Rome from that held by his father and brother. To them, any hint of acceding to Rome's authority smacked of treason and defeatism, but there were those in Macedon, as in every state in Greece, who favored peace and accommodation with Rome, as a means of mere survival, and they began to cluster around Demetrius. Eventually, like the Achaean League, Macedon was split in two, and it almost seemed as though there were two courts, one centered on Demetrius, and the other on Philip and Perseus. Perseus began to wonder whether he would even be able to succeed to the throne. This is all the trigger we need to explain the bad blood between the two: talk of Flamininus explicitly grooming Demetrius is unnecessary, and therefore best explained as propaganda from Perseus' camp, portraying Demetrius as a puppet of the foreign interlopers.

Both camps began a propaganda war of rumor and innuendo. Perseus and Demetrius had different mothers,[21] and Demetrius's camp began to spread slurs against Perseus' mother: that she had been of low birth or had been no more than a concubine, so that Perseus was less legitimate than Demetrius. Perseus did not even resemble Philip, while Demetrius did.[22] This was not an unfamiliar strategy in the Macedonian court: even Alexander the Great had to suffer an accusation of bastardy.[23] But Perseus' mother was an Argive woman of high birth, and Philip's first wife.

The whole affair came to a head at a public ceremony in 182. At the opening of the campaigning season, the Macedonians held an annual festival in honor of the hero Xanthus,[24] at which the main event seems to have been the ritual purification of the army. After the purification, the army divided into two for a mock battle—but this time, with Perseus at the head of one division and Demetrius of the other, the fighting got rather rougher and more serious than usual, falling just short of actual deaths. There matters might have rested, except that in the evening, Demetrius and some of his drinking companions tried to crash in on Perseus' party, and Perseus believed, or pretended to believe, that Demetrius had come to finish off what the mock battle had begun.

Demetrius saw the influence Perseus had with his father and became certain that his days were numbered. He made the mistake of confiding his fears to one of his father's courtiers, a certain Didas, and told him that he was planning to flee to Rome. Didas promptly informed Philip, who tightened the security around Demetrius while waiting for his agents to return from Rome, where they had been trying to find out what they could from that end. And they returned with a letter, purportedly written by Flamininus, but certainly a forgery: how could Macedonians, especially these friends of Philip, have got hold of a copy if it were genuine? It was cleverly written as a series of elliptical responses to a supposed earlier letter of Demetrius, and since it spoke of Demetrius's "lust for the throne" and implied that there was a conspiracy afoot in Rome to have Demetrius succeed Philip, the young prince was damned.[25] At Philip's instructions, Didas poisoned him at a banquet in the winter of 181–180—the only case of dynastic murder throughout the 130 or so years of Antigonid rule of Macedon. And the outcome, of course, was a surge in the mutual hostility between Rome and Macedon.

9.

PERSEUS' CHOICE

IN 179, EVERYTHING WAS ready for the final push that would drive the Dardanians off their land and replace them with the Bastarnae. Philip was poised to realize a long-held Macedonian dream. He had paid off all the warlords and chieftains on the route, and had put together a huge army of Macedonians, allies, and mercenaries (with the Macedonian element presumably not exceeding the limits set by the 196 peace). But he got no further than Amphipolis when he was overtaken by death. In the sixty years of his lifetime, the world had completely changed, with the power of Macedon eclipsed by a "barbarian" nation. He was the first in the eastern Mediterranean to experience the full force of Roman hostility, driven by their lust for the glory of dominance in the Mediterranean. Perseus (see Fig. 9.1) called off the expedition to deal with an opportunistic invasion

FIGURE 9.1

Perseus, the last, doomed king of Macedon, on a silver tetradrachm from the late 170s. The king may well look determinedly forward: he was being forced into war with Rome.

165

by another Thracian tribe, led by Abrupolis, and the Bastarnae, left to their own devices, fell out with their Thracian allies and were ultimately repulsed by the Dardanians.

And so in 179 Perseus became the next king of Macedon under a cloud of suspicion from Rome. As an incoming king must, he immediately began to reaffirm old connections and build new ones. After eliminating a potential rival for the throne, he sent envoys to Rome for recognition of his accession, and this was granted, along with a renewal of his father's treaty with Rome. At the sacred sites of Delphi and Delos, he proclaimed a general amnesty for all Macedonian economic and political exiles. He helped settle troubles in Aetolia and Thessaly, entered into a formal military alliance with the Boeotians, and even very nearly got on good terms with the Achaeans, but pro-Roman Callicrates swung the vote against him. These were bold moves by Perseus; he was making no secret of Macedon's continuing interest in Greece. He tried again with the Achaeans a short while later, but his envoys were not even allowed into the meeting.

In Asia Minor, Perseus' sister married Prusias II of Bithynia (who had succeeded his father to the throne in 182), and in 178 Perseus himself married Laodice, a daughter of Seleucus (who was by then King Seleucus IV), thus repairing relations strained by Macedon's enforced siding with Rome in the Aetolian–Syrian war. Since, by their various treaties with Rome, neither Syria nor Macedon had much of a fleet, and were restricted in their movements, the Rhodians had the honor of transporting Laodice to Macedon, and Perseus handsomely rewarded them. The young Macedonian king had quickly established a useful network of friends in Asia Minor. Naturally, Pergamum was excluded, and, just as naturally, Eumenes played the same role with Perseus that he had with Philip—that is, chief watchdog and sycophantic informant to Rome about alleged transgressions. He persisted in seeing even these first diplomatic moves by Perseus as a form of preparation for war.

Eumenes' insistence that Perseus was positioning himself to restore Macedonian hegemony in the Greek world—the position Rome now reserved for itself—fell on receptive Roman ears. Perseus never really stood a chance against what was now long-standing Roman suspicion of Macedon. Already in 175 the first commission was sent out, in response to a Dardanian appeal, to look into Perseus' connections with the Bastarnae, and as a result Perseus was warned, as his father had been before, not even to give the appearance of transgressing the terms of their treaty. This was a crude attempt to cow a young ruler, and can only have rankled.

The Romans were back again in 174, concerned lest a probably innocent exchange of diplomatic courtesies between Macedon and Carthage was the opening move in a pact such as the one between Philip and Hannibal in 215. But Perseus, in an equally crude attempt to show that he was uncowed, refused to see them, pleading illness. The following year, with the legates still in Greece, Perseus invaded Dolopia, where the Macedonian governor had apparently been tortured to death. Since the invasion aroused no protest, the Romans must have seen the Thessalian Dolopians as Macedonian subjects, so that he was not transgressing the treaty, despite a Dolopian appeal to Rome.

Immediately after the successful conclusion of this campaign, Perseus led his army in a peaceful march on Delphi. It was a kind of overblown parade, a goodwill visit—but under arms—to the sacred center of the Greeks, where his diplomacy had recovered for Macedon seats on the influential and prestigious Amphictyonic Council. The glittering presence of his army sent the message that he was the protector of the Greeks; he was there, at the heart of Greece, and the Romans were not. The Greeks responded favorably, but Perseus had chosen a risky course: by the terms of his treaty with Rome, he was not to take an army out of Macedon, and here he was with an army in Greece, albeit with no overtly hostile intention.

Back in Rome later in 173, the legates accused Perseus of preparing for war with Rome. The Senate sent out another investigatory commission to Macedon, and other legates with various diplomatic tasks, among which one constant was to do their best to stir the Greek states against Perseus. As war edged closer, it was the Romans who were proving themselves the aggressors.

PERGAMUM AFTER APAMEA

Defeat left Antiochus (see Fig. 9.2) very badly off, and matters soon became far worse. During the war, he had withdrawn many men from garrison duty in the eastern satrapies, and this left them vulnerable to the

FIGURE 9.2

Antiochus III of Syria, a bust from the last century BCE or first century CE. Though his eastern campaigns had earned him the title "the Great," his foolhardy resistance to Roman expansion in Greece cost him half his kingdom.

expansionism of the Arsacid dynasty of Parthia (in present-day north-eastern Iran).[1] Antiochus responded, and in the course of plundering a wealthy temple in Elymais, at the head of the Persian Gulf, he lost his life. Elymais was presumably in enemy hands at the time, but, even so, this episode shows that Antiochus's need to maintain his kingdom and repay the indemnity of 15,000 talents was driving him to extremes. Such an act represents a complete reversal of Seleucid policy. Ever since gaining the empire at the beginning of the third century, they had been careful to cooperate with the Zoroastrian priesthood, who were the main power-possessors and landowners apart from the king. The best way to keep the peace, and ensure the compliance of the population as a whole, was never to offend the priests. Antiochus must have been desperate. The man who had come so close to reviving the Seleucid empire left it a fraction of its former self. He was succeeded by his son Seleucus IV (187–175), about whose reign we know little.[2]

The Romans' intention was to stabilize Asia Minor and maintain their remote control there by leaving just two strong states, Rhodes and Pergamum, to keep the peace. But if the system worked quite well at first in Greece, where the Achaeans and Macedon were the two strong states, it was a disaster from the outset in Asia Minor. Eumenes, confident in the protection of Rome, saw Pergamum now as a great power. He formed alliances to the east with Cappadocia and possibly with Armenia, and fought a 3-year war (186–183) against Prusias I of Bithynia, who was displeased at the territorial gains Eumenes had been awarded by the Romans at his expense, and refused to give them up, not least because he was busy expanding his kingdom himself.

Prusias found willing allies in the Galatians, who rebelled against Vulso's settlement, but the Romans allowed the war to rumble on until in 183 Eumenes reported that Prusias was getting aid from Philip. Then Flamininus was sent to pressure Prusias into accepting the settlement of 188. The upshot was a further strengthening of Eumenes' position in Asia Minor. While in Bithynia, Flamininus also found time finally to rid Rome of its greatest bogeyman: he saw to the death of Hannibal, who killed himself to avoid capture by Flamininus's agents. Hannibal had been Prusias's leading military adviser since fleeing there from Antiochus's court.[3] But this was Flamininus's last known act as an officer of Rome; he died in retirement some time after 174. Like his great rival Philip of Macedon, he was just short of sixty years old. Like Philip, he had seen the world change in his lifetime, with himself as an important instrument of that change.

No sooner had this war come to an end than another broke out, engulfing even more of Asia Minor. In 183 King Pharnaces I of Pontus seized the Greek colony of Sinope, which was under Rhodian protection, and also attempted to seize some of Eumenes' territory. Even though up until then Rome had had no contact with Pontus, Pharnaces sent representatives to Rome to justify his actions in the face of complaints from Rhodes and Pergamum. Rome's involvement was again engineered by Eumenes, and over the next few years, the Romans sent several commissions to the area in his support, but to little effect.[4] The problem with remote control is that it is hard by this method to control those who are far removed from the center.

FIGURE 9.3

The Great Altar of Pergamum. The construction of this fabulous monumental altar was one of the uses to which Eumenes II put the prosperity his kingdom gained in part from its long friendship with Rome.

So the war continued until an invasion of Pontus by Eumenes in 179, formidably supported by Ariarathes of Cappadocia and Prusias II of Bithynia (who had come to the throne in 182), brought Pharnaces to his knees.[5] These were the last major wars in northern Asia Minor for several decades. Pergamum entered its peak period of power and prosperity. This is when Eumenes adorned the Pergamene acropolis with monumental structures such as the famous Great Altar of Zeus and Athena (now in the Pergamum Museum, Berlin), in commemoration of his victories. Having defeated the Celts of Galatia, he began to present himself as the protector of Greeks against barbarians, and all his new monuments were immediately recognizable as being quintessentially Greek—as being some of the most perfect examples of Hellenism ever created (see Fig. 9.3).[6]

RHODES AFTER APAMEA

South of the Meander, Rhodes too had never been better off, but, again, there was resistance to the Roman settlement. The Lycians were told in 187 by Roman legates that Lycia had been awarded unconditionally to Rhodes, "as a gift."[7] Seeking clarification of this from the Rhodians, by proposing an alliance, the Lycians were told in no uncertain terms that they were now subjects, not allies; there had long been bad blood between the two states, and the Rhodians were pleased to be able to assert their hegemony with the might of Rome behind them. The Lycians, however, seemed to think that the Romans did not have the right to dispose of Asia Minor at will. When the Rhodians imposed a military government on them, they rebelled, and the rebellion was bloodily extinguished.

Throughout the war, the initial Roman assertion that Lycia was a "gift" to Rhodes was allowed to stand; that was the premise of the war. But in 178, with the last flames of their rebellion sputtering out, the Lycians sent ambassadors to Rome, protesting at the harshness of the Rhodian regime. And the Senate performed a complete volte face. With a deliberate reference back to the legates' statement of 187, the Senate's decision was that Lycia had *not* been awarded to Rhodes as a gift, but as an equal, an ally. By the time the envoys got back to Lycia the war was over, but not surprisingly, on the strength of the Roman reversal, fighting broke out more or less immediately, and continued on and off, without Roman intervention, until the Rhodians finally prevailed in 171.[8]

What we see here is a combination of factors. What looks like Roman carelessness reflects the fact that, after the Peace of Apamea, they really hoped that they could be involved in Asia Minor as little as possible, leaving everything to Rhodes and Pergamum. Even a cursory glance at the record shows why this was important to them. The year 189 was the last time that the consuls were assigned eastern commands until 171. Every year in between, at least one of the consuls, and frequently both, was assigned a command against the Ligurians, a group of tribes inhabiting northwest Italy. In other words, Rome was involved in a major war, part of its ongoing attempt to pacify and ethnically cleanse its northern frontiers. Hence the only other province assigned to the consuls in these intervening years was Istria, where pirates needed further quelling. In the meantime, many of the praetors and promagistrates were sent to Spain, to continue the subjugation of the tribes there, or to Sardinia. There was plenty for the Romans to be getting on with outside of Greece and Asia Minor.

But the deliberate volte face, or lie, in 178 requires a different explanation, and it is to be found not just in Rome's growing determination to give orders rather than drop hints (as Polybius's Callicrates had put it to them in 179), but also in its growing alienation from Rhodes. The trigger, or excuse, for this seems to have been the Rhodians' new friendship with Perseus, as reflected in their escorting his Syrian bride Laodice from Antioch to Pella earlier in 178.[9] This was undoubtedly an innocent action—the Rhodians were always pleased by any rapprochement among the powers of the eastern Mediterranean that would create stable conditions for trade—but the Senate read it as a breach of the moral obligations Rhodes had taken on by being treated so generously by Rome in the Peace of Apamea. Eumenes stirred the pot by reminding the Romans from time to time of this alleged friendship between Perseus and Rhodes—and, indeed, the Rhodians had used the timber Perseus gave them in gratitude for bringing Laodice to build up their fleet to a size that might concern the Senate. The Senate was gaining the impression that the Rhodians were not going to be as compliant as Eumenes, and that was not to its liking. We have seen the same dynamic before: the Romans' hands-off approach gave Greek states enough rope to hang themselves with. They were allowed their freedom, until they were slapped down.

Even our scant evidence shows signs of Perseus and the Romans vying for the friendship of Rhodes. By the time that war between Perseus and Rome was certain, there was clearly a faction in Rhodes that was opposed to Rome, or at least opposed to friendship with Rome if that meant being dragged into warfare. So in 171 both the Romans and Perseus made overtures to the Rhodians. Roman legates toured all the islands of the Aegean, whipping up support for Rome in the coming war, but spent a disproportionate amount of time on Rhodes—because of its importance, but also because it was wavering. It was a successful visit, if the Rhodians were to be believed when they promised to supply forty ships. Perseus too singled Rhodes out for special treatment: he wrote to other Greek states, but sent trusted agents to Rhodes. All they asked was that, in the event of war, the Rhodians should do their best to effect a reconciliation between him and the Romans. This was an unsubtle way of asking them to remain neutral—but the Rhodians were too afraid of the Romans even to be able to promise that.

FLIMSY EXCUSES

There was nothing in Perseus' early activities to alarm the Romans, but they still got alarmed. In part, this was a residue of their old fear of Philip V, and Perseus' enemies played on that fear. The critical embassy from Eumenes came early in 172.[10] The Senate had already debated the possibility of war with Perseus a couple of weeks earlier when assigning provinces to the consuls for the year (though in the end they assigned Liguria to both of them), so Eumenes' information found a receptive audience. The meeting took place behind closed doors, but Livy specifically assures us that the details leaked out, and, as we shall see, we have good grounds for believing him.[11]

Eumenes first recapitulated details that the senators already knew, in order to conclude that Philip had definitely been gearing up for war, and Perseus had simply inherited from his father both his preparations and his resolution. He went on to claim that the years of relative peace since 189 had allowed Macedon fully to recover, and to accuse the Romans of helping to make Perseus strong by their inactivity. After providing the Senate with a list of Perseus' alleged crimes, Eumenes played his trump card: "I felt it would be utterly disgraceful if I failed to reach Italy to warn you before he arrived here with his army."[12] He played on the Romans' familiar fear of invasion—and, as usual, it worked. When Perseus' ambassadors had an audience with the Senate just a few days later, their justifications were rejected out of hand. The Senate was rapidly moving closer to a third war against Macedon.

On his way back to Pergamum from Rome, Eumenes stopped in Delphi for pious purposes. Knowing that he was due there, Perseus arranged for some men to ambush him. Choosing a spot where the king would be vulnerable, since he would be compelled to walk in single file, without the protection of his retinue, they rolled boulders down on him. One struck him on the head and another on the shoulder, and he tumbled unconscious down the slope, while the would-be assassins made their escape. In fact, though, Eumenes was not dead; he was taken to Aegina to recover and, once he was better, he returned to Pergamum and "prepared for war with the utmost energy."[13] A very dramatic episode—and possibly false.

Delphi was, and still is, liable to rockslides, and it is not impossible that Eumenes' court exaggerated a natural accident into a hostile attempt on his life. Still, the Senate investigated the affair, and in the course of their investigations uncovered another alleged plot, to poison leading Roman generals and statesmen as they passed through Brundisium and lodged with a man Perseus thought he could suborn.

Despite the secrecy of Eumenes' conference with the Senate, we can be sure that Livy (following Polybius) has accurately recorded the details. An inscription has luckily survived from Delphi, albeit in a mutilated condition, which preserves the official Roman list of grievances against Perseus, the reasons for war. And the list overlaps to a remarkably high degree with the charges Eumenes was alleged to have brought up in his secret meeting with the Senate and on other occasions, and also with those raised by the Roman legate Quintus Marcius Philippus in 171.[14]

> ... that Perseus, contrary to what is proper, came with his army to Delphi for the Pythian festival; it was plainly wrong for him to be allowed to join in the sacrifices, the contests, or the festival, because he invited in the barbarians from across the Danube, whose foul purpose, on an earlier occasion, had been the enslavement of Greece, and who marched against the sanctuary at Delphi, with the intention of sacking and destroying it, but met a fitting punishment at the hands of the god. And Perseus transgressed the sworn treaty made by his father and renewed by himself. And he conquered the Thracians, who are our allies, and expelled from his kingdom Abrupolis who was included in our treaty with Philip. And he got rid of the envoys sent by the Thebans to Rome to seek an alliance by arranging for their ship to be wrecked. He became so deranged, in fact, that he felt compelled, contrary to the oaths he had sworn, to do away with the freedom given to you by our generals, by throwing all Greece into turmoil and political strife. He caused nothing but trouble and, in an attempt to bring about total chaos by courting the masses and killing the leading men, in his derangement he announced the cancellation of debts and fomented revolutions, which showed the hatred he bore the best men. As a result, catastrophe struck the Perrhaebians and Thessalians, and the barbarian incursions became more formidable. He longed for a major war, so that,

finding you helpless, he should enslave all the Greek cities; and to this end he plotted the murder of Arthetaurus of Illyris and dared to set an ambush for our friend and ally, King Eumenes, who came to Delphi in fulfillment of a vow, which shows how little Perseus cares for the customary ways of worshipping the god practiced by all visitors and how he disregarded the security that your sanctuary has always provided, alike for Greeks and barbarians, since the beginning of time.

The whole inscription is, of course, slanted toward its audience, in this case the Amphictyonic Council of Delphi, so that the Roman author makes out that Perseus' impiety compromised the sanctity of Delphi, as well as having a wider negative effect. At the beginning of the inscription, the Romans tendentiously assimilate the Bastarnae ("the barbarians from across the Danube") to the Celts who a hundred years earlier, in 279–278, had invaded Greece and attacked Delphi, only to be miraculously driven off—or so the Greeks believed.[15]

What is most striking about the inscription—and most sad—is the patent flimsiness of the excuses. The charges consist largely of innuendo, or unproved and unprovable allegations, some of them far-fetched. The tactic is appallingly familiar from our own recent history—from the unproved assertions by prejudiced statesmen that Saddam Hussein of Iraq had "weapons of mass destruction," and sheltered al-Qaeda, and that therefore we had to go to war. It could not be clearer that the Senate had already decided on war, and was casting around for pretexts, when the real reason was that Perseus was making himself the equal of the Romans in Greece. And, eventually, just as in the Iraq War, Roman pressure turned into a self-fulfilling prophecy: Perseus could see that the Romans were intent on war, and so he had to take steps to be ready for them. That was really the only choice he had.

THE 'NEW CUNNING'

The strange thing about all these war noises coming from Rome was that the Romans were more or less unprepared for war. The two consuls for

172 had been assigned Liguria; Brundisium had only the usual Adriatic fleet; no Roman troops had been sent to Illyris. They had already written off 172 by deciding to follow normal procedure and wait for the next consular elections before sending a general east. But it also seems possible that the Romans were playing at brinksmanship, either expecting Perseus to back down, or trying to buy themselves enough time to get ready. The first option—expecting Perseus to back down—was unrealistic: he was a Hellenistic king, and since the choice the Romans were offering him was war or accepting subjection to Rome, he was bound to go to war.

But the Romans did gain some time. The accusation of Eumenes' that rankled most in Rome was that Perseus was winning the Greeks away from them. Their control of Greece depended essentially on the Greek states being cowed into acceptance of their dominance. Diplomacy therefore occupied much of their efforts in this gap year, 172, when war was imminent but no formal declaration had been made.

Some of the Thracian tribes pledged friendship, so that Perseus would be largely surrounded by enemies. The Senate received representatives from Thessaly and Aetolia. Envoys from Issa reported that Genthius of Illyris (who had succeeded Pleuratus in the late 180s) was in league with Perseus. This was not the first round of complaints against Genthius: in 180 the Senate heard that he had been behind a fresh wave of Istrian piracy in the Adriatic, and in the early 170s the Romans had taken steps against both Istrian and Illyrian piracy. This time they sent a team of responsible senators, who warned the king to behave himself; we do not have his answer, but it was no doubt more amenable than Teuta's response to a similar demand in 230. Missions returned from the eastern kings, confirming the loyalty of Eumenes (no surprise there), Antiochus IV (who had succeeded his brother Seleucus IV in 175), Ariarathes of Cappaodocia, and Ptolemy VI. Prusias did the best he could for the Romans given that he was Perseus' brother-in-law, and committed himself to neutrality.

Asia Minor was pretty solidly behind Rome, then—which made the Rhodians' behavior all the more irritating. Although they had let the Romans believe that they would supply forty ships for the war effort, in the end they sent only five, thanks to the resistance of the strong faction there that was opposed to supporting Rome, out of long hatred of its ally Eumenes and a proud reluctance to get involved in Roman wars.

In Achaea, the Romans must have been relying on Callicrates' pro-Roman group to stay in power, because they delivered a resounding insult to the league. Instead of arranging a meeting with the Council and league leaders, they toured the member states, asking each separately for its support. Again, as in the winter of 183–182, they were deliberately inviting each community to act independently of the league—to loosen its ties and possibly even secede, if official Achaean policy towards Rome and Perseus differed from that community's preferred policy.

Meanwhile, an army was recruited and, at the end of the year, sent to Brundisium. Fifty old warships were quickly dusted off and refitted, crews were recruited for them, and the whole advance army was taken across to Apollonia, to garrison border towns in Illyris and Dassaretis, and contain the situation until the official consul arrived in 171. Grain supplies were ordered from North Africa, Sicily, and southern Italy. A home army was raised in Italy, to be deployed if necessary.

Toward the end of 172, a fresh batch of legates was sent to Greece to continue the work of testing the waters and whipping up opposition to Macedon on the pretext—rather tired, by now—of ensuring Greek freedom. Their basic message was a threat: that the Senate was considering war with Perseus and anyone who sided with him. To give the threat concrete form, each of the legates was, unusually, accompanied by an armed retinue. After landing at Corcyra, they separated for their various missions: some went to Genthius to order ships, trusting that he had seen the sense in remaining on good terms with Rome; others went elsewhere. Quintus Marcius Philippus and Aulus Atilius Serranus had successful meetings with both the Epirote and the Aetolian leagues. They found the Epirotes somewhat divided between a pro-Roman party, led by Charops of Chaonia, and a faction led by Cephalus of Molossis that favored neutrality. In Aetolia, the legates were pleased to find that their most vigorous supporter, Lyciscus, was appointed general for the year.

Marcius and Atilius then moved on to Thessaly, where they met with Acarnanian representatives and some Boeotians. The Acarnanians were warned that they had better not side with Macedon again, as they had in the previous two wars. The Boeotians were not official representatives, but exiles: the league had already allied itself with Perseus, so there was nothing they could do except stir up trouble, hoping to bring the league over to Rome or at least undermine its commitment to Perseus. The Thessalians committed themselves to Rome. Each time that a Greek city or state showed itself compliant, the Romans followed up with garrisons. Greece was becoming a Roman fortress, and Perseus was becoming critically short of friends. That was certainly one pragmatic reason why he continued to push for peace.

Throughout this burst of diplomatic activity, the Romans had signally refrained from making contact with Perseus.[16] Since they were simultaneously deploying in Illyris, Dassaretis, and northern Epirus, the tactic is very reminiscent of that employed by Hitler against Poland in 1939: bring an army up to the border and deny diplomatic contact while trying to bully the enemy's allies into neutrality or changing sides. As soon as the Roman legates had arrived in Corcyra, Perseus had written to ask what their purpose was in garrisoning Greek cities, and the Romans had not bothered with a formal written reply, but had just told Perseus' messenger verbally that they were protecting these cities. Since then, they had made no attempt to make contact, and Perseus had to use the lever of family friendship with Marcius to get him to come to a meeting.

The meeting was cordial, but Marcius uncompromisingly repeated all the usual charges. When Perseus replied that the charges were either unprovable or concerned his legitimate attempts, as king, to protect his people, Marcius offered him a ray of hope that war could be avoided, and a period of truce to send envoys to Rome. This was just what Perseus wanted, but Marcius was betraying his "friend" and working only for Rome. This was all he wanted from the meeting—a truce, to buy the Romans time to complete their preparations for war. The episode proves that the Romans actively wanted this war, while Perseus was still trying to avoid it. Whatever Roman propaganda said, Perseus did not inherit his father's confrontational attitude toward Rome, until he had no choice. He wanted peace, but not with dishonor.

While Perseus was briefing his ambassadors for their mission to Rome, Marcius continued on to Euboea, where he found all the cities compliant.

The Boeotians too came and claimed that they were now on the Roman side, but the league was so unstable, so split between pro-Macedonian and pro-Roman factions, that it could hardly be considered a useful ally; at any rate, three Boeotian towns—Haliartus, Thisbe, and Coronea—remained opposed to Rome. After getting the Achaeans to garrison Chalcis, which had been chosen as the Roman headquarters for the war, Marcius and Atilius returned to Rome, where they boasted of how they had deceived Perseus into believing that there was a chance of peace and granting the Romans more time to prepare. They also boasted of how they had dissolved the Boeotian League and so made it a useless ally for Perseus. This "new cunning" (*nova sapientia*) met with disapproval from the more traditional members of the Senate, who remembered when Romans treated their enemies as honored and honorable men, but it had done the trick, and in the end that was what counted with the majority of senators.[17]

So it was no surprise that, when Perseus' envoys arrived, they failed to satisfy the Senate about Perseus' motives and were perfunctorily dismissed. They, and any other Macedonians resident in Italy, were ordered to be gone within thirty days.[18] And so the Romans declared war on Perseus. Publius Licinius Crassus was the consul for 171 who gained Macedon as his province. He would have an army of over 50,000 at his command, including two specially reinforced legions—but then Perseus had almost as many. Livy tallies his army at 43,000 and remarks that no Macedonian king since Alexander the Great was able to field so many men—in other words, that this was the largest army ever to be fielded in defense of Macedon. The outcome of the war was not a foregone conclusion.

Marcius and Atilius returned to Greece as legates—Atilius to garrison Larissa, and Marcius just to keep up the good work. But now diplomatic dissembling would give way to the exercise of force. Gaius Lucretius Gallus took forty of the refurbished ships and made his base at Cephallenia, while his brother Marcus gathered a useful fleet of over eighty ships from their west-coast friends, especially Genthius, Issa, and Apollonia. And then Licinius set out from Italy with the land army.

In Pella, the return of Perseus' envoys from Rome divided his advisers, some arguing for conciliation and concessions, others for war. The latter group was more realistic: concessions now would subjugate the king further to Rome's will, and gradually he would lose his kingdom anyway. But Perseus, of course, would not compromise the greatness of Macedon or his personal honor. The Romans had pushed him too far, and he committed himself to war, more as an attempt just to survive than to continue his father's attempt to restore Macedonian hegemony in Greece. The official Roman version of events (largely followed by both Polybius and Livy) was that the aggressor in this war was Perseus, who had inherited his father's determination to drive the Romans from Greece and even invade Italy. But, as we have seen, this makes little sense: even on the eve of war, Perseus was making conciliatory moves. No, the Romans had decided that the only way to maintain their position in Greece was to have no equals at all, and that meant the removal of the Macedonian monarchy. That was their aim in the Third Macedonian War.

10.

THE END OF MACEDON

IN THE THIRTY YEARS prior to the start of the Third Macedonian War the Romans had crushed the Celts in northern Italy, reduced the Carthaginians and Philip and Antiochus to a fraction of their former power, and imposed their rule on Spain. Mediterranean-wide dominion was, as Polybius saw, the fulfillment of a long-held Roman goal which they had gone about gradually, even intermittently, but with overall determination.[1] Such rapid expansion could only be the fruit of determination. And the purpose of their warfare in Greece was no longer to establish dominion, because they already had it; the point now was only to respond to challenges to their power and authority. The policy of remote control came with stress limits: in response to enough of a challenge—the kind Perseus was felt to be mounting—control would be reasserted by more direct means. There is nothing remote about an army of 50,000 on Greek soil.

The Romans chose to take seriously Eumenes' exaggerations and distortions, and they at last realized that the Macedonian kings, with their long tradition of proud independence and hegemony of Greece, were never going to be Roman puppets. The only solution was the final removal of the Macedonian monarchy, as the Aetolians had argued in the 190s. The Romans wanted this war, and the action of the second consul for 171 is a reflection of that state of mind. Publius Licinius Crassus's colleague was Gaius Cassius Longinus, and he wanted Macedon so badly as his province that he first tried to manipulate the system in his favor, and then, when the provincial lottery gave Licinius Macedon and he was sent against the Celts, he set out east with his army across the north of Italy with the intention of leading his army by land through Illyris to attack Macedon. The Senate was appalled—under no circumstances were consuls allowed to leave their provinces—and Cassius was recalled and severely reprimanded before the quest for personal glory got out of control.[2]

FIRST BLOOD TO PERSEUS

Licinius arrived in Illyris quite late in the summer of 171. Eumenes had joined the Achaeans at Chalcis with his fleet, and with troop-carriers holding 6,000 infantry and 1,000 cavalry. Before long, the bulk of the Roman fleet also moved from Cephallenia to Chalcis. They easily had mastery of the Aegean, so they dismissed all the allied vessels (including the five Rhodian ships), and retained the help only of Eumenes. In this war, they wanted by their side only those whose loyalty was solid. They especially did not want the Rhodians later seeking peacetime advantages on the basis of their wartime performance.

At much the same time, having secured his supply route and assembled his army of Macedonians and Thracians, Cretan and Celtic mercenaries, and a few hundred Greeks (there was the weakness), Perseus advanced south into Thessaly and made camp just south of Mount Ossa. Licinius secured the west coast and marched through Athamania into Thessaly. This in itself was a signal Roman success, a demonstration of how effective their cunning diplomacy of the previous year had been—that they could so easily reach western Thessaly. They had occupied the forward positions and prevented Perseus from doing the same.

Licinius met Atilius at Larissa. He made camp outside the town, by a hill called Callinicus, and was joined there by Pergamene, Aetolian, Achaean, and other Greek reinforcements. Perseus boldly marched right up to the Roman camp, offering battle, and the Romans first sent out only their cavalry and light-armed troops (about 20,000 men), holding the heavy infantry in readiness inside the camp. But Perseus' cavalry and light infantry quickly routed the Roman forces, and he advanced his phalanx to finish the battle. The Romans, however, shocked by their defeat, stayed safe behind their palisade, while Perseus made camp nearby. That night, on Eumenes' advice, Licinius moved his camp north of the Peneus, to put the river between him and Perseus. Over the next few days Roman losses, two thousand men, were made up by the arrival of reinforcements. Perseus, still hoping for peace, offered to pay the Romans' war costs and come to terms based on the prewar status quo, but he was firmly rejected by Licinius, even when he increased the amount of money on offer.

Further skirmishing followed, but the campaigning season was effectively at an end, and Perseus returned to winter quarters in Macedon, leaving garrisons to dissuade any thoughts of pursuit. But the Romans spent the winter brutally punishing the three Boeotian towns that had sided with Perseus. Haliartus was completely destroyed after a siege, with indiscriminate slaughter of civilians; 2,500 men were sold into slavery, and the town remained virtually uninhabited for many decades afterwards. Thisbe and Coronea both surrendered also, but it is hard to tell under what circumstances since our only sources are two fragmentary inscriptions, which seem to suggest that the pro-Macedonians were killed or exiled, their property confiscated, and the pro-Romans strengthened.[3]

Roman savagery, combined with Perseus' success at Callinicus, had a disproportionate effect in Greece. Clearly many Greeks, whether or not they had prudentially affirmed their allegiance to Rome, had actually been holding their breath to see what happened, and now they looked on Perseus as their champion. But mostly they were still too frightened of Rome, especially after the treatment of Haliartus, to translate their pleasure at his victory into practical or long-term support. Still, the Epirote League split: Cephalus led the Molossians and a few smaller tribes into rebellion, while the rest of the league, under Charops, stayed loyal to Rome. Perseus almost gained the Achaeans as well, but in the end they decided to wait and see what was in their best interests. This was Lycortas's proposal, and he was supported by his son Polybius, on one of his first appearances in public life.

PERSEUS RESTORES PARITY

The consul for 170, Aulus Hostilius Mancinus, again seems to have arrived late in the campaigning season, having lingered, perhaps, over his civic duties in Rome. His first job was to shore up the west coast in the wake of the defection of Molossis, and legates were dispatched to Acarnania and Aetolia, as well as the Peloponnese and Boeotia.

On the face of it, their mission was straightforward: they were proclaiming a new decree of the Senate that no one in Greece was to aid the Roman forces except as instructed by the Senate. But the point of this decree was to counteract the bad impression the Romans had made on Greek leaders the previous year. One of Licinius's actions had caused particular resentment: following the defeat at Callinicus, he had scapegoated the leaders of the Aetolians who had fought at his side. After listening to the insinuations of the pro-Roman Lyciscus, the chief Aetolian quisling, that they had deliberately held back in the battle, Licinius had arrested them and sent them to Italy for internment. This heavy-handed assertion of dominance sent shock waves through Greece, as an unequivocal sign that the Romans were prepared to listen to and act on the lies of their supporters. Along with Perseus' success, it was this that prompted Cephalus to lead the Molossians into rebellion.

The Molossian defection forced the Romans to leave troops to defend southern Illyris, and at the same time the garrison on Issa was reinforced (Issa having defected at some point from Genthius to the Romans): even though Genthius had supplied the Romans with ships, they were uncertain of his loyalty. With these measures in place, Hostilius took to the field, but his attempt to invade Macedon from Thessaly came to grief. Perseus' counteroffensive netted him a number of cities in Perrhaebia and Thessaly, and after that he swung back north and crushed the Dardanians, who were working in concert with the Romans. Meanwhile, Lucius Coelius, the legate responsible for Illyris from his base at Lychnidus (modern Ohrid, in the Republic of Macedonia), was badly mauled in an attempt to take Uscanas (modern Kičevo).

At sea, the tally of Roman woes lengthened. Perseus launched a successful raid on the Roman fleet at Oreus, in the course of which he made off with or spoiled a great deal of grain. The Roman fleet, commanded by Lucius Hortensius, was forced to tour the northern Aegean coast in search of supplies. Their stay at Abdera, one of their ally Eumenes' new possessions, was so exacting that afterwards the townspeople sent envoys to Rome to protest. With Eumenes' help, Hortensius's men had stormed the place, killed the ringleaders of the protest, and sold many others into slavery. All the other ports in the vicinity, nominally their friends, promptly closed their harbors against the Romans. Even Chalcis, the Roman headquarters, was unsafe: when the fleet returned, the crews took out their frustration on the local population, looting temples, requisitioning private houses for billets, and selling citizens into slavery. The Senate was understandably furious at the complete unravelling of its attempt to limit the damage caused by Licinius in 171. Hortensius was severely reprimanded, and he was ordered to search out and redeem all those who had been sold into slavery. One of the Romans' great strengths in this war was that they had succeeded in driving a wedge between Perseus and the Greek states; they could not risk alienating their friends or driving the fence-sitters into the Macedonian camp.

It was one setback after another, and the Senate voted to send considerable reinforcements to Greece for 169. Envoys were sent around the Greek states to bolster the pro-Roman factions, but succeeded only in stirring up trouble. The Aetolians were perhaps the most torn: in theory, they were Roman allies, but a strong anti-Roman faction remained. The Roman envoys therefore asked the Aetolians to give them hostages to secure their loyalty. The inevitable effect of this was to set the pro- and anti-Romans at loggerheads, each side denouncing the other, and the Romans left the Aetolians "in a turmoil of mutual suspicion."[4] Much the same happened in Achaea and Acarnania.

Uscanas remained a tempting prize, since it controlled difficult, but passable mountain routes toward Genthius in northern Illyris, toward the Dardanians, and toward the Axius valley. Some time early in the winter of 170–169 the citizens expelled their Macedonian garrison and invited in the Romans, who installed their own garrison of 4,000 Roman troops and 500 Illyrians. But, taking advantage of the isolation of the town in winter, Perseus promptly put it under siege. The unprepared inhabitants were forced to surrender, on terms that allowed the Roman troops to leave, but left the Illyrians to be sold into slavery. The whole area fell under Macedonian control for the remainder of the war and put the Roman garrison at Lychnidus in great danger.

Later that same winter, or in the early spring of 169, Perseus made a surprise attack across the snow-laden Pindus Mountains, with the intention of depriving the Aetolians of the critical border town of Stratus, and returning it, with a Macedonian garrison, to the Acarnanians. It would be a major gain for him, a forward post deep in enemy territory. He was only just foiled: the day's delay caused by having to bridge a swollen river gave the Romans time to garrison the city themselves. On the basis of this stunning winter campaign, Perseus wrote to Genthius for an alliance, but still the Illyrian king hesitated, wanting more money than Perseus was offering.

These were great successes for Perseus, but he was far from attaining a commanding position. All he had done was offset the gains the Romans had made during the period of truce so cunningly arranged at the end of 172. He had restored a degree of parity, and further discouraged the Greek states from assisting Rome, but his situation was no better than that. Ancient wars were very often won by a single decisive battle, and that was what Perseus wanted. He had offered it at Callinicus in 170 but had been refused. Before long, he would have another opportunity.

Given the Romans' failure in the opening seasons of the Third Macedonian War, it is not surprising that Hostilius's command was not extended in 169, and most of his colleagues were recalled as well. The new consul who was assigned Macedon as his province was the veteran Quintus Marcius Philippus, sixty years old and in his second consulship. Marcius intended to embellish his diplomatic coup of 172 with victory over Perseus. His cousin, Gaius Marcius Figulus, took charge of the fleet. Marcius's plan was to push through to the coast of Thessaly with the land army and to link up there with his cousin's fleet for a joint invasion of Macedon.

Anticipating some such move, Perseus had made Dium his base and defended the mountain passes by which Marcius was likely to come, while his cavalry and light infantry patrolled the coastline against raids from the sea. And indeed the Roman army of 30,000 did come up against one of these Macedonian contingents, 12,000-strong, in the pass north of Lake Ascyris. For two days Marcius tried to force his way through, but to no avail. His men had no cover from the elements, and there was no way supplies could reach him in these mountains, so he had to move. Leaving a token force to distract the enemy and catch up later, he boldly led his men through the maquis and down sheer slopes to a valley that gave onto the north Thessalian coastal plain, but which was unguarded, because of the presumed impossibility of reaching it from inland. And indeed the descent was very difficult, especially for the war elephants, which were lowered down on a series of ingenious, gently collapsing platforms. There must have been many moments during this descent when Marcius's men and beasts were vulnerable, but apparently the Macedonians did not fancy their chances. Livy says they were exhausted after the two days of skirmishing.

Livy's description of this hazardous descent, based on a lost passage of Polybius, is especially vivid because Polybius personally accompanied the Roman army. The Achaeans had decided to try to win the favor of the Romans by offering them troops—their entire levy, in fact—and Polybius, their messenger, caught up with Marcius just as he was about to try to break through to Thessaly. Marcius declined the offer: he felt he had enough men to do what was needed, and he recognized the offer for what it was, a last-ditch attempt to ward off Roman reprisals. Some weeks of maneuvering for position, skirmishing, and sabre-rattling followed, during which the Romans succeeded in establishing themselves in Thessaly, where they made their winter quarters, right on the front line, while Perseus retired to Macedon.

Perseus' success in withstanding the Romans for another year finally gained him the allegiance of Genthius. His alliance was critical: Perseus could leave the west coast to the Illyrian's fleet of over 200 *lemboi*, which could play havoc with the Roman supply lines from Italy, while he concentrated on defending Macedon itself. The two kings sanctified their alliance with a splendid ceremony at Dium.

THE BATTLE OF PYDNA

By the end of 169, the Roman position in Greece was precarious, but the arrival in 168 of the new consul, Lucius Aemilius Paullus, with a fresh and generous levy (the result of an investigatory commission organized by

Aemilius himself), put new heart into the Roman army. Aemilius, aged sixty, came with his second consulship and with a reputation from the Spanish wars as an outstanding and honest general.

The first moves came from Genthius, who had spent the winter gathering a formidable army of 15,000 at Lissus. At the beginning of the campaigning season, he advanced south for a confrontation with Lucius Anicius Gallus, the praetor who had been sent to replace Coelius as commander in Illyris. Anicius had brought considerable reinforcements, and the combined Roman army outnumbered the Illyrians by two to one. In June 168 Genthius was beaten at sea and then on land, but he rallied his forces at Scodra (see Fig. 10.1). At Anicius's approach, the Illyrians foolishly emerged from the formidable protection of the fortress for battle; they were soundly defeated and sued for peace. The whole campaign had lasted perhaps thirty days and Livy proudly reports: "This war is unique in having ended before word reached Rome that it had begun."⁵ Genthius

FIGURE 10.1
Scodra, the site of the final defeat of Genthius, which brought the Illyrian monarchy to an end.

and other members of the royal family were arrested and sent to Rome, while Anicius mopped up the rest of Genthius's kingdom by force (as at Pharos) or negotiation (as at Rhizon). Pharos was destroyed so thoroughly that it virtually disappears from the historical record for a century, until re-emerging as the Roman town of Pharia.

Aemilius reached Thessaly early in June with an army of 50,000, and found Perseus well entrenched not far north of Dium. Feeling that his first priority was to dislodge the Macedonians from this position, he dispatched a strong force under Publius Cornelius Scipio Nasica, which fought its way around through the mountains to behind Perseus' position, while Aemilius himself kept Perseus occupied with frontal attacks on his camp. The tactic showed Perseus that his position was not as strong as he had thought, if he could be surrounded in this way, and he moved his army to a new position on the gently undulating plain south of Pydna, facing south, with the sea on his left and rising ground to the right.

Aemilius joined up with Nasica, and together they advanced until they were within sight of the enemy camp. The dust from the Roman army alerted Perseus early to their approach, and he had plenty of time to draw up his men for battle. Aemilius quickly had some of his men form a protective shield while the rest made camp, and he then withdrew all his forces inside the palisade. He had water source near his camp, but was otherwise short of provisions, and from his position Perseus could stop him being supplied from the sea. So Perseus, who could easily be supplied from Pydna, was content to wait, confident that Aemilius would be driven by hunger to make a rash move.

On the night of 21 June there was a lunar eclipse, an event that was held by the Macedonians to portend the eclipse of the king.[6] The next day, Aemilius was reluctant to join battle, but a clash between rival skirmishers gradually led to full battle, as at Cynoscephalae. The Macedonians deployed faster than the Romans, and the phalanx charged the Roman lines while they were still forming up. The slaughter was terrible, but the Macedonian phalanx had become broken up by the uneven ground over which they had advanced. Aemilius saw his chance and seized it. He ordered his men to form small enough units to insert themselves into the gaps in the phalanx and wreak havoc among the phalangites, whose close-quarter weaponry was far inferior to that of the Romans.

While Perseus' phalanx was being cut down in the center, Aemilius used his war elephants to drive back the cavalry and light infantry on Perseus' left wing. He could now attack the phalanx from that flank as well. Aemilius allowed his men to slaughter at will, without taking prisoners. By nightfall, at least 20,000 Macedonians had lost their lives, and the local streams were still running red the following morning. A further 11,000 men were captured over the following days, destined to swell Aemilius's coffers once they had been sold into slavery; only a few thousand cavalrymen and light infantrymen escaped, the cavalrymen riding with Perseus to Pella for refuge. From Pella, Perseus fled with his family, friends, and valuables to the island of Samothrace, where his treasure was stolen by a mendacious ship captain who had promised to help him escape, and the Roman fleet blockaded the island until he surrendered.

It was the end of the Macedonian monarchy—almost the end of Macedonian history—and the military challenge to Rome's supremacy in Greece was over. Polybius chose the following year, 167, the year of the post-Pydna settlement of Macedon, as the end of the process of Roman aggrandizement: "From then on, everyone assumed and regarded as inevitable the fact that they would have to submit to the Romans and let them dictate their futures."[7] The point of this sentence is "everyone": many people had already accepted that position of subordination, but from now on everyone did. After the Third Macedonian War, Rome was the only superpower left in the Mediterranean.

THE SETTLEMENT OF MACEDON

Aemilius's ferocity was not assuaged by the battle. The war had been tough, with the Romans consistently bettered by Perseus for the first two years. Revenge was in order, and he let his men despoil the thousands of dead, plunder Pydna, and ravage the surrounding countryside. Over the following months, other towns were captured and looted on charges of continued resistance that, given the circumstances, must have been specious, or just because they had aided Perseus' forces during the war. In 167, for instance, the small town of Antissa on the island of Lesbos was depopulated, and its leaders executed, for having sheltered Perseus' fleet. Even Pella was plundered (though otherwise spared), as one by one the Macedonian communities surrendered to the conquerors.

Three months after Pydna, Aemilius set off on a tour of Greece with a small retinue. On the face of it, this was a sightseeing and goodwill tour, punctuated by pious sacrifices, but with a distinctly regal flavor to it. At Delphi, for instance, Paullus achieved a second, symbolic victory over Perseus by decreeing that a base that had been destined for a statue group of the Macedonian king was to be used for him instead.[8] If Aemilius intended the gesture, and the frieze (which showed Romans slaughtering Macedonians), to suggest that the Romans had freed the Greeks from Macedonian rule, he must have failed: it surely came closer to suggesting that, as the Aetolians foresaw all those years earlier, the Greeks had exchanged one master for another (see Fig. 10.2). Aemilius took in all the standard sites—Athens, Corinth, Olympia—just like a modern tourist, but with added poignancy: the splendid monuments of past centuries must have contrasted savagely with newer traces of war damage.

But there was more to the tour than tourism: it was also supposed to secure Roman dominion, in the same way that Flamininus had, by making sure that as many cities as possible were governed by Roman friends. The method was even harsher this time: Rome's opponents were to be denounced and eliminated, so that they would never again be a threat. When Aemilius reached Demetrias he was met by news of horrors in Aetolia: Lyciscus and his supporters had, with the help of Roman troops, surrounded the Council chamber and butchered 550 of their opponents. Paullus told the men that he would pass judgment on the case when he was back in Amphipolis, but it was a whitewash: the murderers were acquitted and Aemilius reprimanded only the Roman officer who had let his men be party to the massacre. Before long, Lyciscus was allowed to draw up a further list of his political enemies—those who had survived the massacre—for deportation into exile. After that,

A reconstruction (by Heinz Kähler) of the monument L. Aemilius Paullus erected at Delphi, the sacred center of Greece, to commemorate his victory over Perseus of Macedon.

the pro-Roman factions throughout Greece knew that they could get away with anything.

Amphipolis was the place chosen by Aemilius for the proclamation of the settlement designed by him and the ten legates sent out by the Senate. This was to be the Macedonian equivalent of Flamininus's Isthmian Declaration of 196, and Aemilius ordered ten dignitaries to be present from every major community in Macedon. Even though he knew enough Greek, he chose to speak in Latin and have his words translated, to maintain Roman superiority. And then he announced the dismemberment of Macedon: the monarchy was abolished, every senior Macedonian and every man who had been close to Perseus (and their sons over the age of fifteen) were to be deported to Italy, and the state was split up into four independent republics, called simply and rather sinisterly Sections One, Two, Three, and Four. Bare numbers discourage emotional attachment. The Third Macedonian War had been too closely run for the Romans' liking, and their retribution was intended to be decisive. For the best part of two hundred years Macedon had dominated Greek affairs; that was never to happen again.

The chief towns of the four regions were Amphipolis, Thessalonica, Pella, and Pelagonia (which gained some chunks of Epirote territory too), and each of them was to be administered by a council under an oligarchic constitution dictated by Aemilius. To forestall any move toward reunification, there was to be no intermarriage, no cross-border ownership of land or property, and no trade in salt between any of the sections. Geographically, the republics were isolated by the rivers and mountains that served as their borders. Whereas previously all state revenue, from the mines and forests and so on, had gone to the Macedonian crown, half was now to be paid to the Roman state, and the other half kept to maintain the republics themselves. The copper and iron mines remained open, but the gold and silver mines were temporarily closed (or at least were not allowed to generate any revenue), perhaps while their management was reorganized, or perhaps to discourage short-term economic recovery, but almost certainly because Rome itself was less in need of precious metals at this time.[9] None of the four republics was permitted a proper army or fleet, though they were allowed to garrison troublesome borders. It was an attempt to dismember Macedonian pride, as well as the kingdom.

THE HUMILIATION OF RHODES AND PERGAMUM

Not long before the battle of Pydna, at the time they had made their alliance, Perseus and Genthius had sent an embassy to the Rhodians, inviting them to join their anti-Roman coalition. The attempt was certainly worthwhile: the Rhodians were divided on the question whether their interests were best served by siding with Rome, or with Perseus, or by trying to stay neutral. But they were all agreed that their commercial interests demanded peace, so they told Perseus' envoys that they would be sending a mission to Rome to try to bring an end to the war.

It must have seemed to the Rhodians that they had negotiated a tricky situation rather cleverly, but it all went badly wrong for them. Their peace ambassadors did not reach Paullus in the field until his victory was imminent, or secure an audience with the Senate until after news of Pydna had reached Rome. The Romans, already irritated by the Rhodians' failure to supply them with the full contingent of forty ships they had promised, saw further signs of insincerity, and accused them of not really seeking peace, but wanting only to save Perseus; if they had really wanted peace, they would have tried to negotiate it when Perseus was doing well, not when he was doing badly. But, in fact, Perseus had been doing well when the Rhodians came to their decision; it was just that his fall had been very rapid.

At the same time as approaching Rhodes, Perseus and Genthius also sent embassies to Antiochus IV and Eumenes. They pointed out that the Romans had consistently pitted one monarch against another, and argued that if Macedon fell, the kings of Asia Minor would be Rome's next targets. It would be in their interests, then, either to mediate an end to the war, or to join them against the Romans. But both Eumenes and Antiochus, for their own reasons, said no. Antiochus was involved in the Sixth Syrian War against Ptolemy VI, and hoped to complete his conquest of Egypt while Rome was distracted by the war with Perseus. In this he would be thwarted, as we saw in the Prelude: Rome was not so distracted that it did not send Gaius Popillius Laenas to wield the threat of Roman repercussions and bring the war to an end in 168.

For his part, Eumenes said no just because of his long hostility toward Macedon and friendship with Rome. He still felt himself to be riding high in the Romans' favor, but in fact his position was less sure than he thought, and his enemies in Rome seized this opportunity to slander him. It was said that, rather than rejecting Perseus' approach, he had prevaricated, saying that he would abandon the Roman cause and, depending on how much money he received from Perseus, either remain neutral (cost: 1,000 talents) or try to negotiate peace (cost: 1,500 talents). Gradually, over the months following Pydna, Eumenes lost the favor of the Senate.

Having caught wind of this, Eumenes went in person to Rome in the winter of 167–166 to protest, but he was brushed off with the pretense that the Senate would no longer receive kings in Rome. What had Eumenes done wrong? He seems to have been consistently loyal. In fact, whereas before he had been one of the main beneficiaries of Rome's policy of balancing powers, now he became its victim. The Romans had decided to weaken Rhodes, and so they could not leave Eumenes strong. And Eumenes had recently been showing signs of independence. In 175, for instance, he had helped to place Antiochus IV on the Syrian throne, but the Romans wanted no king-makers in the east apart from themselves.[10]

It was the beginning of the end for Eumenes and, in a repetition of their tactics with Perseus and Demetrius, the Romans openly began to favor his brother Attalus. Tempted at first, Attalus asked for Aenus and Maronea as his own personal domain, and the Senate agreed. But later, when Attalus turned against the scheme, the Senate declared the cities free and autonomous, and lost interest in this kind of direct interference in Pergamene affairs, since Eumenes was behaving himself.[11] Prusias of Bithynia also asked to be rewarded with extra territory, which was refused, despite the fact that he, a king in his own right, abased himself before the senators.

Rhodes was treated just as harshly. There were even those in Rome who thought that war should be declared against the island state while there was still a Roman army in the east. They were an ineffective minority, and were famously opposed by Cato the Censor on both moral and pragmatic grounds,[12] but it still shows how bad things had got. Immediately after the war, Gaius Popillius Laenas stopped off in Rhodes on his way to Alexandria to put an end to the Sixth Syrian War, and, in a ghastly attempt to assuage Rome's hostility, the Rhodians voted to put to death the leaders of the pro-Macedonian faction, as a way of demonstrating their loyalty to Rome. And so they did—those who did not kill themselves first.

Along with every other state in the Greek world, the Rhodians sent emissaries to Rome to offer their congratulations on the victory at Pydna, but they were refused an audience with the Senate, and insultingly denied even hospitality, on the grounds that they were no friends of Rome. The Rhodian envoys took a leaf out of Prusias's book and prostrated themselves before the Senate, but it was no use. They were punished by having almost all the territory they had gained at the end of the Syrian–Aetolian War taken from them.

The Rhodians were further damaged, financially, by the Romans' turning the island of Delos into a free port, under Athenian supervision. The first reasons for this move were commercial rather than political; it was designed not so much to undermine Rhodes as to facilitate Mediterranean trade in general, especially in slaves (Delos rapidly became the center of the slave-trade). Nevertheless, it did seriously deplete Rhodian revenues, by 87 percent, according to one Rhodian spokesman's implausible figure.[13] Rhodes retained its main source of income—brokering the eastern Mediterranean grain trade—because Delos did not have a good enough harbor for the big transport vessels; but, all the same, many traders would now bypass Rhodes and head for the more relaxed regime of Delos. And Rome's hostility damaged the Rhodians' standing in the wider world.

Athens also gained the island of Lemnos, and the farmland of destroyed Haliartus became an Athenian enclave in Boeotia. Athens was rewarded not just for its goodwill towards Rome in the war (an offer of troops and a supply of grain), but because it could safely be strengthened without becoming powerful enough to threaten the balance of power, which was now to be constituted out of a number of equally weak states, rather than a few strong ones, as at the end of the Syrian–Aetolian War.

The humiliation of Rhodes and Pergamum was designed to set an example—to show that Rome's power was now unchallengeable, that it could humble great states without even bothering to go to war. After Pydna, as a way of regularizing their relations with Rome and learning where they stood, the Rhodians repeatedly asked for a formal treaty of alliance, but they were always turned down: the Romans now recognized no equals. It was only once that lesson had been learned, perhaps in 164, that the Romans granted them an alliance, and then it was an unequal treaty, containing the notorious clause about maintaining the greatness of Rome, and allowing Rome to continue to intervene in Rhodian affairs.[14] Meanwhile, Eumenes learnt his lesson more quickly. The rebuff he had received was enough to teach him what behavior the Romans now expected of him, and he apparently found little difficulty in complying. Better that Pergamum should survive as it was than assert itself and be cut down.

11.

IMPERIUM ROMANUM

IN 196, TITUS QUINCTIUS Flamininus, to the almost hysterical delight
of his Greek audience, declared the Greeks free not just from the
Macedonians he had recently conquered, but also from Roman rule—
free to govern themselves and decide their own policies and futures. Only
thirty years later, as we shall see, Lucius Aemilius Paullus unleashed on
Epirus one of the worst atrocities in Roman history. In thirty years, the
Romans moved from benign, if cynical, benevolence to virtual ethnic
cleansing, and from indirect interference to the imposition of regime
changes in Greece, Macedon, and Illyris. The velvet glove had been
stripped off to reveal the assumption of superiority that underlies all
imperialist ventures.

Nothing succeeds like success. After their victories in both the
western and eastern Mediterranean, the Romans began to perceive
themselves as unstoppable. They seemed to just go on winning and
extending their dominion, and the Latin word *imperium* evolved in
tandem. Although it originally meant no more than the power Roman
officials gained on their election to carry out their duties, it gradually
took on a geographical connotation, as "the places under Roman control." In short, "the *imperium* of the Roman people" was evolving into
an empire. And the relative ease and speed with which the Romans
were acquiring an empire made it easy for them to feel that these conquests must have been divinely ordained. Most Romans were sure they
were destined to have a Mediterranean empire.

THE EMASCULATION OF GREECE AND ILLYRIS

Following the whitewash of the Aetolian massacre, every sycophant in Greece put in an appearance at Amphipolis and filled Aemilius's ears with the names of those who had been friends of Perseus. Aemilius encouraged the process, drew up lists based on these allegations, and ordered them all—men from Aetolia, Achaea, Acarnania, Epirus, Thessaly, Perrhaebia, and Boeotia—to be interned in Italy.

This extensive program was designed, obviously, to emasculate political opposition in Greece. The great majority of the thousands of detainees never returned. The Achaean League, as we have seen, had made a late attempt to recover the goodwill of the Romans, but still 1,000 Achaeans were deported for internment in Italy, including Polybius. He had been destined for leadership of the Achaean League, but his 15-year sojourn in Italy worked out well for him: he made powerful friends, especially Scipio Africanus the Younger, the son of Aemilius Paullus; served Rome instead of Achaea as adviser and finally roving ambassador to the Greek cities to help them adjust to the new order of things after 146; and found an alternative life's work as a historian.

The list of condemned Achaeans was drawn up for the Romans by the quisling Callicrates, of course, and consisted simply of his political opponents; Polybius's name will have featured early. Seventeen years later, in 151, the survivors, only three hundred of them, were allowed to return, thanks in part to intervention by Cato the Censor; the league had constantly petitioned the Senate in the meantime, but the restoration of the exiles was determined less by their appeals, or by Polybius's influence in Rome, than by changing Roman policy, as evidenced by the fall from Roman favor of Charops of Chaonia a year or two earlier in the 150s.[1]

At the same time as making these harsh provisions, Aemilius was putting on entertainments, dispensing gifts to both cities and individuals, and receiving petitioners, for all the world as though he were a king. He put on display all the wealth of Macedon in Amphipolis—before shipping it back to Rome. He raised himself high enough to be able to ignore the fact that, at ground level, he was fostering the foulest kind of social manipulation, in which neighbors are encouraged to report their neighbors to the authorities. The overall result was that in Greece Rome was left with "plenty of flatterers, but few friends."[2]

After his rapid victory over Genthius, Anicius occupied northern Epirus, the seat of the Molossians and other Epirote rebels, making Passaron (modern Ioannina) his base. Both Aemilius's and Anicius's commands were extended for another year so that they could work with the commissioners (ten for Macedon, five for Illyris) sent out by the Senate to oversee the settlements. Over the winter of 168–167 all the leading men of Illyris were summoned by Anicius to Scodra to hear their future. Anicius too had his turn at a Flamininus-like proclamation: he declared Illyris free and announced that he would be removing his garrisons at the earliest opportunity. Those communities which had at the last minute surrendered to Rome were to be free from tribute, while everyone else continued to pay the same tribute as before, but now half to Rome and half to maintain themselves. Anyone proscribed by Charops as anti-Roman was executed or sent to Italy. As in Macedon, the monarchy was ended, and northern Illyris was to be divided into three distinct republics—one on the coast down to Lissus; one incorporating Labeatan territory, including Scodra and Lissus; and the third inland and to the north. The three new Illyrian republics were to operate with the same restrictions on trade and intermarriage as the Macedonian states. The southern Illyrians continued as Roman friends, the status they had enjoyed since 228, and Genthius's fleet was divided between Corcyra, Apollonia, and Epidamnus. It was up to them to police the Adriatic.

So the Romans still avoided the expense of turning chunks of Greece into direct provinces of the empire (as in Sicily, Spain, Sardinia, and Corsica) garrisoned by Roman troops. No less a person than Cato spoke against turning Macedon into a permanent province, in favor of leaving it "free."[3] He argued that Rome lacked the resources to hold and defend it, and that it should therefore be left to its own devices. Flamininus's old reason was paramount: it would be incompatible with the "freedom" of the Greeks if they let barbarian hordes in from the north, so Macedon must retain enough strength to be able to act as a bulwark against the hordes.

But, if the Romans avoided creating provinces, they vastly increased the dependency of Illyris and Macedon, above all by making them tributaries of the Roman state (a significant alternative to charging them indemnities). Despite being declared free, the Macedonian and Illyrian republics were left with a strange kind of freedom: no ability to accumulate resources; few men remaining with any experience at administration; their military capacity more or less eliminated. Freedom was supposed to mean self-government, but both places had just had their monarchies forcibly removed and replaced with oligarchic republics. Talk of freedom was spurious; the point of the settlement was only to cripple Macedon and Illyris. The seven new republics were to be governed by their own people, but only under strict Roman supervision, backed by diplomatic missions, the reports of traders, and the threat of force. The Romans had bestowed freedom, and the Macedonians and Illyrians were not to forget that they could take it away as well.

THE REDUCTION OF MOLOSSIS

If the Achaeans, Pergamum, and Rhodes were punished even though they had not taken up arms against Rome, what would happen to the Molossians, who had sided with Perseus? By the autumn of 167 their land had already been occupied by Anicius's army for several months, and state after state had learnt its future, but not Molossis or Epirus as a whole. Whatever happened, it was obviously going to be unpleasant.

Aemilius set out for Epirus not long after his Amphipolis proclamation. One division of the army was instructed to enrich itself by plundering the territory of the Atintani and any Illyrians who had sided with Perseus, and then to meet Aemilius at Oricum for embarkation to Italy. Antigonea, the chief town of the Atintani, was so thoroughly destroyed that the site remained uninhabited for 700 years (see Fig. 11.1). Aemilius himself marched to Passaron, and told Anicius, who was encamped nearby, that he should make no move in response to what was about to happen, because Aemilius had express orders from the Senate that his troops were to be allowed to enrich themselves from Molossis and the other Epirote communities that had sided with Perseus.

FIGURE 11.1
The tumbled stones of this gatehouse at Antigonea still lie where they fell during the terrible Roman
sack of Epirote towns in 167 BCE.

Aemilius sent officers around all the Epirote towns to announce the
imminent departure of the Roman garrisons and their freedom—to lull
them, as it turned out, into a false sense of security. Then he ordered all
private and public treasure and valuables to be collected and stored in
their main towns, presumably as the price of their pardon. Then he sent
his men, under arms, ostensibly just to collect all this treasure. But as
soon as they had taken possession of it, the Roman troops were let loose
on the towns, which were sacked (with all the terror of rape, murder,
looting, the demolition of fortifications, and the burning of public buildings), and 150,000 men, women, and children were seized to be sold into
slavery, or resold if they were already slaves. At a stroke, the population of
Epirus was more or less halved. The league temporarily broke down, and
over subsequent years Epirote coinage virtually ceased, indicating great
poverty. More than a century later, Epirus was visited by the geographer

Strabo, who remarked on how the once populous land was now a wilderness, dotted with decaying and ruined villages.⁴

Archaeological evidence reveals some details of this orgy of destruction. The Epirote region of Thesprotia provides a test case, since its three main towns have all been excavated: Phanote (modern Doliani), Gitana, and Elea. In the war, the Thesprotians appear to have been divided: although we hear of Thesprotians fighting for the Romans, Phanote, on the border between Thesprotia and Molossis, resisted them and was duly punished: it was so reduced that all its remaining inhabitants could fit into what had formerly been just the acropolis of the city, and its fortifications were not rebuilt until the Byzantine period. Gitana too had all its public buildings and fortifications destroyed, and only a fraction of the town was re-occupied afterwards. Elea was more thoroughly devastated, and never inhabited again.⁵

When we have explicit historical evidence that at least some Thesprotians fought for the Romans, and explicit archaeological evidence suggesting that every major Thesprotian town was wholly or partially destroyed, it is hard to resist the conclusion that Aemilius let his men loose indiscriminately on friend and foe alike, or perhaps lost control of them. Then again, Charops' influence may often have been the decisive factor. As far as we can tell, his native Chaonia was spared. If we knew more about his personal likes and dislikes, we would probably see why, elsewhere as well, some were spared and others punished. At any rate, Polybius described him as "the most brutal and unscrupulous monster the world has ever seen," and added that, for a while after the Third Macedonian War, he was effectively the dictator of Epirus.⁶

Seventy towns were said to have been sacked—and there is the rub, because the sum total of communities of any size in Molossis and their allies was far less than seventy. From this perspective too we see that Aemilius's and Charops' purpose was not discriminate destruction, but the kind of savagery that would cow the Epirotes themselves to Charops' regime, and would deter others from contemplating rebellion in the future. The Renaissance thinker Niccolò Machiavelli, commenting explicitly on the Roman conquest of Greece, said: "When the Romans thought to hold Greece by leaving it its freedom and allowing it to be governed by its own laws, they failed, and had to destroy many cities of that Province before they could secure it. For, in truth, there is no sure way of holding other than by destroying."[7]

This was by far the largest slave hunt in the history of Rome, and it was ordered specifically by the Senate, rather than being left, as such decisions usually were, to the commander in the field. This raises a further possibility.[8] A new kind of farming was gathering pace in Italy. Up until the middle of the third century, there was not that great a gap between a general and those of his troops who were better off: they were all farmers, with not much to tell between the sizes of their farms. But the increased prosperity of upper-class families, and the arrival of slaves from Spain and Africa and Greece in quantities that made them more affordable, enabled wealthier men to buy up larger estates and convert their farms from subsistence farming to cattle ranching, or other forms of specialist, labor-intensive agriculture. This, combined with epidemics in the mid-170s, which were serious enough for Livy to talk of piles of unburied slave corpses clogging the roads,[9] is perhaps another reason for the Senate's instructions to Aemilius. A hundred years later, we still find poignant traces of this Epirote slave cull in Latin literature, when a Roman writer on agricultural matters mentions that Epirote slaves were highly valued because they came in family units which made for stability. In some cases, the families that were forcibly plucked from their homes managed to stay together over the generations, uprooted and enslaved, but otherwise intact.[10]

THE TRIUMPHS

So the Romans returned in glory to Rome. Anicius's triumph was marked by the payment of perhaps 20 million *sestertii* into the public treasury, and by the display of a king, Genthius, in chains along with all the members of the Illyrian royal family. Afterwards, Genthius was interned in Iguvium (modern Gubbio, in Umbria), where remains of what has been identified as his tomb can still be seen (see Fig. 11.2).

But Anicius's triumph was nothing compared to Aemilius's, which had taken place a few weeks earlier and became the talk of the town for many

FIGURE 11.2
The remains of the tomb of King Genthius of Illyris, from Gubbio in Italy, where he was interned after his defeat at Roman hands.

years. Aemilius gave so much money to the state treasury that, bearing in mind also that Rome now had regular income from tribute, the Senate indulged in the dramatic gesture of canceling ordinary direct taxation of Roman citizens indefinitely. Faced with the 120 million *sestertii* Aemilius donated to the treasury, his troops complained that they had not been paid enough, but they were so obviously motivated by base greed (their bonus had in fact been very generous) that they were forced to back down when it became clear that Aemilius was not enriching himself at all, but giving everything to his men or the state. Aemilius himself would be enriched by fame alone—or so the Aemilius legend has it.

Aemilius's triumph lasted three days, like Flamininus's; he had a lot to display, having denuded Macedon of its artistic treasures and plundered parts of Greece as well. Over the three days spectators saw paintings and sculptures, countless objects in gold and silver, gorgeous textiles, richly decorated furniture, bullion and coins beyond counting. Macedon had been a wealthy country, and its kings had long patronized the best Greek artists. On the first day, 250 wagons displayed *objets d'art*, great and small. Aemilius seems to have had a fine eye for works of art, and among the many he brought back was a statue of Athena by Pheidias of Athens, the greatest sculptor of the high classical period. On the second day, it was the turn of all the captured arms and armor, cleverly displayed on their floats so that they looked as though they had just fallen on the battlefield, and of silver art objects, bullion, and coinage; there was so much of this that it took 3,000 men to carry it all. The final element in the second day's parade was Perseus' personal ceremonial chariot, laden with the king's arms and armor, with his simple royal diadem laid poignantly on top.

On the third day, Aemilius himself rode in his triumphal chariot, preceded by 120 oxen with gilded horns for an extravagant sacrifice. This third day was dedicated to displaying the most precious objects in gold, including one bowl, studded with gems, that weighed 250 kilograms (550 pounds). But of course the *pièce de résistance* was King Perseus, surrounded by his children, whose innocence aroused the pity of the spectators. It is a true index of the evolution of the Roman desire for dominion that kings had previously been made friends of Rome if they surrendered but were now led in chains before the triumphant general. Perseus was then confined under house arrest in Alba Fucens, an isolated town in central Italy that was often used for the detention of important prisoners. The whole experience was so humiliating that within two years he had starved himself to death. It was his pride that had made him resist Roman bullying in the first place, and now it caused his death.[11]

CULTURE AND IDENTITY

If Aemilius's triumph was remarkable for its splendor and riches, the highlight of Anicius's was a strange theatrical display. The evidence is difficult (and the event may have taken place some years later), but Anicius seems to have deliberately imported the best musicians and dramatic artists from Greece, only to have them fight a chaotic and impromptu musical battle while the audience mocked and hurled insults.[12] The whole event seems to have been deliberately designed to humiliate Greeks by having them make fools of themselves at a Roman's orders and before a Roman audience. It was an assertion of Roman superiority, and this was not an isolated act, or attitude, but takes us right to the core of a profound debate that raged in Rome as a result of more continuous contact with Greek culture.

In the natural course of events, Romans and Greeks had often come into contact before Rome began to send armies east. As excavated pottery fragments attest, trade had been going on between Greece and Italy since about 1500 BCE. The Romans, like everyone else, consulted the oracle at Delphi. Greek loan words began to appear in the Latin language as early as the fifth century. It was said that when the Romans first needed to draw up their legal code, in the fifth century, they looked to Greek models. There were also diplomatic contacts in the fourth and early third centuries—perhaps even with Alexander the Great, but certainly with other kings of Macedon, Egypt, and Syria, and possibly with the Rhodians.[13]

Religion was always a rich field for cross-fertilization, especially given the similarity of the ways in which the major deities of both religions were envisaged. The worship of the Greek god Apollo was established early, in the fifth century. The Romans' fundamental collection of oracles pertinent to their history was the Sibylline Books, written in Greek verse; in the middle of the third century the Greek form of worshipping Demeter (Ceres to the Romans) was grafted onto the Roman version, with Greek priestesses imported from the south; consultation of the Sibylline Books led to the introduction of the worship of the Greek healer god, Asclepius, early in the third century (at a time of plague), to the introduction of Aphrodite of Sicilian Eryx in 217, and to the introduction of the Phrygian Magna Mater (Cybele) in 205.[14]

There was nothing challenging, however, in these early contacts. The fact that legends told of the Twelve Tables being based on Athenian law did not make Romans feel less purely Roman, any more than French influences on the foundations of the United States make its citizens feel less American. That there was a level of accepted intermingling of cultures is shown above all by the multifarious Greek influences on public architecture in Italian cities in the third century.[15] There had long been Greek artists and artisans working in Rome and Italy.

Nevertheless, evidence from our period shows that the influence of Greek culture threw the Romans into some kind of crisis—that it was not always accepted, and not always taken to be an intrinsic and unobjectionable part of some common Mediterranean culture. We will soon consider Cato's opposition to Greek culture, but the very fact that we can say this—that Cato set his face against "Greek culture"—shows that it was considered, at least by Cato and his allies, a detachable block, something distinct and new. Perhaps, then, Marcus Claudius Marcellus was right to boast that the spoils he brought back from the sack of Syracuse in 211 taught the Romans to appreciate Greek art,[16] not just because from then on what had formerly been a trickle became a flood, but more particularly, and more subtly, because, faced with the flood, the Romans became self-conscious about external influences and began to question their value for them.

Now Roman aristocrats not only saw for themselves what Greece had to offer, but acquired the wealth to bring it home, and to use the appropriation of Greek artifacts as a means of asserting their elite status. Given aristocratic competitiveness, if one of their peers earned prestige for being a connoisseur of Greek art, others wanted to keep up with him. Prestige was invariably the name of the game: Greek artists painted scenes from their patrons' victorious battles; Greek sculptors filled the public spaces of Rome with glorifications of their paymasters;[17] Greek architects designed buildings in their patrons' names and inscribed them with accounts of their deeds; Ennius's *Annales* highlighted the achievements of his patron, Fulvius Nobilior, and his family; Marcus Pacuvius (220–130) wrote a play celebrating Aemilius's defeat of Perseus, and Aemilius also brought the philosopher and painter Metrodorus from Athens to commemorate his deeds in pictures and to educate his sons.[18]

Later, noble Romans began to patronize Greek philosophers as a way to rise above their peers, and every great man had Greeks in his entourage. Greek rhetorical skills helped a man stand out and get the better of his rivals in the Senate and law courts. Greek writers and artists had previously been patronized by the Hellenistic kings; now they found a new source. And so they flooded into Rome, as refugees or political prisoners or by choice. By the end of the second century, pretty much all education in Rome was in Greek hands. As Horace, the Roman poet of the late first century BCE, memorably put it: "Captive Greece took her savage conqueror captive and brought the arts to rustic Rome."[19] Sustained contact with Greece was a catalyst for massive shifts in Roman cultural life.

The first phase, then, of the self-conscious appropriation of Greek culture was characterized by a growing familiarity with Greek artifacts, either through the translations of the earliest Latin writers, or through the plunder brought back by victorious generals. From the very start, however, admiration of Greek culture—the kind of admiration that led certain Romans pretentiously to trace their lineages back to Greek heroes and divinities—was tinged with darker feelings. Some Romans of the middle Republic seem to have felt that they were cultural peasants compared with the Greeks, and to have reacted not just with respect but also with attempts, generated by a feeling of inferiority, to seize the high ground. This is the context for Anicius's theatrical fiasco, and also for the fact that, despite the obvious popularity of Greek-style theatrical entertainments, there was no permanent theater in Rome until the middle of the first century BCE, at the earliest. The erection of stages on an ad hoc basis enabled the Senate, as guardian of Rome's morals, to retain control of theatrical productions.

And so the Romans belittled the Greeks, at the same time as admiring their culture. No doubt Cicero, in the first century BCE, was not the first among learned Romans to find a relatively easy way to resolve the tension between admiration and contempt: they could combine respect for the great Greeks of the past with contempt for their contemporaries; or they could acknowledge the superiority of Greek learning, while regretting that it had not helped the Greeks develop a sound moral character.[20] Others, relatedly, valued Hellenism in their private lives, but treated Greeks with contempt in public—when speaking in the Senate and when fighting them abroad. Lucius Aemilius Paullus, a sincere philhellene (he gave his sons a Greek education, for instance), did not let his admiration for Greek culture stop him from destroying it, or at least carrying its artifacts off to Rome. Even the display of Greek artifacts in Rome, in private or in public spaces, was a subtle assertion of dominance: from now on, Rome would be the protector of the Greeks' cultural heritage. Ciceronian contempt for contemporary Greeks undoubtedly fueled Roman plundering, just as it did that of Lord Elgin in the nineteenth century. The underlying sentiment was the same: Greeks nowadays are incapable of looking after their great heritage.

Ironically, the Romans orientalized the Greeks—ironically, because it was the Greeks themselves who, in the fifth century, had "invented the barbarian,"[21] and sketched out the basic terms of orientalism: easterners are effeminate, impulsive, irrational, fond of luxury, servile, and so on. And now the same brush was applied liberally by Romans to them. The traditional focuses of upper-class Roman life had been politics, war, the law courts, and their estates; philosophy, literature, and other forms of Greek leisure seemed frivolous to many.

The process of orientalization started early: already at the end of the third century Greeks in Plautus's plays, for all that the plays were modeled on Greek originals, tend to be effeminate and deranged, and he used words that literally mean "to play the Greek" to imply sexual deviance or general moral weakness. "Go on," he says: "drink night and day, just like Greeks."[22] Greek gymnasia were a particular target for some Romans, who were disgusted by the practice of exercising naked and felt that this was a license for homosexuality.[23] Underlying all the charges was one fundamental feeling: Greeks lack the ballast of Roman *gravitas*. For all their high culture and long history, we Romans are superior because we have the moral basis. It is perhaps worth remembering that the Greeks the Romans knew best were domestic slaves, employed artisans, and diplomats, all classes to whom deference and obsequiousness would simply have been safeguards, and lying sometimes a necessity.

Roman resistance to Greek culture is associated above all with Cato the Censor, thanks to his periodic tirades. But in fact Cato encapsulated the same dilemma that Cicero and others were trying to resolve, the tension between admiration and contempt. On the one hand, he was a learned man, steeped in Greek language, history, and culture; on the other hand, he professed contempt for them as "an utterly vile and unruly race"— this from a letter to his son warning him off all things Greek.[24] His real target, then, was perhaps not Greek culture itself, but those Romans who affected foreign manners and tastes; he found their pretensions repugnant and subversive of traditional Roman morals.[25] Cato's campaign—the task he set himself and unsmilingly went about—was to defend traditional Roman ways, or at least a rather whimsical and idealized version of early Rome as a community of robust farmers with austere and frugal lives. As the virtual founder of Latin prose literature, he sometimes went too far in downplaying his Greek predecessors.

Contact with Greek culture made it urgent for Rome to find its place in the wider cultural life of the Mediterranean, and to do so in a way that left its sense of dominance intact. They believed that it was their moral superiority that had awarded them the backing of the gods and ensured their success in warfare. Drawing on an age-old imperialist tenet, they felt that superiors were bound, by natural law, to rule inferiors and, illogically affirming the consequent, they felt that the fact that they ruled Greece proved their superiority.[26] It was, of course, a self-fulfilling prophecy, in the sense that, once conquered, the Greeks were bound to behave more like subjects.

From time to time, the assertion of superiority took a more direct, but more paranoid form. In 186 the Senate decided to suppress the worship of Dionysus (Bacchus to the Romans), the god of wine and ecstatic liberation. This was carried out brutally, with many adherents of the cult executed, and further persecution over the next few years. But the worship of Dionysus had been long established, and it was certainly no more outlandish or immoral than, say, the worship of the Cybele, which was widely believed to involve ritual self-castration.[27] The fundamental issue was, as much as anything, the fact that this form of worship of Bacchus had crept into Rome without being sanctioned by the Senate (unlike, say, the introduction of Cybele), and there was felt to be a danger that worshippers might identify themselves more with their cult than with the public rituals that made up civic religion and supported Roman citizenship. The reason given for the suppression was that the Bacchic cult had degenerated into sexual excess and even ritual murder, but this sounds like propaganda and justification of an act prompted by panic and prejudice. The burning in 181 of Pythagorean books, which had allegedly been found in a chest belonging to an early king of Rome, stemmed from the same concerns about religious unorthodoxy and about foreign teaching corrupting Roman morals. The same goes for the equally public expulsion of Greek philosophers and teachers of rhetoric in 161 and 154, while individual senators cultivated Greek philosophers and found Greek teachers for their sons.[28]

A good example of the way in which the Romans simultaneously borrowed from Greece and tried to improve on what they learned is afforded by the type of sculpture called "veristic" ("lifelike"). There were no competent Roman sculptors and artists—in fact, there was a strain of contempt for art as a profession; it was felt to be unsuitable for Romans[29] —so all the artists involved in this movement were Greeks, but they were working to Roman commissions. The coin portrait of Flamininus on p. 85 is a good example of verism, and a very early one. There is no attempt to portray Flamininus as any kind of ideal, but presumably an attempt, crude in this case, to portray him as he actually was. By the time the veristic fashion was in full swing, we find truly remarkable warts-and-all sculptures of Roman dignitaries. They show middle-aged or elderly men with all their wrinkles, creases, and defects made prominent, even exaggerated. They seem to be gazing forward earnestly, with a presence that is often very intense. The bust of Scipio Africanus on p. 107 is a relatively low-key veristic sculpture.[30]

Greek sculpture of the time was given to a similar degree of realism in its portrayal of lowly subjects such as slaves, children, foreigners, and animals, but it still tended to idealize kings and other great men, as did the vast majority of Roman sculpture too. Clearly, however, the instructions the veristic sculptors received for their Roman commissions were along the lines of "No fancy stuff. Just show us as we are." The impression the sculptures are supposed to convey is of battle-hardened, mature, responsible men, who had earned their wrinkles in uncompromising service to the state. The message was that Greek art was to be in the service of Rome. So the Romans did not merely imitate Greek art, but they also emulated it; they did not just take it over, but made it their own. The Hellenization of Rome went hand in hand with its Romanization, the development of Roman forms on a Greek foundation. The Roman poet Ovid made the point most cleverly, by inverting Horace's tag. "Not yet," he wrote, referring to early Rome, "had Greece surrendered its conquered arts to the conquerors."[31] In his version, the Romans took over Greek culture and made it their own.

Sustained contact with Greek culture made the Romans aware of the poverty of their own tradition; they had little to teach the Greeks, but much to learn from them. There was very little native Latin literature—no epics, no love poetry, little in the way of tragedy or comedy—and even in other spheres, such as architecture, it was contact with Greece that pushed the Romans to develop their own forms for the first time. Of course the Romans were literate before they came into contact with Greece, and they had their own songs, poetry, lowbrow plays, and poetic competitions, perpetuated largely orally. The change is a change of register, up the scale toward highbrow: hence Cato, with his emphasis on plain Roman virtues would disparage it, and for some decades many subjects—medicine, geography, science, philosophy—were available only in Greek texts.

The influx of Greek culture forced the Romans to think about what it was to be Roman: Cato expressed Roman-ness in one way, senatorial expulsions in another. Thus the Hellenization of Rome impelled the Romans to find their own identity and create their own art forms: Hellenization and Romanization occurred together as a constantly evolving process. The Romans were learning to be "bilingual," both literally and figuratively (fluent in both languages, and in both cultures). But bilingualism is a limited metaphor, since it implies that the two cultures sat side by side, just as someone with both languages may switch at will from one to the other. Apart from language, culture does not behave like that: much of it is absorbed, not learned, and so one cannot simply switch from one cultural mode to the other. When Russian high society went overboard for French taste in the eighteenth and nineteenth centuries, what it was to be Russian included a liberal and inseparable admixture of French habits. The same went for Rome. Grafting is a more accurate metaphor than bilingualism. But Rome did not thereby become less Roman; it just became more Greek.

12.

THE GREEK WORLD AFTER PYDNA

O NCE AGAIN, AFTER PYDNA, the Romans withdrew their forces. Given the nature of Roman dominion in the east, however, the presence or absence of an army was not a particularly significant factor. Annexation is not the only form of imperialism: "Empire...is a relationship, formal or informal, in which one state controls the effective sovereignty of another political society. It can be achieved by force, by political collaboration, by economic, social or cultural dependence. Imperialism is simply the process or policy of establishing or maintaining an empire."[1]

The Romans had weakened every state in the Balkan peninsula and in Asia Minor until none of them could launch a credible threat on its own, and they kept a close enough eye on events to be sure of hearing if any kind of coalition was forming. They sent regular missions, but they also had informers in every city, league, and state—the quisling yes-men whose power they had so ruthlessly fostered. The seven Macedonian and Illyrian republics were tributaries of Rome, and every state in Greece and Asia Minor was now governed by pro-Romans; open opposition had been more or less entirely eliminated. Perseus was crushed at Pydna in the same year that Popillius Laenas curbed Antiochus IV by threat alone;[2] opposition could and would be ended by either military or diplomatic means, especially since anyone dealing with a Roman diplomat knew that he bore an implied threat of force.

And so the Greek states learned further lessons in sycophancy; they approached Rome with caution and humility, and occasionally with abject servility. Immediately after the Third Macedonian War, a number of states in Greece rushed to honor the Roman victors: the Achaean

League erected a statue of Marcius Philippus at Olympia; even the undisciplined Hortensius was awarded a golden crown by Delos.[3] It had long been the practice of the Greek states to look back on their glorious past in the hope of its revival; such sentiments were merely embarrassing now. Mastery of the Mediterranean had passed into other hands.

DEFERENCE TO ROME

Even kings looked to Rome to shore up their regimes and awarded the newcomer a prudent degree of deference. After Popillius had stopped Antiochus IV taking Egypt, obsequious envoys were dispatched from Antioch to Rome to say that "a peace that pleased the Senate seemed more desirable to Antiochus than any victory," and that he had obeyed Popillius's order "as he would an order from the gods." Shortly after gaining the throne in 163, Ariarathes V of Cappadocia not only persuaded the Romans to recognize his rule, as a hedge against the hostility of Demetrius I of Syria, but obsequiously bought their continuing favor with bribes. In 161, he even put aside his bride because she was Demetrius's sister and the widow of Perseus. And Demetrius himself found deference the way to recover, to some degree, the Romans' favor after his escape in 162 from internment in Italy. Prusias II of Bithynia sent his son to be brought up in Rome and educated in Roman ways. In 156, when Attalus II of Pergamum was contemplating action against the Galatians, he found it prudent to get the Senate's approval first. In 155 even Pharnaces I of far-flung Pontus, with whom the Romans had had negligible dealings, urged himself and a treaty partner to "maintain their friendship with the Romans and do nothing contrary to them."[4]

Kings and states had to exercise fine judgment: they needed the backing of Rome to gain power over their neighbors, but if they grew too strong they risked incurring Rome's wrath. They had seen what happened to Philip, Perseus, and Eumenes. The ultimate in kingly deference to Rome came in 155 when Ptolemy VIII bequeathed his satellite kingdom of Cyrenaica to Rome; he was followed in 133 by Attalus III, who bequeathed the entire kingdom of Pergamum to Rome.[5]

Nevertheless, for a while Asia and Asia Minor were still remote, and Roman policy was applied fitfully. For a while, kings could get away with conduct that would otherwise have displeased Rome. So Eumenes fought the Galatians from 168 to 166, and the Romans did nothing until the war was over, when they ordered him to respect Galatian autonomy and withdraw his forces from their territory. Or again, in 156, Prusias II of Bithynia persevered in his war against Pergamum even after the Senate had made its displeasure known, and was persuaded to end it a couple of years later only when the Romans canceled the treaty between them and him, threatening armed intervention.

Roman mastery was maintained not just by grand gestures such as war, the cancellation of treaties, and diplomatic threats, but also still by interference in local events, a tactic we have seen them pursuing from the start. Individual cities and towns in both Asia Minor and Greece were granted alliances. In no case do we know why, but one effect will have been to enable these places to achieve or maintain local dominance. Asia Minor was largely left to its own devices, but Greece was closer to the center and already had a longer history of Roman management. Hence Rome intervened, for instance, in disputes between Athens and Delos, between Sparta and Megalopolis, and between Sparta and Argos.[6] Kings in Asia Minor may have retained some freedom of movement, but there was considerably less for the Greek leagues and states.

INDIFFERENCE OR REMOTE CONTROL?

Having disciplined both Eumenes and the Rhodians, Rome was content to trust in the balance of powers and leave Asia and Asia Minor largely to their own devices. Legates were occasionally sent, usually with a combination of specific and general commissions—to sort out a particular problem, to keep an eye on things, to prop up the supposedly self-sustaining peace. In 165, for instance, Titus Sempronius Gracchus was the head of an embassy that visited Pergamum, Cappadocia, Syria, and Rhodes. In 163, Gnaeus Octavius headed up another embassy, with a long list of important jobs: the Macedonians were finding it hard to adjust to their new situation, and disputes there needed settling; Cappadocia and Galatia were at loggerheads; in Egypt the two warring Ptolemy brothers were to be reconciled.

Most importantly, Octavius and his colleagues were to settle Syria "according to the Senate's wishes." One of the reasons Sempronius had been sent to Syria in 165 was that Antiochus IV had held a huge military parade the year before, and the Romans were concerned that he might be building up his armaments beyond the limits imposed by the Peace of Apamea. He was indeed, and the Senate, while pretending to turn a blind eye for a while, was in fact helping his enemies. Above all, they supported a Jewish rebellion led by Judas Maccabeus (167–160), provoked by Antiochus's foolish attempt to get the Jews to worship Greek gods. But the Senate now decided to disarm the Syrian king. As his near success in Egypt a few years earlier demonstrated, he was strong enough to threaten the balance of powers, and the Roman legates were to see that his navy was burned and war elephants crippled.[7]

The upshot of this massive interference was that in 162, after having successfully hamstrung Syria's military capability, Octavius was murdered there. In 230, the murder of a Roman ambassador prompted the invasion of Illyris; what would the Romans do about Octavius's death? The envoys of Antiochus V, the boy king who had succeeded his father to the Syrian throne in 164, tried to convince the Senate that the king had had nothing to do with the business. The Senate was skeptical, but chose to let Syria sort out its own affairs. The assassination of Octavius had left Antioch in great turmoil, and the Senate, or a powerful group of senators, hoping to gain influence in Syria, connived at the "secret" escape of Demetrius from Italy in 162.[8] Demetrius was welcomed on his return to Antioch, where he killed his young cousin and took the throne for himself. Justice was done, in so far as the buck for Octavius's murder stopped at Antiochus. Demetrius also sent the ringleaders of the murder to Rome for trial, but again the Senate took a canny course. They merely returned the murderers for Demetrius to deal with, and cherished their outrage as a stick to beat successive Syrian kings into submission, for instance over their chronic tardiness in paying tranches of the indemnity imposed after the Syrian–Aetolian War. The whole affair shows the Senate manipulating events in Syria from afar, without lifting a finger or committing Rome to anything except continued paternalistic dominance.

These are, of course, good examples of the exercise of remote control, and they clearly display the Senate's continuing determination to do as little as possible, short of endangering their dominion. The same policy was also employed in Greece, where the Senate increasingly tended to insist on compulsory mediation for conflicts, either by themselves or, more usually, by some suitable third party.[9] The Romans had Greece sewn up pretty tight, and that drastically reduced their need for direct interference. When Lyciscus, the leader of the pro-Roman faction in the Aetolian League, was killed in 159, for instance, the Romans did nothing. They did not need to, because Lyciscus's death did not jeopardize anything. In fact, the downfall of the pro-Roman faction brought an end to civil strife in Aetolia, and the same thing happened in Boeotia, Acarnania, and Epirus. The Romans did nothing in all these cases because there was nothing to be done, not because they were indifferent to what was going on. They no longer needed men like Lyciscus and Charops.

THE FOURTH MACEDONIAN WAR

Not surprisingly, given the severity of the Roman solution in their case, the worst trouble came from the Macedonian republics, or "sections." The gold and silver mines were reopened in 158 (Rome had need of precious metals again), but the country had been devastated and plundered in the wake of Pydna, and poverty was widespread. The reopening of the mines would in any case chiefly help only Sections One and Two, where they were located. The enormous royal estates had been taken over by Rome, and men must have been sent out, or appointed from within Macedon, to manage them, but it is likely that there was an extended period when production from farming and forestry was far lower than it had been. All competent administrators had been removed to Italy for internment, countless others had fled abroad, and inexperienced inefficiency must have characterized the republics in their first decade.

To make matters worse, Aemilius had helped himself to all surplus grain and oil, and had given it away to individuals and states by way of reward.[10] Prices will have risen. Transhumant pasturage, a mainstay of peasant life in the Macedonian mountains, may have been interrupted by the new borders. For quite a while, before Roman money started trickling back east in trade, there were those who, out of desperation or loyalty, longed to see their country reunited under a king. In the years between Pydna and the outbreak of the Fourth Macedonian War there was trouble on at least two occasions.[11]

Then, in 152, a young Macedonian mercenary officer called Andriscus, in the employ of Demetrius of Syria, emerged with the claim that Perseus was his father, and that he had been biding his time until the moment was right. He attracted a growing following among other Macedonians resident in Syria, and eventually asked Demetrius to help place him on the Macedonian throne. But Demetrius, as always, needed to find ways to please the Romans, so he had the pretender arrested and sent to Rome.

Andriscus probably was Perseus' son (he was the spitting image, apparently), but his mother was most likely a concubine.[12] Before long he had escaped from Rome and returned east. He made his way to several other Macedonian émigré strongholds, especially Byzantium and Miletus, where he continued to attract followers and build up a small army. Finally, he went to Thrace, where Perseus' sister was married to a Thracian king, and so far from disowning him, she and her husband encouraged him in his aspirations, though without supplying him with many troops.

The Macedonian sections had been left with only small militias, and before long Andriscus had gained control of Pella and was acclaimed king, giving himself the royal name Philip VI. He had met with resistance on the borders, and his rule was far from universally popular, especially since many of the émigrés in his train returned with claims to land that had for at least ten years been in others' hands. But there was enough anti-Roman feeling, and conservative sympathy for the monarchy, to keep him afloat for the time being.

A team of legates under Publius Cornelius Scipio Nasica was sent out to investigate, and to settle matters by negotiation if they could, but that proved impossible and Nasica wrote in alarmist terms back to the Senate. In the meantime, as a Macedonian king should, Andriscus had launched a campaign to recover Thessaly. The Thessalians appealed for help to the Achaean League, who could get troops to them quickly, and Nasica found himself drawing on his experiences from the Pydna campaign to organize the defense of Thessaly by the Achaeans.

In response to Nasica's report, the Senate dispatched the praetor Publius Juventius Thalna with one legion, but soon after his arrival in 148 he was annihilated in battle by Andriscus, with the loss of almost all his men and his own life. It was a brilliant Macedonian victory, the worst defeat the Romans had ever suffered in the east, and it must have hugely improved Andriscus's standing in Macedon—but, of course, it was bound to bring the might of Rome down onto his head.

Following Juventius's defeat, the Senate quickly sent out another praetor, Quintus Caecilius Metellus, with a considerably larger army and the support of the Pergamene fleet. Andriscus was soon defeated and fled to Thrace. This time he was more successful at raising an army there, and he returned to the fray, only to be defeated once more by Caecilius. In due course of time he featured as the most notorious captive in Caecilius's triumph, and Caecilius proudly gained the *agnomen* Macedonicus. So ended the Fourth Macedonian War, the final Macedonian bid for independence. It had delivered a real shock to the Romans—and then two further pretenders emerged, in 147 and 143, re-emphasizing, even though their attempts failed, the unpopularity of the Roman settlement and the persistence of Macedonian pride.

A NEW DISPENSATION FOR MACEDON

Much of Illyris too had been sectionalized, as we have seen, but the only trouble there arose further up the Dalmatian coast when the northern Illyrians began to raid Roman friends such as Issa. Legates were sent in 158, but they were treated so insultingly that the Romans took military action to punish the offenders. As usual for this post-Pydna period, we know too few details, but the Third Illyrian War took the campaigning seasons of both 156 (under Gaius Marcius Figulus) and 155 (Publius Cornelius Scipio Nasica); in contrast with the brevity of its two predecessors, it looks as though, as with Andriscus in Macedon, the Romans met stiffer resistance than they had expected. But after that there was peace in Illyris for many years.

Macedon, however, seemed unlikely to adjust to its new situation. There were still too many dissidents, and even pretenders to the throne. And there was no telling what the effect of a resurgent Macedon might be on the Greeks further south; rebellion in Macedon could be just the first rumble of a major avalanche. The Romans could now either reunite Macedon, so that it had the strength to resist incursions such as Andriscus's on its own, or they could assume direct control. The fact that they were engaged on the Third Punic War, the final elimination of Carthage, inclined them towards the latter course, as the swiftest and easiest solution. And so for the first time in Greece remote control was abandoned, and an army of occupation was installed, with a military governor. From the time of Caecilius's departure in 146, a Roman commander and troops (probably no more than a single legion) were sent out every year to Macedon;[13] policing the troubled northern borders was now the job of Roman garrisons, who were also available to respond rapidly to any perceived emergencies further south.

It was the beginning of the process of turning Macedon into a permanent province of the Roman Empire, joining Sicily, Corsica/Sardinia, Cisalpine Gaul, and Spain, where the process was further advanced. Little was done immediately beyond the installation of the army and governor—the four sections remained in place, for instance, and no colonies were planted, despite a land shortage in Italy—but a new calendar was introduced, indicating a new era. Although the governor's primary responsibilities were military, he also oversaw the collection of tribute and responded to the local petitions that came now to his door, not that of the Senate in Rome; and so, over the years, his administrative duties became as important and time-consuming as his military duties. Gradually, all major Macedonian policy decisions began to be taken by Romans alone, or at best in consultation with senior Macedonians. Gradually, the Roman governor came to see Macedon as a whole, overarching the four republics, and administrative structures evolved that enabled Macedon to become a formal province of the empire, perhaps by the end of the second century.

THE ACHAEAN WAR

The major event in Achaean political life of the 160s and 150s was the internment of 1,000 of their leading men as part of the Roman settlement of Greece following their victory at Pydna. As already mentioned, their petitions were eventually successful, and the surviving exiles returned, if they wanted to, in 151.[14] But if this was a sign of Roman favor for the league, the position would very quickly alter; if the Romans thought that they no longer needed the hostages as a stick with which to keep the Achaeans toeing the line, they were soon proved wrong. The underlying problem was perhaps simply that twenty years had passed since Callicrates had seen the prudential necessity of compliance with Rome; a new generation of Achaean hardliners gained influence within the league, presumably with the support of at least some of the exiles returning from Italy.

So when Sparta seceded once more from the league, the event was bound to set rival Achaean political groups against each other. In 149 the Achaean envoys—they included the aged Callicrates, but he died in mid-embassy—who had journeyed to Rome to consult with the Senate over the Spartan question came back with divergent messages. Some, the inheritors of Philopoemen's independence faction, insisted that the Romans had left it up to the league to sort out its own internal affairs, and others insisted that the Spartans were now free to leave the league if they wanted, with Roman blessing.

The Spartans duly seceded, and the Achaeans duly responded by attacking the rebel city, despite the warning of Roman envoys sent from Macedon by Caecilius to wait for Roman commissioners to come and settle the affair. The war continued into 147, and when Lucius Aurelius Orestes eventually arrived to announce the Roman decision, feelings were running high. His announcement that not only Sparta, but Corinth, Argos, Heraclea near Thermopylae, and one or two other places were free to leave the league and govern themselves, reduced the meeting to violence and chaos.

As long ago as 182 the Romans had revealed their intention to use fragmentation as a way of keeping the league weak; they had made further such attempts in 172, and again in 164, in supporting the secession of the Aetolian town of Pleuron from the league. The pretext was always the same: the alleged incompatibility between the "freedom" of the cities and their membership in the league.[15] Renewed Achaean independence following Callicrates' death now resurrected this senatorial policy, though their reasons for picking on these particular places, apart from Sparta, are obscure. Perhaps it was no more than a bluff: it did not matter which places were mentioned, because the point was only to cow the Achaeans before Rome's authority, to remind them that they were not actually free.

But the Romans must have known that Aurelius's message was sheer provocation, especially given that just the previous year the Achaeans had been prepared to help the Romans against Andriscus. Aurelius was inviting the Achaeans to connive at their own political suicide! The Corinthian delegates stalked out, showing their contempt for Aurelius's suggestion, and Aurelius barely escaped with his life (or so he claimed on his return to Rome). The Romans had badly miscalculated, and their next envoy later in the year, Sextus Julius Caesar,[16] adopted a more conciliatory tone and spoke only about Sparta. The underlying message remained unchanged, however—that Rome had the right to dictate the future of the league—and Caesar's mission was really no more than a stop-gap. It was too late in the year for the Romans to send out an army, so they used diplomacy instead.

Critolaus, the current Achaean general, came to power on the wave of anti-Roman feelings that these clumsy attempts provoked. Caesar returned to Rome in disgust, and Critolaus immediately declared war on Sparta, knowing that this was the same as declaring war on Rome itself. Perhaps he assumed that the Romans would be too preoccupied by their siege of Carthage and warfare in Spain to respond until the re-incorporation of Sparta was an accomplished fact and he could present the Romans with a peaceful and unified Peloponnese. Or perhaps this was just a magnificent gesture in the face of certain doom.

Critolaus spent the winter of 147–146 trying to raise allies, but he succeeded only in gaining the rump Boeotian League, Chalcis in Euboea, and a few other towns from central Greece. They never stood a chance. In 146 the Romans declared war and ordered Caecilius south from Macedon. Caecilius defeated the rebel army near Thermopylae (where they had been trying to recover Heraclea, which had indeed seized the moment and seceded from the league) and then again at Chaeronea. He offered the Achaeans peace, but they had nothing to lose now since the league was as certain to be broken up by such a peace as by defeat.

And so in 146 the consul Lucius Mummius arrived to finish the job with a battle at the Isthmus. The Achaean hardliners died on the field or by their own hands. After the battle, Corinth and its inhabitants were designated by Mummius as a sacrificial offering to the gods of the under-world, and the city was sacked: its inhabitants murdered or sold into slav-ery, its antiquities looted by the victorious Roman and Pergamene troops, its fortifications and major public buildings destroyed, and its territory made the public property of Rome and rented out to Sicyon. No atrocity on this scale had been seen in Greece for almost two hundred years, since Alexander the Great had razed Thebes. In the past, Roman wars in Greece had ended with treaties; that time was truly over.

Thebes and Chalcis had their fortifications demolished, and leading anti-Romans were executed, but otherwise the rebels were not so badly punished. Corinth was singled out because the Achaean League had been the ringleader in this war, and because possession of Corinth had always been a token of the strength of the league. It was also famously wealthy, so that Mummius could expect plenty of plunder, and indeed we are told that "most, and certainly the best, of its public monuments" were looted.[17]

The Achaeans had to be taught a lesson, but the lesson was also meant to be learned by everyone else in Greece: "We will not tolerate challenges to our supremacy." We have seen the Romans acting in this way before, but two factors make the Achaean War especially significant. First, the Achaeans were the last Greeks with even the remotest chance of resisting the Romans, so this war was the last flicker of Greek independence for a long while. Second, the Senate had shown that it expected Roman troops stationed in Macedon to be used further south, and so the more realis-tic among the Greek statesmen now expected an increase in the level of direct rule. So, for instance, when there was trouble in Achaean Dyme shortly after the end of the war, the Roman governor of Macedon stepped in.[18] With the end of the Achaean League, Greek pride was extinguished. There was no one left to stop the Romans doing exactly what they wanted.

THE SETTLEMENT OF GREECE

Ten commissioners were, as usual, sent out from Rome to assist Mummius with the postwar settlement of Greece; in fact, so confident were the Romans of the successful conclusion of the war that the commissioners were dispatched before Mummius's final victory. Again, as with Macedon, the Senate held back from making Greece a full province of the empire. In both places, provincialization occurred gradually, not at a stroke of the commissioners' pen, but it was their job to begin the process. They focused on those parts of Greece which had dared to take up arms against Rome. So, for instance, the Dyme inscription referred to just above reveals that the town had a new constitution imposed on it by the Romans. Over the winter of 146–145 the commissioners laid down the broad principles, and left it to Polybius and other Roman friends "to visit the cities and adjudge any disputes, until the people became accustomed to the new political system and regulations."[19]

The Achaean and other leagues were dissolved into their constituent cities. Achaea and Boeotia "came under the sway of the people of Rome," which probably means, in practical terms, that they were placed more directly under the supervision of the governor of Macedon.[20] The newly "freed" cities had oligarchic administrations imposed on them, and were to pay tribute to Rome; a few also had to pay wartime indemnities. No one was to own property beyond the borders of his native city or city of residence. Great swaths of land were confiscated as the public property of Rome and rented out.[21] It was a foretaste of the provincialization of Greece.

These drastic, broad arrangements are as much of the immediate settlement of Greece as our meager sources allow us to reconstruct; at its heart lay the idea that the Greeks should have limited powers of self-administration, under the firm guidance of Rome, and even more limited military capabilities. It was not a success. Within ten years or so, several of its provisions had to be undone: the leagues were partially reconstituted (presumably to increase the chances of wealth-creation by allowing cross-border ownership of property), and indemnities were canceled. It seems that the hardship produced by the settlement was severe enough to compel the Senate to change its mind. Perhaps there had been a year or two of bad harvests as well. Widespread impoverishment in Greece is also suggested by the fact that cancellation of tribute became the best way in subsequent decades for the Romans to show favor to a city.[22] However, the restrictions implied by the physical presence of a Roman army, even a small one, in Macedon, and by the right of the governor of Macedon to intervene in Greece to the south, remained in place. Fortunately, such interventions were rarely needed in the decades immediately following 146.[23] It would be several decades before Greek pride recovered enough to put up any kind of resistance to Rome.

ROME IN GREECE

The Achaean War and the Fourth Macedonian War were the last gasps of Greek independence, and they more closely resemble rebellions than wars of one independent power against another. Afterwards, Caecilius and Mummius were obsequiously honored by the Greek states.[24] They also both received triumphs back in Rome, but there are no extant descriptions of them. The single year 145 saw not only the triumphs of Caecilius and Mummius (who took the *agnomen* Achaicus), but also that of Publius Cornelius Scipio Aemilianus over Carthage, and all three are said to have been among the most spectacular ever seen in Rome.[25] An idea of the enormous wealth of the two Greek triumphs may be gained from the fact that some of Caecilius's gains were spent on adorning two temples back in Rome with porticoes and a number of fine statues, including Lysippus's famous 25-piece bronze statue group celebrating Alexander the Great's victory over the Persians at the Granicus river in 334, plundered from Dium. Mummius similarly built and refurbished public buildings up and down Italy, such as the temple of Apollo at Pompeii, and even in Greece and Asia Minor. Now that the subjugation of Greece was complete, there was no need for him to scatter monuments that would stress Roman hegemony; he was free to present himself as a more benign and sensitive conqueror.[26]

The subjugation of Greece was indeed complete, and it has been one of the principal purposes of this book to bring out how it was achieved. It was not achieved by treaties, colonialism, provincialization, and the imposition of permanent taxes and an army of occupation. It was a stripped-down, cheap form of imperialism, which depended only on the ability of the Senate and the Roman people to get foreign kings and states to acknowledge their power and comply with their wishes. But it would be a mistake to think this a weak form of empire; as long as the subject states remained deferential, and as long as they remained aware of Rome's ability to field brutally destructive armies, it worked very well indeed. It made no difference that the Romans withdrew their armies after every military intervention; their hegemony was never withdrawn.

And it would also be a mistake to think that the Romans went about it in a haphazard and uncommitted fashion; it is of course impossible to tell precisely when the policy of control over the Greek world became taken for granted in Rome, but it was not long after they first set foot on Greek soil. Even before the First Macedonian War, some senators must have known they would have to curb Macedon. And certainly by the end of the Second Macedonian War (which was just a continuation of the interrupted first one), the Romans were committed to hegemony not just in Greece but in Asia Minor as well. Imperialist hegemony was the point of the wars in Greece against Philip V, Antiochus III, the Aetolians, Perseus, and the Achaeans; and it was equally the point of manipulating Pergamum and Rhodes into submission in Asia Minor.

After 146, the system did not immediately change to any great degree: there was still no universal payment of tribute, no permanent colonial administrative structures, and no army of occupation beyond a few thousand men in Macedon. The Greek cities still had some independence; they were not merely cogs within a vast imperial machine, with administrations designed only to provide tribute and manpower for the maintenance of the empire. Oppression remained indirect, and continued to be achieved by the imposition of administrations friendly to Rome and by diplomacy.

Of course, this relatively benign form of imperialism could not last. When Mithridates VI of Pontus rose up against Rome in 89 BCE, in by far the most successful attempt to throw off Roman dominion, he was joined by Athens and some other Greek states. It took Rome twenty-five years to defeat Mithridates, but considerably less to devastate Athens and Greece. Only then did permanent provincial structures begin to be put in place in Greece and Asia Minor, and again the process was not abrupt. Tribute-payment was gradually extended, and that went hand in hand with the creation of provinces with governors, armies, and a Romanized civil service. It was not until 27 BCE that governors were regularly sent out to govern the province of Greece, which the Romans called "Achaea."

ECONOMIC EXPLOITATION

Since 229, Rome had taken vast amounts of plunder from Greece, and after 146 it was open for commercial exploitation by Roman and Italian traders. Exploitation of the resources of Greece and Asia Minor (apart from plundering) had been slow to take off. Roman traders had, as always, profited from the wars—they formed the army's commisariat[27] —but now peacetime exploitation became an attractive prospect. Plenty of land in Greece and Macedon, now the property of the Roman state, needed managers and farmers; tribute and indemnities had to be collected; there were public works to be financed and undertaken, and commodities to be traded. In 158 the gold and silver mines of Macedon were reopened; their Spanish equivalents had been a good source of profit for Roman and Italian businessmen since the 190s. In the 130s construction began on the Via Egnatia, a trunk road running for over 1,100 kilometers (700 miles) right across northern Greece from the Illyrian coast to Byzantium, and designed for commercial traffic as well as armies (and also as a potent token of Roman control). Senators were the ones with the money to make money, and they must have begun to look for business opportunities in the east, though they used agents to retain their dignity and not soil their hands with filthy lucre. Businessmen stepped in: they always did and they always will.

Unfortunately, it is virtually impossible to track the process. The system worked smoothly enough that traders and financiers were rarely remarked on. We hear of cases only when they made headlines. In 141 Decimus Junius Silanus was the praetor responsible for Macedon. He was found guilty of accepting bribes and of plundering resources while in office (we know no more than that) and committed suicide.[28] But this was an isolated misdemeanor by an official; the grand days of imperialist peculation in the east were yet to come (though they had already arrived in Spain, and a special court was set up in 149 to deal with cases of illegal asset-stripping of provinces by Roman officials).

As for businessmen, at the time of the massacres by Mithridates VI of Pontus in 88 BCE, there were tens of thousands of Italians, traders and others, in Asia Minor.[29] They must already have been in Greece by the 150s, but we rarely hear about them or their activities. The occasional inscription or literary reference records the presence of Romans or Italians in the Greek world from the middle of the third century onwards. A richer harvest of inscriptions comes from the island of Delos, especially after it became a free port in 166.[30] But all we can say is that they were there, and that they must have been as important as generals and armies in forming the Greeks' impressions of the Romans as conquerors. Since they rarely made a mark on the historical record, we can assume that they treated the Greeks well and were treated well in return. In some cases, they may even have been seen less as exploiters than as assistants in the recovery of devastated economies. In their way, they were as important as the legion for planting and securing Roman influence in the east.

POST-CONQUEST GREECE

The literary sources give us an unrelievedly bleak picture of Greece in the decades immediately following the Roman conquest. Polybius is a contemporary witness. In a passage criticizing attempts to blame the gods for things that are men's doing, he takes as his example the current ("in my own lifetime"—that is, most of the second century) depopulation of Greece and the consequent barrenness of the land. He blames this on poverty: people cannot afford big families any more, so they produce only one or two children, and the chances are that one or both of those will be carried off by sickness or warfare. Then again, one of Cicero's correspondents, writing from Athens in 45 BCE, describes what he saw on a recent voyage: "Behind me was Aegina, before me Megara, to my right Piraeus, to my left Corinth, towns once of the greatest prosperity, but now leveled and ruined." Livy happens to mention the impoverishment, by looting, of Epidaurus.

We have already seen the description by the geographer Strabo, writing at the end of the first century BCE, of the desolation of Epirus; the picture he paints of Arcadia is just as frightening—another district of Greece so devastated by war that it is hardly better than a desert—and Laconia was not much better. A century later Dio Chrysostom confirmed the desolation of Arcadia and added Thessaly, and Plutarch suggested that the decline in the consultation of oracles in Greece was to be attributed to the fact that there were simply not enough people for it to be worth keeping the shrines open. At much the same time, Pausanias described over sixty towns in Greece as abandoned or in a ruinous condition.[31]

But there are problems with this evidence—except in the case of Epirus, of course, which could have vouched for the truth of the famous saying of the later Roman historian Tacitus: "The Romans create a wilderness and call it peace."[32] First, the evidence is contaminated by the sentimental theme of "Greece's Glorious Past." Second, most of these testimonies date from after the sack of Greece in the course of the Mithridatic War, and/or after the Roman civil wars (in the 40s and 30s BCE), many of the battles of which were fought on Greek soil. It is impossible to determine how much devastation was caused by these later events, rather than the fifty or sixty years of the initial Roman conquest. Archaeology is therefore a better source of reliable information, and it gives us a more nuanced picture, although establishing precise chronological parameters for the results is rarely easy.[33]

Many areas—especially Boeotia, Euboea, Attica, Arcadia, the Argolid, Thessaly, and the Cyclades—saw a dramatic drop in rural occupation between the late third century BCE (when this book begins) and the early years of the Common Era (150 or so years after this book ends). Small farms were abandoned (larger ones survived better), and people clustered more in towns and cities. Phocis and Locris suffered a more gradual decline in rural occupation within the same period. Aetolia, on the other hand, flourished at first, and then went into decline, presumably after its reduction in the Syrian–Aetolian War. Much of this change was started by the wars and hardship in our period: as peasant soldiers were killed or maimed in battle, or were sold into slavery, their land was abandoned, or confiscated by Rome. Except in the case of troubled Boeotia, there was not much decline in population, merely displacement of some or much of the rural population. This process would have accelerated once the Romans started to tax Greece as a province of the empire: as a result of the extra financial pressure on farmers, and of the political stability provided by the *pax Romana*, a subsistence economy gave way to market production, with its corollaries of agricultural specialization and increased urbanization.[34]

It is clear that the coming of the Romans caused considerable disruption and change. The full effect of the change, the redistribution of economic resources, did not emerge for a while, but the trend towards a widening of the gap between the rural rich and the rural poor was well begun in our period. In due course of time, it would lead to the takeover of large stretches of agricultural land by owners (Greeks or Romans) of increasingly large estates. The utter devastation of Epirus laid it open to this development earlier than other parts of Greece; Cicero's friend Titus Pomponius Atticus was one of those who seized the opportunity for a land grab. At the same time, increased concentration of resources in towns and cities favored the elite, who tended to monopolize such resources, and further widened the gap between rich and poor. The poor, bereft of their traditional smallholding occupation, saw changes in their working habits, as they divided their time between casual agricultural labor and other jobs.

That, really, is as far as we can go in assessing the initial impact of the Roman conquest on Greece. By the time Greece was a province of the empire, further and greater changes would take place: large-scale resettlements and territorial realignments, such as the movement of the populations of Ambracia and other Acarnanian towns and villages to Nicopolis, after its foundation by the emperor Augustus, and the foundation of new colonies (as, for instance, Gaius Julius Caesar, *the* Caesar, founded a colony at Corinth shortly before his murder in 44 BCE, revitalizing the town). Under the empire, local boundaries meant less, and larger administrative units were created: "Macedonia" consisted of all northern Greece, incorporating Thessaly and Epirus; the rest was "Achaea." These were the Greek provinces of the empire (with "Illyricum" to their northwest), and one of the main ways they altered Greek lives was that the interstate rivalries that had characterized Greek history for centuries mostly became redundant. Greece became more nearly a nation state than at any time in its past. If this is a good thing, it is ironic that it began with the destruction, by warfare and looting during the Roman conquest, of many local infrastructures—rural, urban, administrative, and sacred.

But the greatest change is also, in a sense, the hardest to describe. Simply put, the Greeks learned to be subjects. Plutarch, himself a Greek, thought not only that Philopoemen was "the last of the Greeks," but that Aratus's capture of Corinth in 243 was the last significant action undertaken by Greeks.[35] After that there was just a decline until the end of Greek history. The lesson of subservience lasted a very long time: Greece was in turn part of the Roman Empire, the Byzantine Empire, and the Ottoman Empire, until it gained its freedom in 1832 CE. It is still a young country.

SOUL-SEARCHING IN ROME

Roman senators, as we have seen, competed among themselves for the kind of glory that was to be won by warfare. At the same time, however, it is clear that the Senate was also concerned to maintain an overall balance in order to preserve its own authority, if for no other reason. The downfall of the Scipios in the 180s should be seen in this context. Africanus, especially, had complemented his victory over Hannibal with a share of the defeat of Antiochus III; he was adored by the common people of Rome and Italy, and had shown himself on several occasions to be capable of flouting the regulations, most famously when, at the age of twenty-five, in 211 BCE, he offered to take command of the war against the Carthaginians in Spain.[36] The Senate could not tolerate a man who placed himself above the law, and who made it hard for his fellow senators to have their day in the sun.[37]

The task of preventing one or a few men from gaining extraordinary power in the Republic had become urgent by the 180s and 170s. The reason was Greek money from Sicily, Greece itself, Macedon, and the Asian kingdoms. In a scene set in 182, Livy could still describe the appearance of Rome as somewhat humble, but it would not be for long.[38] Wealth poured into Rome and transformed both the capital and many towns throughout Italy, with grand new structures from temples to mausoleums, and large-scale engineering projects such as bridges, roads, aqueducts, and a major upgrading of Rome's sewers. Generals returned from the east with enough money to stand out from their peers by undertaking public works, by creating jobs and putting money into circulation, and by providing entertainments, and these expenditures gave them the potential to disrupt the smooth running of the republican system.

Spearheaded by Marcus Porcius Cato, the Senate launched a coherent and well-organized attack on luxury and extravagance, the basic premise of which was that too much wealth undermined the traditional values that had made Rome great. This became one of the burning issues of the day, and the kind of worried reaction that we noted to both Vulso's 188 triumph and that of Fulvius Nobilior in 187 was far from uncommon.[39] As Polybius noted, with explicit reference to Rome:[40]

> When a state has warded off many serious threats, and has come to attain undisputed supremacy and sovereignty, it is easy to see that, after a long period of settled prosperity, lifestyles become more extravagant, and rivalry over political positions and other such projects becomes fiercer than it should be.

Because of the close link between personal excess and political ambition, the war to curb increased competitiveness and individual glory could be disguised as a war on extravagance. The opening salvo came with the difficulties experienced by Vulso and Fulvius in gaining their triumphs. Both of them finally got their way, but they and others had been reminded not to aim too high and not to milk their provinces so much that resentment built up among Rome's subjects. This was followed by a series of largely futile laws attempting to curb displays of wealth in the home, tax luxuries, and crack down on excessive distribution of cash and gifts as a way to influence elections. At the same time, in 181 the number of praetors per year, which had been raised from four to six in 197 (and from two to four only in 227) to cope with increased demand for officers abroad, was reduced so that there would be four or six in alternate years. The measure was no real solution (officers were still needed abroad) and did not last long, but its reason was that every single praetor wanted next to become a consul, and their competitiveness was one of the main engines of extravagant electioneering, and of the corruption needed to fund it. The regularization, in the 190s and 180s, and slowing of the process by which a man gradually ascended to high office, was part and parcel of the same desire for moderation and collective conformity, as opposed to individualism.

So one of the main effects of the conquest of the east was that it provoked a period of soul-searching in Rome—searching for the true heart of Roman-ness. And this links us back to the quest for Roman identity that we have already noted as a result of contact with Greek culture. The famous aphorism of Horace about captive Greece capturing its savage captor belongs precisely in this context, with its contrast of sophisticated Greece and primitive Rome. Cato and his allies believed that primitive Rome was truer to itself, and that sophisticated luxury undermined not just their credibility in the eyes of others, but even their ability to conquer and administer an empire.

But Cato and his allies were fighting a losing battle. Hellenism had arrived in Rome, and it was not to be dislodged even by acts of desperation such as the expulsion of philosophers and suppression of the worship of Dionysus.[41] These were very public acts, and perhaps that was the point: to let Roman citizens know that Greekness was not favored at an official level by the Senate, however much individual senators might affect Greek styles. The messages were that the Senate was in control, and that Greek culture was always to be secondary to the traditional culture of Rome. And it worked: Rome never became a Greek city, and before long Roman writers and artists began to develop specifically Roman forms of expression, on the foundation of Greek learning. So the glory that was Greece passed, while Rome grew fat and confident on the material and immaterial spoils of its conquest of the Mediterranean.

The soul-searching took another form too. In various texts we find traces of a debate about the rights and wrongs of empire, which must have begun soon after 146, if not earlier. Polybius shows that while some Romans thought the destruction of Macedon and Carthage were justified, others saw it as rank and brutal imperialism. Then, in the first century BCE, we find the debate echoed one-sidedly in Cicero's claim that Rome's empire was won only by defending the weak, and in these proud lines of Virgil's *Aeneid*:

> These will be your special skills, Roman: to make peace unexceptional,
> To pardon the defeated, and to wage relentless war on the arrogant.

The "arrogant" presumably being all those who opposed Rome's rule. And elsewhere the poet writes, again in prophetic mode (Jupiter is speaking):

> I place no bounds in space or time on their realm;
> My gift is dominion without end.

This is empire as divinely ordained destiny, an empire to be proud of. Cicero's evidence is especially telling. In *Philippics* he spoke at one point of the Romans as "those who, by the decree of the immortal gods, shall rule over all peoples." In *On the State*, he developed the theory that imperialism is natural, and good for the subjects: "Nature gives rulership to the superior for the advantage of the inferior"—an argument that was a gift to later European imperialists. But there was another side to the coin, as the Romans knew; it was not just paternalistic benevolence. For instance, Livy has a character tell a Roman official: "You Romans always conceal your dishonesty under some specious pretext of right and justice." Sallust has Mithridates VI attribute Roman imperialism simply to a deeply rooted desire for dominion and wealth. And Polybius recognized that, after a certain point, the pretense that it was all being done for altruistic motives is singularly unconvincing.[42] A Ciceronian shepherd looks after his sheep—but only in order to increase his own profits.

If we accept Cicero's far-fetched thesis, it follows that empire is in conformity with natural justice only if conquered nations enjoy better conditions than they did before they were conquered. But did Greece enjoy better conditions before or after the Roman conquest? How does one measure "better"? By Greek standards, self-determination was a critical aspect of living well. Another consequence of Cicero's thesis is that imperialism is unjust if it is imposed on peoples who are in fact capable of looking after themselves—who are not "natural subjects." The Greek states during the period of the Roman conquest were as fractious as usual, but did that make them incapable of independence or somehow deserving of external rule? It seems to me that with these and other patronizing arguments the Romans were attempting to obfuscate the issue and justify their occasionally appalling treatment of Greeks and others. Empire is sought and held because it is to the advantage of the imperialists, not their subjects. For all that remote control is an unusual form of imperialism, the Romans cannot be accused of altruistic benevolence. To believe otherwise is to succumb to their own propaganda.

KEY DATES

Rulers of more-or-less unified Illyris

Ardiaean dynasty

Agron (?–231)
Teuta, regent for Pinnes (231–228)
Demetrius of Pharos, regent for Pinnes (228–219)

Labeatan dynasty

Scerdilaidas, regent for Pinnes/king (c. 216–c. 207)
Pleuratus (c. 207–c. 182)
Genthius (c. 182–168)

Rulers of Macedon (Antigonids)

Demetrius II (239–229)
Antigonus III Doson (229–222)
Philip V (222–179)
Perseus (179–168)
Philip VI Andriscus (149–148)

Rulers of Syria (Seleucids)

Seleucus II (246–225)
Seleucus III (225–223)

Antiochus III the Great (223–187)
Seleucus IV (187–175)
Antiochus IV (175–164)
Antiochus V (164–162)
Demetrius I (162–150)

Rulers of Pergamum (Attalids)

Attalus I (241–197)
Eumenes II (197–159)
Attalus II (159–138)
Attalus III (138–133)

Rulers of Egypt

Ptolemy III Euergetes (246–221)
Ptolemy IV Philopator (221–204/3)
Ptolemy V Epiphanes (204/3–180)
Ptolemy VI Philometor (180–145)

Rulers of Bithynia

Prusias I (228–182)
Prusias II (182–149)

TIMELINE

753	traditional foundation of Rome
323	death of Alexander the Great
280–274	Pyrrhus of Molossis in Italy and Sicily
272	death of Pyrrhus
264–241	First Punic War
250s–230s	consolidation of Aetolian and Achaean leagues
241-197	Attalus I of Pergamum
240	first works of Latin literature by L. Livius Andronicus
230s	Agron unifies much of Illyris

239–229	Demetrius II of Macedon
235–222	Cleomenes III of Sparta
232	overthrow of Aeacid monarchy in Epirus
220s	further expansion of Aetolian League
229–221	Antigonus III Doson of Macedon
229–222	Cleomenean War
229	First Illyrian War
227	creation of Roman provinces of Sardinia/Corsica, and of Sicily
226–222	Rome vs. Celts
224	Antigonus Doson founds Common Alliance of Greek leagues
223–187	Antiochus III the Great of Syria
221–204	Ptolemy IV Philopator of Egypt
221–179	Philip V of Macedon
220–217	Social War in Greece
219	Second Illyrian War
219–217	Fourth Syrian War
219–201	Second Punic War
217	Battle of Trasimene; Peace of Naupactus
216	Battle of Cannae
215	treaty between Hannibal and Philip V
214–211	siege of Syracuse
214–205	First Macedonian War
211	alliance between Rome and Aetolian League
206	peace accord between Aetolia and Macedon
205	Peace of Phoenice ends First Macedonian War
204–180	Ptolemy V Epiphanes of Egypt
204	Antiochus III in Asia Minor
202	'secret' pact between Philip V and Antiochus III; Battle of Zama ends Second Punic War
202–200	Philip V in Thrace, Hellespont, and Aegean
201–199	Fifth Syrian War
200–c. 118	Polybius
200	siege of Abydus

200–197	Second Macedonian War
198	T. Quinctius Flamininus takes command of the war; alliance with Achaeans
197	Battle of Cynoscephalae; Peace of Tempe ends Second Macedonian War; two Spanish provinces created
196	Isthmian Declaration by Flamininus; settlement of Greece and Macedon
195	war against Nabis of Sparta
194	Roman evacuation of Greece
192	murder of Nabis; Antiochus lands in Greece
192–188	Syrian–Aetolian War
191	Battle of Thermopylae
190	battles of Myonessus and Magnesia
189	Vulso vs. Galatians
188	peace with Aetolia; Peace of Apamea ends Syrian War; Asia Minor divided between Pergamum and Rhodes; Sparta forced into Achaean League
187–171	Lycian war of rebellion against Rhodes
186–183	war between Pergamum and Bithynia
183–179	war between Pergamum and Pontus
183	Philip V withdraws from Aenus and Maronea; death of Hannibal
182	death of Philopoemen
180	Callicrates' mission to Rome; Philip V kills son Demetrius
179–168	Perseus of Macedon
172	Eumenes II of Pergamum in Rome and Delphi; Marcius Philippus's mission to Greece; Boeotian League dissolved
171–168	Third Macedonian War
170–168	Sixth Syrian War
169	Molossians and northern Illyrians join Perseus; death of Ennius
168	Battle of Pydna ends Third Macedonian War; defeat of Genthius; humiliation of Antiochus IV by Popillius Laenas

167	Macedon and Illyris divided into republics; deportation to Rome of Greek political prisoners; mass plundering and enslavement in Epirus
162	Murder of Cn. Octavius in Syria
156–155	Third Illyrian War
151	Achaean political prisoners released from Italy
149–148	Philip VI Andriscus of Macedon
149–146	Third Punic War
148	Fourth Macedonian War
147	military governorship of Macedon begins; Aurelius Orestes authorizes secessions from Achaean League
146	Achaean War; destruction of Corinth and Carthage

Sparta and the Achaean League

Sparta joined the Achaean League in 192; left later in 192 or early in 191; rejoined in 191; left in 189; rejoined in 188; left in 182; rejoined in 182; and finally left in 148, triggering the Achaean War.

aedile   4 were elected annually, responsible especially for the maintenance of public buildings and public order, and overseeing public festivals. The usual *cursus honorum*—hierarchical ladder of official positions—ran: tribune, quaestor, aedile, praetor, consul.

Amphictyonic Council of Delphi   an ancient council of states established to protect the interests of the sacred centers at Delphi and Thermopylae; membership was prestigious, and therefore shifted somewhat with the political tides of Greece.

censor   the most prestigious appointment in Rome, but not the most powerful. Two censors were elected every 5 years, for 18 months, to conduct a census, contract out public works, and, as guardians of Rome's morals to decide on entry and expulsion from the Senate. Cato the Censor had indeed been a censor (in 184–183), but he retained the nickname because of his hard line on morals.

consul   one of 2 annually elected military/political leaders of Republican Rome; the highest office, and the object of intense aristocratic rivalry.

hoplite   a heavy footsoldier, armed, typically, with a helmet, a corselet with a short protective skirt, bronze greaves for the shins (if he could afford them), and above all a large, round, concave shield, about 90 cm. in diameter, made of bronze-covered wood with a rim of bronze. He carried a long thrusting spear with an iron head, and an iron sword.

league   an institution allowing previously independent cities to band together under a common constitution to increase their overall power, especially in foreign relations. By the time the Romans came to Greece, almost all the cities there had formed such federations. The most successful leagues were the Aetolian and Achaean, both of which grew beyond their original geographical and ethnic boundaries.

legate   a Roman officer attached to the staff of a general at the general's own request (rather than as a result of election) and generally used as an adviser and envoy; an officer sent out by the Senate on a particular mission or set of missions.

legion   literally "levy," the main military unit of the Roman army, consisting of citizens; a regular Republican legion (though they were often larger) consisted of 3,000 heavy infantry, 1,200 light infantry, and 300 cavalry. Consuls were usually assigned two legions.

lembos   a small, fast warship, with single bank of oars, capable of transporting 50 footsoldiers (or prisoners and other plunder) as well as the crew.

maniple   a tactical subunit of a legion, consisting of 60 or, more usually, 120 soldiers. See p. 129.

phalanx   a corps of heavy infantry in the Greek world, armed either in the Macedonian manner (see p. 128), or as hoplites.

philhellenism   admiration for things Greek and/or expertise in contemporary Greek language, politics, law, and customs.

pomerium   a strip of consecrated land running around a city, such as Rome, and acting as the symbolic boundary between it and the outside world. The Roman *pomerium* was supposedly first ploughed by Romulus himself, the legendary founder of the city.

praetor   the second highest military/political office in Rome; from 197 BCE, 6 were elected (previously 4); 2 were responsible for civic justice, but the rest were military appointments.

proconsul, propraetor   a consul or praetor whose command has been extended for a further year, usually for military purposes.

province   a task or theater of military operations assigned by the Senate to a consul or praetor; later, an administrative unit of the empire.

quaestor   10 were elected annually; a junior post largely responsible for finances.

Senate   see pp. 14–15.

tribune a middle-ranking officer in the Roman army; there were 6 tribunes in each legion. It was the traditional first rung on the *cursus honorum* for a politically ambitious young aristocrat.

tribune of the people 10 were elected each year, with the duty of protecting the rights of the ordinary people, as opposed to the Senate. They had the right to veto proposals by other elected officials and even a decree of the Senate.

triumph see pp. 34–37.

ROMAN AND GREEK MONEY

Greek: 36,000 obols = 6,000 drachmas = 60 mnas = 1 talent. In the ancient world, coined money was not fiduciary, but was intrinsically worth its weight. A talent weighed almost 26 kilograms (c. 57.5 lbs.). Possession of four or five talents made an individual very rich.

Roman (at this period of the Republic): 10 *asses* (copper or bronze) = 4 *sestertii* (silver) = 1 *denarius* (silver). 1 *denarius* was roughly the weight of 1 Greek drachma, so that 6,000 *denarii* was equivalent to 1 talent.

It is virtually impossible to arrive at a meaningful estimate of the value of Roman money at this period. The only sensible way would be to find the cost of certain staples and compare them to the cost of staples today, and compare both with equivalent wages. But information about costs and wages at this period is very scarce. Here is a scatter of items that may give some idea: a footsoldier received about 120 *denarii* per year, a cavalryman about 360. Ten days' worth of wheat cost about 4 *asses*. Repairs to the Roman sewer system in 184 BCE cost 6,000,000 *denarii*. For large-scale costs such as warfare, see ch. 5, n. 12.

NOTES

ABBREVIATIONS

Ager	Ager 1996 (see the "Inscriptions" section of the Bibliography, p. 264).
Austin	Austin 2006 (see the "Inscriptions" section of the Bibliography, p. 264).
BD	Bagnall and Derow 2004 (see the "Inscriptions" section of the Bibliography, p. 264).
Briscoe C 1, 2, 3, 4	Briscoe, J., *A Commentary on Livy Books XXXI-XXXIII, Books XXXIV-XXXVII, Books 38-40, Books 41-45* (Oxford: Oxford University Press, 1973, 1981, 2008, 2012).
Burstein	Burstein 1985 (see the "Inscriptions" section of the Bibliography, p. 264).
CIL	T. Mommsen et al. (eds.), *Corpus Inscriptionum Latinarum* (1853– ; updated by the Berlin-Brandenburgische Akademie der Wissenschaften).
ORF	H. Meyer (ed.), *Oratorum Romanorum Fragmenta* (3rd ed., Turin, 1953).
RDGE	Sherk 1969 (see the "Inscriptions" section of the Bibliography, p. 264).
Sherk	Sherk 1984 (see the "Inscriptions" section of the Bibliography, p. 264).
*Syll.*³	Dittenberger, W., *Sylloge Inscriptionum Graecarum* (3rd ed., Leipzig, 1915–1924).
Walbank C 1, 2, 3	Walbank, F., *A Historical Commentary on Polybius*, 3 vols. (London: Oxford University Press, 1957, 1967, 1979).
Welles	Welles 1934 (see the "Inscriptions" section of the Bibliography, p. 264).

NOTES TO PREFACE

1. Polybius 1.1.5.

2. Quoted by Julian Go, http://www.upf.edu/iuhjvv/_pdf/jgo-empires.pdf.

NOTES TO PRELUDE

1. Rome the center: Polybius 1.3.4-5. The moment: 5.105.4.

2. Polybius 5.104. On speeches in Polybius, see Champion 1997. On the general issue, see J. Marincola, "Speeches in Classical Historiography," in id. (ed.), *A Companion to Greek and Roman Historiography* (Oxford: Blackwell, 2007), 118–132.

3. The image of "clouds in the west" is repeated in another speech at 9.37.10, applied unequivocally to the Romans.

4. Polybius 29.27; Livy 45.12.1-6; Diodorus of Sicily 31.2; Velleius Paterculus 1.10.1-2; Appian, *The Syrian Wars* 66; Justin 34.3.1-4; Plutarch, *Essays* 202f. Ager 122 supplies context.

CHAPTER 1

1. The Bora, the northerly wind of the Adriatic, used to force ancient ships to hug the eastern coastline (which also has far more natural coves and islands for shelter), not the Italian side, and made them sitting ducks: J. Morton, *The Role of the Physical Environment in Ancient Greek Seafaring* (Leiden: Brill, 2001), 49–50. The Dalmatian coastline had been awash with pirates for at least 120 years (Diodorus of Sicily 16.5.3).

2. There are considerable inconsistencies in our sources for this affair, chiefly Polybius 2.8 and Appian, *The Illyrian Wars* 7 (with Pliny, *Natural History* 34.24, adding the implication that *both* ambassadors were killed, since they both received statues, as was usual for envoys who died in the line of duty). And there are reasons for preferring each of them. I combine the two accounts where possible. The trigger for the Roman embassy in Appian was an appeal from Issa, in Polybius an appeal from Italian traders: these can be combined. In Polybius, the meeting between Teuta and the Roman brothers is critical, whereas in Appian it never happened because the murder took place before the meeting: these cannot be combined.

3. Polybius's sketch of Teuta (2.8) is spoiled by his prejudices against both women and Illyrians. As a symbol of Illyrian independence, she is now depicted on the modern Albanian 100 leke coin. Pinnes was actually Agron's son by another wife, Triteuta, who as the mother of the heir apparent should have been senior. There must have been some compelling reason for passing her over.

4. The name 'Passaron' is usually attached to a large hill fortress northwest of Ioannina, but recent archaeological work by Georgia Pliakou of the Ioannina Archaeological Museum is beginning to suggest that it might be Ioannina itself.

5. Chiefly fish and wine. According to Agatharchides of Cnidus (second century BCE), Issaean wine was the best in the world: fr. 18 Jacoby. In a good year, the island could produce two million liters (Kirigin and Vickers, 27). On Pharos's unique coastal plain (since 2008 a Unesco protected World Heritage site), see B. Kirigin, *Pharos: An Archaeological Guide* (Stari Grad: Centre for Culture, 2003).

6. The sailing season usually began in March and ended in November, not just because of the increased risk of storms, but because of decreased visibility and shorter days.

7. On the aggressive and imperialist nature of this phase of Roman expansion, see Cornell, Oakley, and Rowland.

8. Rosenstein 2012, 73.

9. Dionysius of Halicarnassus, *Roman Antiquities* 19.5.

10. For what little can be known about Molossian political structures, see Davies.

11. This was the third in a sequence of Roman–Carthaginian treaties: Polybius 3.22-27 with Walbank *C* 1.349.

12. It was the overthrow of his descendants in 232 that caused the chaos in Epirus referred to above.

13. We will find traces of this fear from time to time. Three clear cases of overreaction are Livy 35.23.3 (taking steps against a supposed invasion of Sicily by Antiochus III), Livy 42.13.11 (fear of invasion by Perseus), and Appian, *The Mithridatic Wars* 102 (fear of invasion by Mithridates VI). It was Pyrrhus's success that triggered the fear: the presence of Archidamus III of Sparta in 342-338 or Alexander I of Molossis in 334, both also summoned by Tarentum, generated no such shock waves.

14. Sena Gallica, Hadria, and Castrum Novum were founded in the 280s, and then Ariminum (268), Firmum Picenum (264) and Brundisium (244). On trade at this time in the Adriatic, see Čašule and Marasco.

15. Livy 24.21.9.

16. For more on Roman constitutional matters, see Lintott 1999, and essays in Flower 2004, and in Rosenstein and Morstein-Marx 2010.

17. See the Glossary (pp. 243–245) for these and other recurrent technical terms.

18. Hopkins and Burton.

19. The Roman year began, at this period, in our March. April or May was, then, the earliest that Roman armies appeared in the field abroad, when the weather was good enough for sailing. Very often, however, a consul would delay the start of his campaigning season by lingering in Rome over domestic duties.

20. Livy 31.6.5.

21. Livy 42.32.6. Likewise, at 35.4, Polybius remarks on the reluctance of men to be called up in 151 BCE, as if it were a new phenomenon.

22. It was a notorious case: Livy 38.50-60; Polybius 23.14.

23. This is not to say that senators did not have them: the *Lex Claudia* of 218 (Livy 21.63.3-4), which prohibited any senator from owning cargo vessels capable of holding more than 300 amphoras, shows that such interests already needed curbing as a possible source of administrative corruption.

24. On the limited profitability of large-scale agriculture, see Rosenstein 2008, and Hopkins 1978 on the increase in large estates in this period.

25. See J. D'Arms, *Commerce and Social Standing in Ancient Rome* (Cambridge: Harvard University Press, 1981).

26. Sherwin-White 1984, 15. On the profitability of warfare for Rome, see also Harris 1984, 68–74. Not every war made a profit: Rosenstein 2011 (though he does not take indemnities into consideration). See ch.5, n. 12 for correspondences between modern and ancient costs.

27. Hopkins 1978, 33. Roughly 21 percent of the British male population served in World War I.

28. Livy 41.28.8-9.

29. Harris 1984, 102–103. See also Polybius 1.11.2: the Senate gained recruits for the First Punic War by holding out the prospect of enrichment.

30. Austin 1986; Eckstein 2006, chs. 4, 6. On the bloody births of the Successor kingdoms after the death of Alexander the Great, see R. Waterfield, *Dividing the Spoils: The War for Alexander the Great's Empire* (New York: Oxford University Press, 2011).

CHAPTER 2

Main primary sources: Appian, *The Illyrian Wars* 2.1-8; Cassius Dio 12.19-20; Justin 29.1-3; Livy, *Periochae* 20; Polybius 2-5.

1. Justin, 28.1-2, reports a somewhat earlier appeal to Rome by the Acarnanians, but this embassy is likely to be fictitious or at least out of place: Oost 1954, 92–97.

2. Polybius 2.11.5.

3. The evidence for Oricum's having accepted Roman protection is weak, but Zonaras 9.4.4 says that in 213 the Romans "recovered" Oricum, as if it had been theirs before.

4. Epidamnus, as modern Durres, is still a major port town. A change in the course of the Aous ended Apollonia's days as a port. Oricum is still in use, as a joint Albanian–Turkish naval base.

5. On Epirote development under Pyrrhus, see Hammond 1967, 572–588.

6. Rich 2008.

7. A little is known of the constitution of the Common Alliance: Hammond and Walbank, 352–353.

8. See, e.g., Larsen 1968, 326–358; Scholten 2000, 200–228; Walbank 1940, 24–67.

9. Cassius Dio 12.53. Teuta, formerly Pinnes' guardian, must have died—but then, why did Triteuta not take over the regency for Pinnes, who was, after all, her own child? This is the second time (see ch. 1, n. 3) we have found Triteuta being passed over. Between giving birth to the heir and the death of Agron, some accident must have happened to make her unacceptable as a ruler.

10. Polybius 3.16.3, with Walbank *C* 1.324-5.

11. Polybius 3.16.2; Appian, *The Illyrian Wars* 8.

12. For the poverty of Rhizonian coinage around this time, see D. Morgan, "Autonomous Coinage of Rhizon in Illyria," http://independent.academia.edu/DubravkaUjesMorgan/Papers/550112/Autonomous_Coinage_of_Rhizon_in_Illyria.

13. Polybius 3.19.9.

14. A recent ally, just as, one week before Hitler invaded Poland in September 1939, Britain signed an agreement with Poland for mutual assistance in the event of invasion by "a European power."

15. Polybius (3.16.3) makes much of the fact that Demetrius (and Scerdilaidas) had sailed south of Lissus with their ninety *lemboi* in 220, apparently in transgression of the 229 Lissus pact with its specification that no more than two *lemboi* were to pass this point; but that is probably a red herring. Not, as Badian thought (1952a, 14), because the 229 pact was made with Teuta, not with Demetrius: it was made with Pinnes, with Teuta the proxy, and now Demetrius was Pinnes' proxy. But they must have sailed south of Lissus before. For instance, in 222 when Demetrius took 1,600 troops south to help Doson at Sellasia, he is very unlikely to have made the arduous journey by land.

16. Polybius agrees (3.16.4)—and for this campaign, he could rely on information passed down by the consul L. Aemilius Paullus himself, because Polybius became a close friend of Aemilius's grandson, P. Cornelius Scipio Aemilianus.

17. Polybius 7.11.8.

18. Livy 22.33.5.

19. Rich 1993, 50.

20. Harris 1984, 32.

21. The first triumph on the Alban mount was held in 231, apparently in protest at the Senate's quibbling refusal of a triumph. It was possibly a revival of the original form of triumph, before the Senate became involved at all. After a few cases, it fell into disuse after 172.

22. Frontinus, *Stratagems* 4.1.45. Livius was fined and retired to his country estates: Suetonius, *Tiberius* 3; Livy 27.34.3.

23. Polybius 9.35.3; 18.37.9.

24. Polybius 4.25 on the aims of the war; 5.102 on Philip's haste.

25. Polybius 5.101.6-10.

26. Polybius 5.102.1. But news could have leaked out afterwards. Livy certainly felt that Philip, at the end of his life, was contemplating invasion: 40.21.7; 40.57.7.

27. Polybius 5.10.10; see Walbank 1993.

28. *Palatine Anthology* 9.518.

CHAPTER 3

Main primary sources: Appian, *Macedonica* 3; Cassius Dio 13–17; Diodorus of Sicily 26–27; Justin 29.4; Livy 21–29.12; Pausanias 8.49-50.3; Plutarch, *Life of Aratus* 49–54; *Life of Philopoemen*; Polybius 3; 5.106-11; 7–11.

1. Polybius 3.117.1-4.

2. This is one of only three known occasions in the Republic: Eckstein 1982.

3. *On the Agrarian Law* 2.73; on the Latin colonies, see Rosenstein 2012, 91–93.

4. The idea of an orderly withdrawal is mine. Polybius, who did not like Philip, has him panicking: 5.110.1-5.

5. Full details at Polybius 7.9.

6. Livy 23.38.9.

7. Livy 24.44.5. His command was extended the following year as well, for 212.

8. Earlier approaches: Livy 25.23.9; 26.24.1. Text: Adcock and Mosley, 263–264; Austin 77; BD 33; Sherk 2.

9. We hear no more of Pinnes; perhaps the young man had died.

10. Galba had a distinguished career. He was elected consul in 211 despite having not held high office previously. Then he had a 5-year run in Greece; he was wartime dictator in 203, and consul again in 200, when he returned to Greece for the Second Macedonian War. He was the remote ancestor of Servius Sulpicius Galba, emperor of Rome in 68–69 CE.

11. Polybius 22.8.9-10. The island remained an Attalid possession until the end of the dynasty in 133 BCE.

12. Polybius 8.12.2; Plutarch, *Life of Aratus* 52; *Life of Philopoemen* 12.2; Pausanias 8.50.4. Philip's involvement is not impossible, because Aratus had refused to let Achaean troops be used for the attack on Apollonia in 215, and Philip may well have wanted to check such fledgling signs of Achaean independence. Plutarch also reports that Philip seduced Aratus's daughter-in-law, giving a personal edge to the political rupture. He later married her.

13. In what follows, I broadly follow the reconstruction of Rich 1984; see also Eckstein 2008, 85–116; Lazenby, 157–168. For a thorough analysis of the efforts of diplomats during this war, see Eckstein 2002.

14. Livy 29.12.14. The presence of the Athenians is hard to explain and may be an annalistic invention.

15. Attalus wanted the Trojans included to cement his relationship with Rome by claiming kinship: as well as the well-known foundation story of Romulus and Remus, the story that Aeneas of Troy had founded Rome was also becoming popular at this time. See Erskine 2001 and, in general, C. P. Jones, *Kinship Diplomacy in the Ancient World* (Cambridge: Harvard University Press, 1999).

16. Anticyra: Polybius 9.39.2-3. Aegina: Polybius 9.42.5-8. Oreus: Livy 28.7.4. Dyme: Livy 32.22.10. General barbarianism: Polybius 9.37.5-6; 9.39.1-5; 11.5.6-8; 18.22.8; Livy 31.34.8 (= Plutarch, *Life of Flamininus* 5.6; *Life of Pyrrhus* 16.5).

17. Polybius 10.15.4-5; Ziolkowski 1993.

18. Lendon in Sabin et al. (eds.), 510. See also p. 133.

19. Melos: Thucydides 5.116.4. Phthiotic Thebes: Polybius 5.100.1-8; Diodorus of Sicily 26.9. The change of name did not last long.

20. Livy 29.12.16; Justin 29.4.11; Derow 1979, 6–7. Hence Polybius (3.32.7) astutely saw the first two Macedonian wars as really a single entity.

21. Gruen 1984a, 317–321.

22. *Syll.*³ 393 = *RDGE* 33; Sherk 4; BD 36.

23. Momigliano, 16. The passage in Lycophron (*Alexandra* 1226-31) on how a Trojan-born race will take revenge on the Greeks for their sack of Troy is certainly a later interpolation: West 1984. Lycophron was writing c. 250 BCE.

24. John of Stobi, *Anthology* 3.7.12. Bowra 1957; Erskine 1995 suggests that the hymn might have been part of the order of service for worship of Roma. For "Roma" as "strength," see also ch. 5, n. 16.

25. Diodorus of Sicily 3.47.7-8. Rome is not specifically mentioned, just the Arabians' remoteness, but Rome is certainly meant.

26. *Roman Antiquities* 1.89-90; 10.51.5.

27. Phlegon of Tralles fr. 36.III.6-14 Jacoby.

CHAPTER 4

Main primary sources: Appian, *Macedonica* 4; Cassius Dio 18; Diodorus of Sicily 28.1-7; Justin 30.3; Livy 31; Plutarch, *Life of Flamininus*; *Life of Philopoemen*; Polybius 13–16.

1. One member of this commission seems to have tried to wage a private war against Philip: Twyman 1999. When Philip complained, he was told that if he was trying to provoke war, he would find it: Livy 30.42.7.

2. For the date, see Briscoe *C* 1.130. Others prefer late in 202 (Holleaux 1921, 293–297) or late in 201 (Derow 1979, 7–8).

3. Polybius 18.54.7-11.

4. Polybius 13.5.1; Polyaenus, *Stratagems* 5.17.2; Berthold, 107–108; Dmitriev 2011a, 433–436; Walbank *C* 2.415-16. The war was largely a success for the Rhodians.

5. Livy 33.18.16; details in Ma, 78.

6. There are doubts about the ordering of the battles of Chios and Lade, and Philip's invasion of Pergamum: see Walbank *C* 2.497-501. For accounts of the battles, see Murray.

7. Polybius 16.24.4.

8. Polybius 3.2.8; 15.20; Livy 31.14.11; Appian, *Macedonica* 4. The existence of the pact has been denied (Magie 1939; Balsdon 1954; Errington 1971b), but vaguenesses in our sources can be explained by the fact that the pact was, in origin, secret, even if it soon became common knowledge. Events certainly seem to bear it out. According to Justin (30.2.8), the existence of the pact was confirmed in Rome by Egyptian emissaries.

9. Polybius 16.1.8-9; 16.24.6.

10. Polybius 15.10.2.

11. Livy 31.7.

12. Livy 31.8.5 on the veterans; 31.13 on the loans, with Eckstein 2006, 285–286.

13. Polybius 16.34.7.

14. Livy 31.18.9. There is a gap of several months between the war vote in Rome and Galba's arrival (in October? Livy 31.22.4) in Illyris. A whole campaigning season was effectively lost. The delay is probably to be explained by complications in recruiting, and because, having chosen to recruit as few veterans as possible (p. 68), the men needed to be trained before being sent abroad: Rich 1976, 82.

15. Plutarch, *Life of Aemilius Paullus* 28.11. On Roman collectors: Pollitt 1986, 159–162.

16. Cicero, *Against Verres* 2.4.129.

17. Badian 1972, 30.

18. Pollitt 1978, 170–171.

19. Lysippus: Strabo 10.2.21; Pliny, *Natural History* 34.40. Fabius tried to take another of Lysippus's works from Tarentum, but was unable to remove it from its stand. He later set up his own statue next to the "Labors of Heracles," for personal aggrandizement. Zeuxis: Pliny, *Natural History* 35.66.

20. Pliny, *Natural History* 35.26; 35.70.

21. Resentment: Polybius 9.10. Sack of Macedon: Livy 34.52.4-5. Sack of Ambracia: Livy 38.9.13; 39.5.15; Polybius 21.30.9. Sack of Tarentum: Livy 27.16.7-8. Sack of Achaea: Pliny, *Natural History* 34.36; 35.24. Sack of Syracuse: Plutarch, *Life of Marcellus* 21.1. Polybius's view: 9.10. In general: Cicero, *Against Verres* 2.1.55.

22. Livy 31.45.16.

CHAPTER 5

Main primary sources: Appian, *Macedonica* 5–9; Cassius Dio 18; Diodorus of Sicily 28.8-11; Justin 30.3-4; Livy 32–33.35; Plutarch, *Life of Flamininus*; Polybius 18.1-48.

1. Plutarch, *Life of Cato the Elder* 17.

2. *Syll.*³ 393 = *RDGE* 33; Sherk 4; BD 36. On the weaknesses (disputed by Armstrong and Walsh, 34–35), see Sherk at *RDGE*, 199. We know nothing of Flamininus's personal appearance beyond the ambiguous evidence of the coin portrait on p. 85.

3. Livy 32.7.8-12, with Briscoe *C* 1.180.

4. Briscoe *C* 1.188.

5. Eretria plundered: Livy 32.16.16.

6. Livy 36.31.8; 36.35.4.

7. Founding colonies: Appian, *The Iberian Wars* 38. Making kings: Livy 30.15.11; 30.17.8. Nemean Games: Plutarch, *Life of Flamininus* 12; Polybius 10.26.1. Consuls like monarchs: Polybius 6.11.12. Kings in council: Plutarch, *Life of Pyrrhus* 19.6.

8. There is no physical feature there that remotely resembles a dog's head, even after Hammond encourages us to think of the long, flat snouts of Greek sheep-dogs (1988, 80–81). I suggest that what the name is describing is the sequence of five or six low hills that thrust their prows or heads forward in a southwesterly direction from the ridge at Ano Khalkiades (Philip's camp) towards Zoodokhos Pigi (Flamininus's camp), as hunting dogs strain forward when aroused but still on their leashes. See the map at Hammond and Walbank, 439.

9. Plutarch, *Life of Flamininus* 9.

10. Polybius 18.39.1.

11. See ch. 3, n. 8.

12. It has been estimated (cited in Harris 1984, 68) that at this period it cost 2,400,000 HS (*sestertii*) a year to keep a single legion in the field. 2.4 million HS = 9.2 million *denarii* = (in Greek terms) 9.2 million drachmas = c. 1,500 talents. Hence this indemnity was enough to keep two-thirds of a legion of 4,500 men in the field for one year. The cost of maintaining 4,500 infantry soldiers in the field per year today has been estimated at c. \$4,000,000,000 (Center for Strategic and Budgetary Assessments website). Two-thirds of that is c. \$2,750,000,000. When assessing large-scale military costs such as indemnities, therefore, I have assumed that 1,000 talents = \$2,750,000,000, so that 1 talent = \$2,750,000. This does not mean that the talent or its fractions are worth the same in other contexts.

13. Hostage-taking was becoming a favored tool of Roman diplomacy. See D. Braund, *Rome and the Friendly King* (London: Croom Helm, 1984), 10–16, for the fairly lenient conditions of the internment of noble or royal hostages. The purpose, as much as anything, was to indoctrinate them into Roman ways; Demetrius was 11 when he went to Italy and 17 when he returned—formative years.

14. Ager 76.

15. *Syll.*³ 591 = Austin 197; BD 35; Sherk 5.

16. Sherk 18, 41; Gruen 1984a, 178, 187; Larsen 1968, 245–246. All the places that came to worship Roma are listed in Mellor 1975, 27–110. See Erskine 1995 on all the fascinating ramifications of the fact that "Roma" means "strength" in Greek.

17. Livy 32.8.13; 33.20.8. He gained this status probably in 200: Briscoe *C* 1.283.

18. Polybius 18.46.5; Livy 33.32.5; Plutarch, *Life of Flamininus* 10. The lack of mention of the Acarnanians is odd, but it must mean that their status as free was already as clear as it was for the others not mentioned, the Achaeans and so on: Oost 1954, 53–54.

19. Livy 31.29.6-16, 32.21.32-7.

20. Gruen 1984a, 147–149; Badian 1970, 54, on the lack of evidence for Flamininus's personal philhellenism.

21. Sherk 6 collects the inscriptions; coins were struck in his name (fewer than ten survive; we do not even know who minted them); at Argos and Gytheum games were instituted in his name; at Chalcis he received divine honors. See also Briscoe *C* 1.28, n.1; Walbank *C* 2.613-14; Gruen 1984a, 167. At Gytheum and Chalcis, he was still receiving cult honors in the first century CE: Erskine 2010, 65; Plutarch, *Life of Flamininus* 16.

22. Livy 33.24.3. The Isthmian Declaration was so famous that it dictated the whimsical choice by the emperor Nero in 67 CE of the Isthmian Games to declare Greece free and exempt from taxation: Suetonius, *Life of Nero* 24.2.

23. From where did Flamininus get the freedom slogan? Representative views: Badian 1958a, 69–74; Briscoe 1972; Dmitriev 2011a, ch. 5; Eckstein 1987, 296–297; Ferrary 1988, 83–84; Gruen 1984a, 132–157; Seager; Walsh 1996. Talk of "freedom" is always in the air when one power is trying to detach a satellite from another power. The Romans declared the states of southern Illyris free in 229; in the First Macedonian War the Romans were portrayed as enslavers; and in general Roman propaganda was portraying Philip as a despot. Talk of freedom was natural. Flamininus plucked the concept out of the air and let it flourish.

24. Livy 35.16.2.

25. Plutarch, *Life of Flamininus* 12.6.

CHAPTER 6

Main primary sources: Appian, *The Syrian Wars* 1–21; Cassius Dio 19; Diodorus of Sicily 28.12–29.4; Justin 31.1-6.5; Livy 33.36–36.21; Pausanias 8.50.7-51.3; Plutarch, *Life of Flamininus*; *Life of Philopoemen*; *Life of Cato the Elder*; Polybius 18.49–20.8.

1. The recovery of his ancestral kingdom was the core of Antiochus's policy, his "Great Idea": Ma, chs 1-2. In fact, though, Seleucus I had extended his empire to Europe for only a few weeks in 281 before being assassinated.

2. Polybius 18.51-52; Ager 77; Badian 1959, 119–121; Grainger 2002, 85–97. The suggested Rhodian arbitration seems never to have taken place.

3. Livy 33.44.8.

4. Livy 34.31-32, with Briscoe *C* 2.98-99.

5. Livy 34.52.4-9. Further details in Plutarch, *Life of Flamininus* 13.9. On the precision of the figures, see Beard, 171–172. Armenas was never released and died in custody: Polybius 21.3.4.

6. No historian, but *Syll.*³ 585 is the evidence for the visit to Delphi: one of Antiochus's envoys, Hegesianax, was created spokesperson for Delphi in Antiochus's court, a largely honorific role. Burstein 70 translates some of this inscription.

7. Livy 36.31.10–32.9; Gruen 1984a, 470–471.

8. Livy 38.32.6-8; 39.37.9-17.

9. Plutarch, *Life of Philopoemen* 1.7; *Life of Aratus* 24.2. Compare Pausanias 8.52.1.

10. Polybius 20.8.1-5; Livy 36.11.1-4; 36.17.7; Appian, *The Syrian Wars* 16; Diodorus of Sicily 29.2; Plutarch, *Life of Philopoemen* 17.1; *Life of Flamininus* 16.1-2. Ogden, 137–138.

11. Acarnania: Livy 36.11-12; Appian, *The Syrian Wars* 16. Boeotia: Polybius 20.7.3-5; Livy 36.6.1-5. Epirus: Polybius 20.3.1-4; Livy 36.5.3-8. The Epirotes were later officially pardoned for their lack of active support for Rome: Livy 36.35.11.

12. Diodorus of Sicily 29.1.

13. Livy 36.1-2. Calendrical problems exacerbate the usual difficulties in the exact timing of events. It is even possible that the Romans declared war before they knew of the deaths at Delium, though this is contradicted by Livy 35.51.2. See, e.g., Grainger 2002, 209; Eckstein 2006, 304.

14. To judge by the poem of Alcaeus translated on p. 92, Philip's failure in this respect was notorious, and must have rankled.

15. *ORF*, Cato 20—a neat inversion, since the charge was usually made of the Athenians, not their enemies. Despite his familiarity with Greek, Cato chose to speak in Latin, probably as an assertion of cultural dominance.

16. This was the emergency that caused Amynander to put the island of Zacynthos up for sale: see p. 114.

17. Herodotus, *Histories* 7.202-233.

18. Astin 1978, 58.

CHAPTER 7

Main primary sources: Appian, *The Syrian Wars* 22–44; Cassius Dio 19; Diodorus of Sicily 29.5-13; Justin 31.6-8; Livy 36.22–38.41; Plutarch, *Life of Flamininus*; *Life of Philopoemen*; *Life of Cato the Elder*; Polybius 20.9–21.45.

1. Polybius 20.9-10; Livy 36.27-29; Gruen 1982a; Eckstein 1995; Dmitriev 2011a, 237–263.

2. Livy 1.38.2. Livy is reporting an ancient ritual, but Polybius 36.4.1-2 confirms that it was still being carried out in the same way.

3. Florus 1.24.13; more sober analysis by Murray, 215–218; Steinby, ch. 6.

4. The Galatians were relative newcomers to Asia Minor. They were a loose confederation of La Tène Celts, refugees from central Europe. See B. Maier, *The Celts: A History from Earliest Times to the Present* (Notre Dame: University of Notre Dame Press, 2003), ch. 7.

5. This is an inference from the fact that we hear no more about Hannibal's fleet. The evidence (from a hieroglyphic document) for the Egyptian attack on Aradus is given in Grainger 2002, 362–363.

6. Polybius 21.15; Livy 37.34; Diodorus of Sicily 29.8. Briscoe *C* 2.339.

7. Tolstoy delivers a wonderful rant against the possibility of any "science" of warfare in *War and Peace*, vol. 3, part 1, ch. 11.

8. Ancient historians too liked to compare the two formations: Polybius 18.28-32; Livy 32.17-18.

9. Livy 31.34.4.

10. Livy 37.59.

11. Livy 39.7.1-5. Thracian brigands: Livy 38.40-41.

12. Livy 39.6.7-9. But then Livy (as he shows in the Preface to his history) believed that the whole history of Rome was one of gradual decline. Pliny thought that Scipio's triumph the previous year was the source of corruption: *Natural History* 33.148. Cato the Censor of course weighed in on the issue with a couple of speeches: *De Pecunia Regis Antiochi* and *De Praeda Militibus Dividenda*. On the rhetoric of luxury in Rome, see C. Edwards, *The Politics of Immorality in Ancient Rome* (Cambridge: Cambridge University Press, 1993).

13. Though not unparalleled: Rich 1993, 57–58; M. Pittenger, *Contested Triumphs: Politics, Pageantry, and Performance in Livy's Republican Rome* (Berkeley: University of California Press, 2008); see Richardson 1975, 58, n.55, for a convenient list of contested triumphs. Cato the Censor delivered a speech on the issue, *De Falsis Pugnis*.

14. Livy 36.34.8-9; Plutarch, *Life of Flamininus* 15.

15. The triumph nearly did not happen: Glabrio had passed his troops on to L. Cornelius Scipio, and that could on occasion (see, e.g., Livy 39.29.5) be a reason for refusing a triumph, on the grounds that if the army was still in the field, the war was not over.

16. Polybius 21.26-30; Livy 38.3.9-7.13; 38.9.4-6, 13. Linderski 1996; Habicht 1976.

17. Polybius 21.32.2. Livy (38.11.2.) has *imperium* and *maiestas*—"the rule and greatness" of Rome. On the concept of *maiestas*, see Lendon 1997, 275–276. At *Pro Balbo* 35–36, Cicero specifically identifies the inclusion of this clause in treaties as a deliberate instrument of subordination. See also Bederman, 191, n.347; Gruen 1984a, 26–32.

18. Livy 41.25.1-4.

19. A little later in the 180s, the Senate granted Ambracia the right to set its own harbor dues— provided that the grateful citizens exempted Italian traders from them altogether (Livy 38.44.4). This is an isolated instance, and nothing should be made of it in terms of Roman economic policy. It did Ambracia little good.

20. Nicely brought out by Gruen 2014.

21. Livy 36.34.8-9.

22. Livy 39.23.9.

23. Amynander died a short while later, and Athamania became a republic.

24. List of new possessions: Walbank *C* 3.104.

25. Livy 44.16.5-7.

26. See Swain.

27. L. Jonnes and M. Ricl, "A New Royal Inscription from Phrygia Panoreios: Eumenes II Grants Tyraion the Status of a Polis," *Epigraphica Anatolica* 29 (1997), 1–30; BD 43; Austin 236.

28. *Syll.*³ 601 = Austin 199; BD 39; *RDGE* 34; Sherk 8; Ma 38; K. Rigsby, *Asylia: Territorial Inviolability in the Hellenistic World* (Berkeley: University of California Press, 1997), 153.

29. Polybius 21.19-21; Livy 37.53.

30. Livy 42.13. Compare the obsequiousness of King Masinissa of Numidia at Livy 45.13.12-14.9 (168 BCE).

31. Aetolians: Livy 37.49.1-4. Carthaginians: Livy 42.23.10. Prusias: Polybius 30.18; Livy 45.44.19-21.

32. Sallust, *Histories* 4, fr. 67.8 (McGushin).

33. Combining Polybius 21.23.4 and Livy 37.54.

34. Livy 35.32.9.

CHAPTER 8

Main primary sources: Justin 32.1-2; Livy 38.42–40.24; Pausanias 8.51.4-8; Plutarch, *Life of Philopoemen*; Polybius 22–24.13.

1. On the normality of armed intervention in the Greek world, see Low, ch. 5.

2. Livy 34.49.7-11.

3. Burton 2011 is essential reading on diplomatic friendship; see also Gruen 1984 and Eckstein 2008, indexes, s.v. *amicitia*. For friendship as a longstanding concept in Greek diplomacy too, see Low, 43-6. Polybius 28.3.6 is an example of Greek paranoia.

4. E.g., Livy 38.32.6-8, 39.37.9-17.

5. Livy 39.37.13.

6. Polybius 21.17.11-12.

7. Polybius 23.17.4.

8. The developed Roman empire, under the principate, relied on only a few hundred administrators to govern about 50,000,000 subjects. They could not have done so without the cooperation of local elites.

9. Livy 34.51.6.

10. E.g., Livy 39.46.7-8. Ager 106 lists the complaints.

11. *Syll.*³ 609 = *RDGE* 37; Sherk 12; Ager 88.

12. Diodorus of Sicily 29.33.

13. *Syll.*³ 612 = *RDGE* 1; Sherk 15. *Syll.*³ 611 = *RDGE* 38; Sherk 16.

14. Livy 39.26.14; 39.29.1-2. But in fact Philip still had a few places outside: Briscoe *C* 3.315-16.

15. Livy 39.26.9; Diodorus of Sicily 29.16.

16. Livy 42.12.10.

17. Polybius 23.1.9. Senate glad to hear complaints: Livy 39.46.7-8.

18. See p. 93.

19. Polybius 23.3.6-8, suppressed by Livy as part of his rehabilitation of Flamininus.

20. Livy 39.53.15-16.

21. This was, in Daniel Ogden's terms, a pretty standard "amphimetric" dispute—that is, a dispute for the throne between two sons of the same father, the king, but different mothers. Perseus' mother was called Polycrateia, but we do not know the name of Demetrius's.

22. Livy 39.53.3; Plutarch, *Life of Aratus* 54.3; *Life of Aemilius Paullus* 8.7.

23. Plutarch, *Life of Alexander* 9.7-8.

24. Polybius 23.10.17; Livy 40.6-7. "Xanthus" is a name with equine associations, and the hero received a sacrifice of warhorses, but other than this we have little to go on: Walbank *C* 3.233-4.

25. Livy 40.20-24; 40.54-57.

CHAPTER 9

Main primary sources: Appian, *Macedonica* 11; Justin 32.3-4; Livy 40.54–42.50; Polybius 24.14–27.6.

1. Appian, *The Syrian Wars* 21.

2. For a survey of Seleucid history after Apamea, see Gruen 1984a, 644–671.

3. Ager 112 on Flamininus's mission. Hannibal's death: Plutarch, *Life of Flamininus* 20–21; Appian, *The Syrian Wars* 11; Livy 39.51; Diodorus of Sicily 25.19; Justin 32.4.3. Briscoe 1972, 23–24.

4. Ager 114.

5. For an alternative dating of the war, see Dmitriev 2007. The war is "singularly ill documented" (Sherwin-White 1984, 27). I follow Burstein 1980.

6. For a survey, see Pollitt 1986, ch. 4. For more precise information and theories: F. Queyrel, *L'Autel de Pergame: Images et pouvoir en Grèce d'Asie* (Paris: Picard, 2005). My generalization about Pergamene Hellenism is rightly, but only lightly, qualified by A. Kuttner, " 'Do You Look Like You Belong Here?' Asianism at Pergamon and the Makedonian Diaspora," in E. Gruen (ed.), *Cultural Borrowings and Ethnic Appropriations in Antiquity* (Stuttgart: Steiner, 2005), 137–206.

7. Polybius 22.5.7; Ager 102. Details of the Lycian League: Larsen 1968, 240–263.

8. Polybius 21.24.7; 25.4-5; 27.7.6; 30.31.4; Livy 41.6.8-12; 41.25.8; 42.14.8; Berthold, ch. 8.

9. See p. 166. Polybius 25.4.7-8.

10. Livy 42.11-13; Appian, *Macedonica* 11.1-2.

11. Livy 42.14.1.

12. Livy 42.13.11.

13. Livy 42.18.4.

14. Livy 42.11-13; 42.40. The inscription is *Syll.*³ 643 = *RDGE* 40; Sherk 19; BD 44; Austin 93. The chief problem caused by the mutilation is that we do not know how long the lines were: *RDGE* and Austin follow Pomtow's version with longer lines than Colin's, which is preferred by Sherk and BD. I have translated the shorter version. In a somewhat circular fashion, some of the restorations of the inscription are derived from Livy's lists of Eumenes' complaints.

15. Pausanias 10.20-23; Justin 24.6-8; *Syll.*³ 398 (= BD 17; Austin 60). Some of these Celts ended up in Galatia: see ch. 7, n. 4.

16. Along with the majority of scholars, I consider the embassy of Livy 42.25 to be an annalistic justificatory invention. For a convenient list of diplomatic missions prior to the Third Macedonian War, see Briscoe *C* 4.15-18.

17. Livy 42.47.4-9; Diodorus of Sicily 30.1.

18. Livy 42.36; 42.48; Polybius 27.6; Appian, *Macedonica* 11.9, with poignant scenes of the suffering involved.

CHAPTER 10

Main primary sources: Appian, *Macedonica* 12–19; *The Illyrian Wars* 2.9; Cassius Dio 20; Diodorus of Sicily 29.30–30.24; Justin 33; Livy 42.50–45; Pausanias 7.10; Plutarch, *Life of Aemilius Paullus*; Polybius 27–30.

1. Polybius 1.3.6; 3.2.6; 3.32.7; 8.1.3; 9.10.11.

2. Livy 43.1; 43.5. For Cassius's actions as typical of the times, see Adams 1982, 249.

3. *Syll.*³ 646 = *RDGE* 2; Sherk 21; *RDGE* 3 = Sherk 20. Haliartus: Livy 42.63; Alcock, 97.

4. Polybius 28.4.13.

5. Livy 44.32.5.

6. Livy 44.37.5-9; Polybius 29.16. The chief historical importance of this eclipse is that "the calendar date given by Livy (§8), together with that for the eclipse of 190 (37.4.4), forms the basis for all reconstructions of the Roman calendar in this period" (Briscoe *C* 4.585).

7. Polybius 3.4.2-3; cf. 1.1.5; 6.2.3.

8. The base has survived (*Syll.*³ 652a), as have fragments of the frieze that accompanied Aemilius's monument, on which see Pollitt 1986, 156–157. The Latin inscription (Sherk 24) reads: "Lucius Aemilius, son of Lucius, general, took this from King Perseus and the Macedonians."

9. Crawford 1977, 97–98 (in Champion [ed.] 2004). For the suggestion that the Senate closed the mines to spite Italian businessmen, see Badian 1972, ch. 2. On the contrary, businessmen must have flourished in the lax regime of Macedon, with no direct rule and no Roman governor to answer to, yet with protection guaranteed by Roman influence there.

10. Burstein 38; Appian, *The Syrian Wars* 45.

11. Attalus succeeded his brother to the throne anyway, on Eumenes' death in 159.

12. *ORF*, Cato 163–169; Astin 1978, 273–281; Dmitriev 2011a, ch. 8. Some fragments are translated by Bringmann, 101–102.

13. Polybius 30.4-5; 30.31.9-12; 30.21; 31.4-5; Livy 44.15.1; 45.10; 45.20.4-25; Diodorus of Sicily 31.5. Delos was also a Panhellenic sacred island (sacred to Apollo and Artemis), and control of it carried much the same international prestige as control of Delphi. Rhodian income was further depleted by the removal of Caunus and Stratoniceia at this time: Polybius 31.21; 31.31.6-8. For assessments of how badly Rhodes was hurt, see Sherwin-White 1984, 30–36; Berthold 1984, 205–209. It has to be borne in mind that Rhodes was suffering anyway: just the previous year (169) it had had to import grain (Polybius 28.2.5).

14. See ch. 7, n. 17. Cicero, *Letters to Friends* 12.15.2; Sherwin-White 1984, 31.

CHAPTER 11

Main primary sources: Plutarch, *Life of Aemilius Paullus*; Diodorus of Sicily 31.1-15.

1. Pausanias 7.10; Polybius 30.6-7; 32.6; Plutarch, *Life of Cato the Elder* 9.2-3.

2. Polybius 24. 10.5.

3. *ORF*, Cato 161–162.

4. Strabo 7.7.6; 7.7.9.

5. Livy 43.21.4; 45.26.2. E. Kanta-Kitsou, *Doliani Thesprotia, Archaeological Guide* (Athens: Ministry of Culture, 2008); E. Kanta-Kitsou, *Gitana Thesprotia, Archaeological Guide* (Athens: Ministry of Culture, 2008); G. Riginos and K. Lazaris, *Elea Thesprotia: The Archaeological Site and the Neighbouring Region* (Athens: Ministry of Culture, 2008).

6. Polybius 30.12; 32.5-8; Diodorus of Sicily 31.31. Roof-tiles have been found bearing a stamp that, instead of naming the town (in this case Gitana) or saying "public property," says simply "property of Charops" (Igoumenitsa Archaeological Museum).

7. Machiavelli, *The Prince* (trans. N. H. Thomson), ch. 5; see also ch. 3 for further analysis of the Roman conquest of Greece.

8. Ziolkowski 1986.

9. Livy 41.21.

10. M. Terentius Varro, *De rerum rusticarum* 1.17.5. The literary critic Q. Caecilius Epirota, a former slave freed in the first century BCE by Cicero's friend T. Pomponius Atticus, was perhaps a descendant (Suetonius, *On Grammarians* 16.1).

11. Plutarch, *Life of Aemilius Paullus* 30–38; Diodorus of Sicily 31.8.10-9.7; Livy 45.36-40; Polybius 18.35.4-5; 31.22; Pliny, *Natural History* 34.54.

12. Polybius 30.22.

13. Early visits to Delphi: e.g., Livy 1.56.4-13; 5.28.1-2. Legal code: Dionysius of Halicarnassus, *Roman Antiquities* 10.51.5; Livy 3.31.8. Diplomacy: Strabo 5.3.5; Pliny, *Natural History* 3.57; Cleitarchus fr. 31 Jacoby; Polybius 30.5.6; Gruen 1984a, 62–65. I have already dismissed as fictional an Acarnanian embassy of much the same time: ch. 2, n. 1.

14. Demeter: Cicero, *Pro Balbo* 55; Pliny, *Natural History* 35.154. Asclepius: Livy 10.47.6-7. Aphrodite of Eryx: Livy 22.9.7-10. Cybele: Burton 1996; Erskine 2001, 205–218. Her temple was dedicated in 191: Livy 36.36.3-4.

15. See essays in Zanker.

16. Plutarch, *Life of Marcellus* 21.

17. There came to be so many statues (both looted and newly commissioned) cluttering the center of Rome that the Senate had some of them removed in 179 and then again in 158.

18. Pliny, *Natural History* 35.135.

19. Horace, *Epistles* 2.1.156.

20. Cicero, *Letters to His Brother Quintus* 1.1.16, 27; Petrochilos, 63–67.

21. The title of a famous 1989 book by Edith Hall is *Inventing the Barbarian*. For the term "orientalism," see Edward Said, *Orientalism* (new ed., London: Penguin, 1995).

22. Plautus, *Mostellaria* 22.

23. For Republican Roman loathing of homosexuality, see Champion 2004, 58–60.

24. Quoted by Pliny, *Natural History* 29.13. See also Plutarch, *Cato the Elder* 23.

25. Astin 1978, 157–181.

26. See, e.g., Dionysius of Halicarnassus, *Roman Antiquities* 1.5.2, trying to convince his fellow Greeks (at the end of the first century BCE) to suffer their subjection equably.

27. Beard, North, and Price, 1.97-8, 1.164-6. The worship of Bacchus was suppressed not just in Rome, but throughout Italy.

28. Livy 39.8-18; *CIL* I 196; Briscoe *C* 3.230-50. Briscoe *C* 3.480-3 on the Pythagorean books.

29. E.g., Cicero, *On Obligations* 1.151.

30. A likely influence on Roman veristic sculpture, but impossible to assess for lack of evidence, was Roman funerary masks: see Polybius 6.53.

31. Ovid, *Fasti* 3.101-2.

CHAPTER 12

Main primary sources: Appian, *The Illyrian Wars* 10–11; *The Syrian Wars* 45–47; Diodorus of Sicily 31.16-32; Justin 34–36; Livy, *Periochae* 46–52; Pausanias 7.11-16; Polybius 31–39; Zonaras 9.24-25, 28, 31.

1. M. Doyle, *Empires* (Ithaca: Cornell University Press, 1986), 45.

2. In fact, the arrival of the news of Pydna probably emboldened Popillius to wield the threat.

3. Gruen 1984a, 169–170, with further examples.

4. Antiochus: Livy 45.13.2. Ariarathes: Polybius 31.3; 31.7-8; 31.32; Diodorus of Sicily 31.28. Demetrius: Polybius 31.2; 31.11-15; 31.33; 32.2-3; Diodorus of Sicily 31.29-30; Appian, *The Syrian Wars* 47. For more on his escape: Gruen 1984a, 663–665. Prusias: Livy 45.44.13. Attalus: Welles 61; Austin 244; Sherk 29; BD 50. Pharnaces: Sherk 30.

5. Cyrenaica: Austin 289; BD 51; Burstein 104; Sherk 31. Pergamum: Austin 251; *RDGE* 11; Sherk 40.

6. Individual alliances: Gruen 1984a, 731–738. Athens and Delos: Polybius 32.7 (Ager 140); *Syll.*³ 664 (= *RDGE* 5; Burstein 75; Sherk 28). Sparta and Megalopolis: *Syll.*³ 665; Ager 135; cf. Polybius 31.1.7. Sparta and Argos: Pausanias 7.11.1-2 (Ager 136).

7. Polybius 30.25-6; 31.2.9-14; 31.8.4-8; Appian, *The Syrian Wars* 46; Diodorus of Sicily 31.16. Maccabeus: I Maccabees 8; II Maccabees 11:34-8; Sherk 43, 44.

8. For the standard view of Demetrius's escape, see e.g. Badian 1958, 107–108; Walbank *C* 3.478.

9. E.g., Ager 152–164.

10. Livy 45.33.3-4; Plutarch, *Life of Aemilius Paullus* 28.2-3.

11. Polybius 31.2.12; 35.4.11.

12. Ogden, 189–192.

13. Kallet-Marx, ch. 1.

14. We hear nothing about the other detainees, from Acarnania and so on. It would be nice to think they were eventually allowed home too.

15. 182: p. 156; 172: p. 177; 164: Pausanias 7.11.1-3.

16. Great-uncle of the unborn future dictator.

17. Strabo 8.6.23. An inscription exists—*CIL* I² 626 = *CLE* 3—in which Mummius boasts of destroying Corinth. Accounts of its destruction became exaggerated by assimilation to the Romans' more total destruction of Carthage in the same year, 146.

18. *Syll.*³ 684 = *RDGE* 43; Sherk 50; BD 52. On this inscription, see R. Kallet-Marx, "Q. Fabius Maximus and the Dyme Affair," *Classical Quarterly* n.s. 45 (1995), 129–153.

19. Polybius 39.5.2.

20. Cicero, *Against Verres* 2.1.55.

21. Pausanias 7.16.9-10, our chief source for the settlement, leaves its extent and nature controversial: for a minimalist view, see esp. Kallet-Marx, chs. 2–3.

22. E.g., *RDGE* 23; Pausanias 10.34.2.

23. Kallet-Marx, 52–55.

24. Polybius 39.6; Gruen 1984a, 171; Kallet-Marx, 91–92.

25. Eutropius (fourth century CE) 4.14.

26. Caecilius: Velleius Paterculus 1.11.3-5; Cicero, *Against Verres* 2.4.126. Mummius: Gruen 1992, 123–129; Yarrow 2006; Wallace-Hadrill 2008, 131–133.

27. E.g., Livy 44.16.1-4, an example taken from Greece.

28. Livy, *Periochae* 54; Cicero, *On Moral Ends* 1.24.

29. Appian, *The Mithridatic Wars* 22–23; Plutarch, *Life of Sulla* 24.7; Memnon fr. 22.9 Jacoby.

30. Gruen 1984a, 170–171, 302–303. Romans in the Adriatic region: Čašule, 218–226.

31. Polybius 36.17.5-9; Cicero, *Letters to Friends* 4.5; Livy 45.28.3; Strabo 8.4.11; 8.8.1; Dio Chrysostom, *Speeches* 33.25; Plutarch, *On the Decline of Oracles* 413f-414a. Pausanias: Alcock, 146. For further ancient testimony, see Alcock, 26–27.

32. Tacitus, *Agricola* 30, in the mouth of a Caledonian chieftain. The tag was used by Robert F. Kennedy against the Vietnam policy of Lyndon Johnson, in a speech at the University of Kansas, March 18, 1968.

33. For the archaeological evidence, see especially Alcock. For Boeotia, see also A. Snodgrass, 'Survey Archaeology and the Rural Landscape of the Greek City', in O. Murray and S. Price (eds.), *The Greek City from Homer to Alexander* (Oxford: Oxford University Press, 1990), 113–136. For the southern Argolid, see M. Jameson et al., *A Greek Countryside: The Southern Argolid from Prehistory to the Present Day* (Stanford: Stanford University Press, 1994).

34. Hopkins 1980.

35. Plutarch, *Life of Aratus* 24.2. See also Plutarch's essay "Precepts of Statecraft," where more than once (e.g. 824e-f) he remarks on the powerlessness of the Greeks and advises the would-be politician to aspire for no more than deference to Rome and instilling concord in his fellows.

36. Livy 26.18.6-11.

37. The first hint of an attack on the Scipios is the fact that, after their successes in Asia Minor in 190, neither Lucius nor Africanus had his command extended. This was probably due to the family's astonishing arrogance: Wallace-Hadrill 2008, 220–223. Then they launched political attacks on both Vulso's and Fulvius's triumphs, and this prompted a counterattack. Lucius was accused of keeping for himself an enormous sum of Antiochus's money, at which Africanus, with incredible arrogance, publicly tore up his brother's accounts and asked the Senate why they were concerned about 4,000,000 sestertii when his brother had added fifty times that amount to the exchequer (Livy 38.55-60). The fall of the Scipios was more or less complete with the death of Africanus in 183. Astin 1978, 60–73; Briscoe C 3.170-9; Scullard 1973, 290–303. The vigor of the line was briefly resurrrected by the adoption, c. 170, of a son of Aemilius Paullus Macedonicus (the two families had long been political allies), who became P. Cornelius Scipio Aemilianus Africanus, or Scipio Africanus the Younger, the general tasked in 146 with the destruction of Corinth, and the friend of Polybius. See H. Etcheto, *Les Scipions: Famille et pouvoir à Rome à l'époque républicaine* (Bordeaux: Ausonius, 2012).

38. Livy 40.5.7.

39. Pp. 135, 141. Pliny (*Natural History* 33.148), however, thought that Scipio Asiagenes' triumph in 189 started the rot. Cato seems to have blamed the influx of Syracusan treasure in 211: Livy 34.4.4. Cf. 25.40.2. See also Polybius 31.25.3-5. Briscoe C 3.225-6; Lintott 1972. All of them blame the loot, not the looters.

40. Polybius 6.57.5.

41. See p. 211.

42. Polybius 36.9. Cicero, *On the State* 3.33-35; *Philippics* 6.19; Virgil, *Aeneid* 6.852-3; *Aeneid* 1.278-9; Livy 9.11.7; Sallust, *Histories* 4.67 (McGushin); Polybius 31.10.7. Further relevant texts in Brunt 1978; Gruen 1984a, 274–275; Champion (ed.) 2004; Erskine (ed.) 2010.

BIBLIOGRAPHY

Ancient Sources

Literature

The most important ancient historian is Polybius (c. 200–c.118 BCE), who covered much the same period as this book of mine, but in forty books. Only the first five of these survive in their entirety, but substantial fragments remain of the rest. I recommend my own translation (*Polybius: The Histories* [Oxford University Press, 2010]), which has an introduction and notes by B. McGing. The most important fragments not included in my translation may be found in the several volumes of the Loeb Polybius (Harvard University Press), translated by W. Paton, and revised by F. Walbank and C. Habicht. The essential academic companion to Polybius is F. Walbank, *A Historical Commentary on Polybius*, 3 vols. (London/Oxford: Oxford University Press, 1957–1979).

After Polybius, the next most important ancient historian is Livy (T. Livius, 59 BCE–17 CE). Though writing in Latin (Polybius was a Greek), Livy's importance lies not least in his preservation of otherwise lost Polybian material. His work covered Roman history from the foundation of the city (supposedly in 753 BCE) until 9 BCE, in 142 books, of which only 1–10 and 21–45 survive (up to 167 BCE). The most relevant of these to our purposes are books 21–45. The best translations of these books are J. Yardley, *Livy: Hannibal's War. Books 21–30* (Oxford: Oxford University Press, 2006); J. Yardley, *Livy: The Dawn of the Roman Empire. Books 31–40* (Oxford: Oxford University Press, 2000); and J. Chaplin, *Livy: Rome's Mediterranean Empire. Books 41–45 and the* Periochae (Oxford: Oxford University Press, 2007). There are good academic commentaries by J. Briscoe: *A Commentary on Livy Books XXXI–XXXIII, Books XXXIV–XXXVII, Books 38–40, Books 41–45* (Oxford: Oxford University Press, 1973, 1981, 2008, 2012). Also relevant are five volumes of commentary on Books 36–40 by P. Walsh (Warminster: Aris & Phillips, 1991–1996).

Apart from these two major sources, there is important information to be found in a number of other historians. In book 9 of his *Roman History*, Appian (an Alexandrian Greek historian of the second century CE) covered Macedonian affairs; fragments remain of this narrative, and his account of the Illyrian Wars (originally an appendix to book 9) is complete; the beginning of his work on the Syrian Wars (from book 11) is also relevant. There is a thorough commentary on the *Illyrica*: M. Šašel Kos, *Appian and Illyricum* (Ljubljana: National Museum of Slovenia, 2005). And the relevant part of *The Syrian Wars* has been edited by K. Brodersen, *Appians Antiochike (Syriake 1,1–44,232). Text und Kommentar* (Munich: Editio Maris, 1991).

The fragments that remain of the later books of Diodorus of Sicily's *Library of History*, written probably late in the first century BCE, contain further snippets: the relevant books, 25–32, may conveniently be found in translation in F. Walton, *Diodorus Siculus, Library of History, Books 21–32* (Cambridge: Harvard University Press, 1957).

Cassius Dio (early third century CE) is another historian the relevant part of whose work survives only in fragments, particularly as summarized by John Zonaras in the twelfth century CE. Nevertheless, the remains of Books 13–21 of his *Roman History* sometimes open further windows on the period, and are available in the Loeb Classical Library, translated by E. Cary.

The digest by Justin (M. Junianus Justinus, 3rd century CE) of books 28–34 of the *Philippic History* of Pompeius Trogus (late 1st century BCE) is occasionally useful, and is available in translation: J. Yardley, *Justin: Epitome of the Philippic History of Pompeius Trogus* (Atlanta: Scholars Press, 1994).

Fragments of other historians and the work even of more literary authors cast rare but precious extra light.. But the most important not-strictly-historical source is Plutarch, the essayist and biographer of the late first and early second centuries CE. His Lives include a number of relevant biographies: *Philopoemen and Flamininus* (paired together as parallel Lives), *Cato the Elder*, *Pyrrhus, Aemilius Paullus*, and *Aratus. Cato the Elder* and *Aemilius Paullus* were included in my *Plutarch: Roman Lives* (Oxford: Oxford University Press, 1999), while the rest will be included in my *Plutarch: Hellenistic Lives* (Oxford: Oxford University Press, 2014).

Inscriptions

The most important inscriptions are available in translation in the following sourcebooks, some of which also contain excerpts from ancient literary and/or papyrus sources:

Ager, S., 1996, *Interstate Arbitrations in the Greek World, 337–90 BC* (Berkeley: University of California Press).

Austin, M., 2006, *The Hellenistic World from Alexander to the Roman Conquest: A Selection of Ancient Sources in Translation* (2nd ed., Cambridge: Cambridge University Press).

Bagnall, R., and P. Derow, 2004, *The Hellenistic Period: Historical Texts in Translation* (2nd ed., Oxford: Blackwell) (1st ed. title: *Greek Historical Documents: The Hellenistic Period*).

Burstein, S., 1985, *The Hellenistic Age from the Battle of Ipsos to the Death of Kleopatra VII* (Cambridge: Cambridge University Press).

Sherk, R., 1969, *Roman Documents from the Greek East: Senatus Consulta and Epistulae to the Age of Augustus* (Baltimore: Johns Hopkins University Press).

Sherk, R., 1984, *Rome and the Greek East to the Death of Augustus* (Cambridge: Cambridge University Press).

Welles, C., 1934, *Royal Correspondence in the Hellenistic Period: A Study in Greek Epigraphy* (New Haven: Yale University Press; repr. Chicago: Ares, 1974).

Secondary Literature

Atlases

Metallinou, G. (ed.), 2008, *Historical and Geographical Atlas of the Greek–Albanian Border* (Athens: Ministry of Culture).

Talbert, R., 2000, *Barrington Atlas of the Greek and Roman World* (Princeton: Princeton University Press).

Bibliography

Books and Articles

I have marked with an asterisk those English-language books that I consider indispensable launch-pads for further enquiry. Where a collection of essays gains an asterisk, I have not separately listed the essays it contains.

Adams, W. L., 1982, "Perseus and the Third Macedonian War," in W. Adams and E. Borza (eds.), *Philip II, Alexander the Great and the Macedonian Heritage* (Washington, DC: University Press of America), 237–256.

Adams, W. L., 1993, "Philip V, Hannibal and the Origins of the First Macedonian War," *Ancient Macedonia* 5, 41–50.

Adcock, F., and D. Mosley, 1975, *Diplomacy in Ancient Greece* (London: Thames and Hudson).

Ager, S., 1992, "Rhodes: The Rise and Fall of a Neutral Diplomat," *Historia* 40, 11–41.

Ager, S., 2009, "Roman Perspectives on Greek Diplomacy," in C. Eilers (ed.), *Diplomats and Diplomacy in the Roman World* (Leiden: Brill), 15–43.

*Alcock, S., 1996, *Graecia Capta: The Landscapes of Roman Greece* (Cambridge: Cambridge University Press).

Allen, R., 1971, "Attalos I and Aegina," *Annual of the British School at Athens* 66, 1–12.

*Allen, R., 1983, *The Attalid Kingdom: A Constitutional History* (Oxford: Oxford University Press).

Armstrong, D., and J. Walsh, 1986, "*SIG*³ 593: The Letter of Flamininus to Chyretiae," *Classical Philology* 81, 32–46.

Astin, A., 1978, *Cato the Censor* (London: Oxford University Press).

*Astin, A., et al. (eds.), 1989, *The Cambridge Ancient History*, 2nd ed., vol. 8: *Rome and the Mediterranean to 133 BC* (Cambridge: Cambridge University Press).

Austin, M., 1986, "Hellenistic Kings, War and the Economy," *Classical Quarterly* n.s. 36, 450–466.

Badian, E., 1952a, "Notes on Roman Policy in Illyria (230–201 BC)," *Papers of the British School at Rome* 20, 72–93; repr. in id., *Studies in Greek and Roman History* (Oxford: Blackwell, 1964), 1–33.

Badian, E., 1952b, "The Treaty between Rome and the Achaean League," *Journal of Roman Studies* 42, 76–80.

Badian, E., 1958a, *Foreign Clientelae (264–70 BC)* (London: Oxford University Press).

Badian, E., 1958b, "Aetolica," *Latomus* 17, 197–211.

Badian, E., 1959, "Rome and Antiochus the Great: A Study in Cold War," *Classical Philology* 54, 81–99; repr. in id., *Studies in Greek and Roman History* (Oxford: Blackwell, 1964), 113–139.

Badian, E., 1968, *Roman Imperialism in the Late Republic* (Oxford: Blackwell).

Badian, E., 1970, *Titus Quinctius Flamininus: Philhellenism and* Realpolitik (Cincinnati: University of Cincinnati Press).

Badian, E., 1971, "The Family and Early Career of T. Quinctius Flamininus," *Journal of Roman Studies* 61, 102–111.

Badian, E., 1972, *Publicans and Sinners: Private Enterprise in the Service of the Roman Republic* (Oxford: Blackwell).

Badian, E., 1984 "Hegemony and Independence: Prolegomena to a Study of Rome and the Hellenistic States in the Second Century BC," in J. Harmatta (ed.), *Actes du VIIe Congrès de la F.E.I.C.* (Budapest: Akadémiai Kiadó), 397–414.

Badian, E., and R. M. Errington, 1965, "A Meeting of the Achaean League (Early 188 BC)," *Historia* 14, 13–17.

Badian, E., and S. Oost, 1960, "Philip V and Illyria: A Reply," *Classical Philology* 55, 182–186.

Balsdon, J. P. V. D., 1954, "Rome and Macedon, 205-200 BC," *Journal of Roman Studies* 44, 30–42.

Balsdon, J. P. V. D., 1967, "T. Quinctius Flamininus," *Phoenix* 21, 177–190.

Balsdon, J. P. V. D., 1979, *Romans and Aliens* (London: Duckworth).

Barchiesi, A., 2009, "Roman Perspectives on the Greeks," in G. Boys-Stones et al. (eds.), *The Oxford Handbook to Hellenic Studies* (Oxford: Oxford University Press), 98–113.

Baronowski, D., 1987, "Greece after 146 BC: Provincial Status and Roman Tribute," *Monographies en Archéologie et Histoire de l'Université McGill* 6, 125–138.

Baronowski, D., 1988, "The Provincial Status of Mainland Greece after 146 BC: A Criticism of Erich Gruen's Views," *Klio* 70, 448–460.

Baronowski, D., 1991a, "The Roman Awareness of Their Imperialism in the Second Century BC," *Cahiers des Études Anciennes* 26, 173–181.

Baronowski, D., 1991b, "The Status of the Greek Cities of Asia Minor after 190 BC," *Hermes* 119, 450–463.

Barré, M., 1983, *The God List in the Treaty between Hannibal and Philip V of Macedon* (Baltimore: Johns Hopkins University Press).

Beard, M., 2007, *The Roman Triumph* (Cambridge: Harvard University Press).

Beard, M., J. North, and S. Price, 1998, *Religions of Rome*, 2 vols. (Cambridge: Cambridge University Press).

Bederman, D., 2001, *International Law in Antiquity* (Cambridge: Cambridge University Press).

Berthold, R., 1976, "The Rhodian Appeal to Rome in 201 BC," *Classical Journal* 71, 97–107.

*Berthold, R., 1984, *Rhodes in the Hellenistic Age* (Ithaca, NY: Cornell University Press).

Bickermann, E., 1932, "*Bellum Antiochicum*," *Hermes* 67, 47–76.

Bickermann, E., 1945, "*Bellum Philippicum*: Some Roman and Greek Views concerning the Causes of the Second Macedonian War," *Classical Philology* 40, 137–148.

Bickermann, E., 1952, "Hannibal's Covenant," *American Journal of Philology* 73, 1–23.

Bickermann, E., 1953, "Notes sur Polybe," *Revue des études grecques* 66, 479–506.

Bowra, C. M., 1957, "Melinno's Hymn to Rome," *Journal of Roman Studies* 47, 21–28.

Bragg, E., 2005, "Illyrian Piracy—Ancient Endemic or Historical Construct?" *Daedalus* 5, 19–33.

Braund, D., 1982, "Three Hellenistic Personages: Amynander, Prusias II, Daphidas," *Classical Quarterly* n.s. 32, 350–357.

Brennan, T. C., 1996, "Triumphus in Monte Albano," in Wallace and Harris (eds.), 315–337.

*Bringmann, K., 2007, *A History of the Roman Republic*, trans. by W. Smyth (Cambridge: Polity Press).

Briscoe, J., 1964, "Q. Marcius Philippus and *Nova Sapientia*," *Journal of Roman Studies* 54, 66–77.

Briscoe, J., 1967, "Rome and the Class Struggle in the Greek States, 200–146 BC," *Past and Present* 36, 3–20; repr. in M. Finley (ed.), *Studies in Ancient Society* (London: Routledge, 1974), 53–73.

Briscoe, J., 1969, "Eastern Policy and Senatorial Politics, 168–146 BC," *Historia* 18, 49–70.

Briscoe, J., 1972, "Flamininus and Roman Politics, 200–189 BC," *Latomus* 31, 22–53.

Briscoe, J., 1978, "The Antigonids and the Greek States, 276–196 BC," in P. Garnsey and C. Whittaker (eds.), *Imperialism in the Ancient World* (Cambridge: Cambridge University Press), 145–157.

Briscoe, J., 1982, "Livy and Senatorial Politics, 200–167 BC: The Evidence of the Fourth and Fifth Decades," in H. Temporini and W. Haase (eds.), *Aufstieg und Niedergang der römischen Welt* 2.30.2 (Berlin: de Gruyter), 1075–1121.

Briscoe, J., 1992, "Political Groupings in the Middle Republic: A Restatement," in C. Deroux (ed.), *Studies in Latin Literature and Roman History* 6 (Brussels: Latomus), 70–83.

Brizzi, G., 2001, "*Fides, Mens, Nova Sapientia*: Radici greche nell'approccio di Roma a politica e diplomazia verso l'Oriente ellenistico," in M. Bertinelli and L. Piccirilli (eds), *Linguaggio e terminologia diplomatica dall'antico oriente all'impero bizantino* (Rome: L'Erma di Bretschneider), 121–131.

*Broughton, T. R. S., 1951, *The Magistrates of the Roman Republic*, vol. 1 (New York: American Philological Association).

Brown, P., 1986, "The First Roman Literature," in J. Boardman, J. Griffin, and O. Murray (eds.), *The Oxford History of the Classical World* (Oxford: Oxford University Press), 437–453.

Brunt, P., 1978, "Laus Imperii," in P. Garnsey and C. Whittaker (eds.), *Imperialism in the Ancient World* (Cambridge: Cambridge University Press), 159–191.

Buraselis, K., 1996, "*Vix Aerarium Sufficeret*: Roman Finances and the Outbreak of the Second Macedonian War," *Greek, Roman, and Byzantine Studies* 37, 149–172.

Burstein, S., 1980, "The Aftermath of the Peace of Apamea," *American Journal of Ancient History* 5, 1–12.

Burton, P., 1996, "The Summoning of the Magna Mater to Rome," *Historia* 45, 36–63.

Burton, P., 2009, "Ancient International Law, the Aetolian League, and the Ritual of Surrender during the Roman Republic: The Constructivist View," *International History Review* 31, 237–252.

*Burton, P., 2011, *Friendship and Empire: Roman Diplomacy and Imperialism in the Middle Republic (353–146 BC)* (Cambridge: Cambridge University Press).

Cabanes, P., 1976, *L'Épire de la mort de Pyrrhos à la conquête romaine (272–167 av. J.C.)* (Paris: Les Belles Lettres).

Cabanes, P., 1988, *Les Illyriens de Bardylis à Genthius (IVe –IIe siècles avant J.-C.)* (Paris: Sedes).

Campbell, B., 2002, "Power without Limit: 'The Romans Always Win'," in A. Chaniotis and P. Ducrey (eds.), *Army and Power in the Ancient World* (Stuttgart: Steiner), 167–180.

Carawan, E., 1988, "*Graecia Liberata* and the Role of Flamininus in Livy's Fourth Decade," *Transactions of the American Philological Association* 118, 209–252.

Cartledge, P., and A. Spawforth, 2002, *Hellenistic and Roman Sparta: A Tale of Two Cities* (2nd ed., London: Routledge).

Čašule, N., 2012, "'In Part a Roman Sea': Rome and the Adriatic in the Third Century BC," in Smith and Yarrow (eds.), 205–229.

Champion, C., 1997, "The Nature of Authoritative Evidence in Polybius and Agelaus' Speech at Naupactus," *Transactions of the American Philological Association* 127, 111–128.

Champion, C., 2000, "Romans as *Barbaroi*: Three Polybian Speeches and the Politics of Cultural Indeterminacy," *Classical Philology* 95, 425–444.

Champion, C., 2004, *Cultural Politics in Polybius' Histories* (Berkeley: University of California Press).

*Champion, C. (ed.), 2004, *Roman Imperialism: Readings and Sources* (Oxford: Blackwell).

Champion, C., 2007, "Empire by Invitation: Greek Political Strategies and Roman Imperial Interventions in the Second Century BCE," *Transactions of the American Philological Association* 137, 255–275.

Coppola, A., 1993, *Demetrio di Faro* (Rome: L'Erma di Bretschneider).

Cornell, T., 1995, *The Beginnings of Rome: Italy and Rome from the Bronze Age to the Punic Wars* (London: Routledge).

Cornell, T., 2000, "The City of Rome in the Middle Republic (400–100 BC)," in J. Coulston and H. Dodge (eds.), *Ancient Rome: The Archaeology of the Eternal City* (Oxford: Oxford University Press), 42–60.

Crawford, M., 1977, "Rome and the Greek World: Economic Relationships," *Economic History Review* 30, 42–52.

Crawford, M., 1992, *The Roman Republic* (2nd ed., London: Fontana).

Davies, J., 2000, "A Wholly Non-Aristotelian Universe: The Molossians as Ethnos, State, and Monarchy," in R. Brock and S. Hodkinson (eds.), *Alternatives to Athens: Varieties of Political Organization and Community in Ancient Greece* (Oxford: Oxford University Press), 234-58.

Deininger, J., 1973, "Bemerkungen zur Historizität der Rede des Agelaos 217 v. Chr. (Polyb. 5, 104)," *Chiron* 3, 103–108.

Dell, H., 1967a, "The Origin and Nature of Illyrian Piracy," *Historia* 16, 344–358.

Dell, H., 1967b, "Antigonus III and Rome," *Classical Philology* 62, 94–103.

Dell, H., 1970, "Demetrius of Pharus and the Istrian War," *Historia* 19, 30–38.

Dell, H., 1977, "Macedon and Rome: The Illyrian Question in the Early Second Century BC," *Ancient Macedonia* 2, 305–315.

Dell, H., 1983, "The Quarrel between Demetrius and Perseus: A Note on Macedonian National Policy," *Ancient Macedonia* 3, 67–76.

Derow, P., 1973, "Kleemporos," *Phoenix* 27, 118–134.

Derow, P., 1979, "Polybius, Rome, and the East," *Journal of Roman Studies* 69, 1–15.

Derow, P., 1991, "Pharos and Rome," *Zeitschrift für Papyrologie und Epigraphik* 88, 261–270.

Dmitriev, S., 2003, "Livy's Evidence for the Apamean Settlement (188 BC)," *American Journal of Ancient History* n.s. 2, 39–62.

Dmitriev, S., 2007, "Memnon on the Siege of Heraclea Pontica by Prusias I and the War between the Kingdoms of Bithynia and Pergamum," *Journal of Hellenic Studies* 127, 133–138.

Dmitriev, S., 2010, "Attalus' Request for the Cities of Aenus and Maronea in 167," *Historia* 59, 106–114.

Dmitriev, S., 2011a, *The Greek Slogan of Freedom and Early Roman Politics in Greece* (Oxford: Oxford University Press).

Dmitriev, S., 2011b, "Antiochus III: A Friend and Ally of the Roman People," *Klio* 93, 104–130.

Dorey, T., 1957, "Macedonian Troops at the Battle of Zama," *American Journal of Philology* 78, 185–187.

Dorey, T., 1959, "Contributory Causes of the Second Macedonian War," *American Journal of Philology* 80, 288–295.

Dorey, T., 1960, "The Alleged Aetolian Embassy to Rome," *Classical Review* n.s. 10, 9.

Dorey, T., and S. Oost, 1960, "Philip V and Illyria: The Annalistic Point of View," *Classical Philology* 55, 180–181.

Dzino, D., 2010, *Illyricum in Roman Politics, 229 BC–AD 68* (Cambridge: Cambridge University Press).

Eckstein, A., 1976, "T. Quinctius Flamininus and the Campaign against Philip in 198 BC," *Phoenix* 30, 119–142.

Eckstein, A., 1982, "Human Sacrifice and Fear of Military Disaster in Republican Rome," *American Journal of Ancient History* 7, 69–95.

Eckstein, A., 1987a, *Senate and General: Individual Decision-making and Roman Foreign Relations, 264-194 BC* (Berkeley: University of California Press).

Eckstein, A., 1987b, "Polybius, Aristaenus, and the Fragment 'On Traitors,'" *Classical Quarterly* n.s. 37, 140–162.

Eckstein, A., 1987c, "Nabis and Flamininus on the Argive Revolutions of 198 and 197 BC," *Greek, Roman, and Byzantine Studies* 28, 213–233.

Eckstein, A., 1988, "Rome, the War with Perseus, and Third Party Mediation," *Historia* 37, 414–444.

Eckstein, A., 1990, "Polybius, the Achaeans, and the 'Freedom of the Greeks,'" *Greek, Roman, and Byzantine Studies* 31, 45–71.

Eckstein, A., 1994, "Polybius, Demetrius of Pharus, and the Origins of the Second Illyrian War," *Classical Philology* 89, 46–59.

Eckstein, A., 1995, "Glabrio and the Aetolians: A Note on *Deditio*," *Transactions of the American Philological Association* 125, 271–289.

Eckstein, A., 1999, "Pharos and the Question of Roman Treaties of Alliance Overseas in the Third Century BC," *Classical Philology* 94, 395–418.

Eckstein, A., 2002, "Greek Mediation in the First Macedonian War (209–205 BC)," *Historia* 52, 268–297.

Eckstein, A., 2005, "The Pact between the Kings, Polybius 15.20.6, and Polybius' View of the Outbreak of the Second Macedonian War," *Classical Philology* 100, 228–242.

*Eckstein, A., 2006, *Mediterranean Anarchy, Interstate War, and the Rise of Rome* (Berkeley: University of California Press).

*Eckstein, A., 2008, *Rome Enters the Greek East: From Anarchy to Hierarchy in the Hellenistic Mediterranean, 230–170 BC* (Oxford: Blackwell).

Eckstein, A., 2009a, "The Diplomacy of Intervention in the Middle Republic: The Roman Decision of 201/200 BC," *Veleia* 26, 75–101.

Eckstein, A., 2009b, "Ancient 'International Law,' the Aetolian League, and the Ritual of Surrender during the Roman Republic: A Realist View," *International History Review* 31, 253–267.

Eckstein, A., 2010, "Macedonia and Rome, 221–146 BC," in J. Roisman and I. Worthington (eds.), *A Companion to Ancient Macedonia* (Oxford: Wiley-Blackwell), 225–250.

Edson, C., 1935, "Perseus and Demetrius," *Harvard Studies in Classical Philology* 46, 191–202.

Edson, C., 1948, "Philip V and Alcaeus of Messene," *Classical Philology* 43, 116–121.

*Errington, R. M., 1969, *Philopoemen* (London: Oxford University Press).

Errington, R. M., 1971a, *The Dawn of Empire: Rome's Rise to Power* (London: Hamish Hamilton).

Errington, R. M., 1971b, "The Alleged Syro-Macedonian Pact and the Origins of the Second Macedonian War," *Athenaeum* 49, 336–354.

Errington, R. M., 1974, "*Senatus consultum de Coronaeis* and the Early Course of the Third Macedonian War," *Rivista di filologia e d'istruzione classica* 102, 79–86.

Errington, R. M., 1988, "Aspects of Roman Acculturation in the East under the Republic," in P. Kneissl and V. Losemann (eds.), *Alte Geschichte und Wissenschaftsgeschichte: Festschrift für Karl Christ* (Darmstadt: Wissenschaftliche Buchgesellschaft), 140–157.

Errington, R. M., 1990, *A History of Macedonia*, trans. by C. Errington (Berkeley: University of California Press).

*Errington, R. M., 2008, *A History of the Hellenistic World* (Oxford: Blackwell).

Erskine, A., 1994, "The Romans as Common Benefactors," *Historia* 43, 70–87.

Erskine, A., 1995, "Rome in the Greek World: The Significance of a Name," in A. Powell (ed.), *The Greek World* (London: Routledge), 368–383.

Erskine, A., 1996, "Money-loving Romans," *Papers of the Leeds International Latin Seminar* 9, 1–11.

Erskine, A., 2000, "Polybios and Barbarian Rome," *Mediterraneo Antico* 3, 165–182.

Erskine, A., 2001, *Troy between Greece and Rome: Local Tradition and Imperial Power* (Oxford: Oxford University Press).

Erskine, A., 2003a, "Spanish Lessons: Polybius and the Maintenance of Imperial Power," in J. Yanguas and E. Pagola (eds.), *Polibio y la Península Ibérica* (Vitoria: Gasteiz), 229–243.

Erskine, A., 2003b, "Distant Cousins and International Relations: *Syngeneia* in the Hellenistic World," in K. Buraselis and K. Zoumboulakis (eds.), *The Idea of European Community in History*, vol. 2 (Athens: National and Capodistrian University of Athens), 205–216.

*Erskine, A. (ed.), 2003, *A Companion to the Hellenistic World* (Oxford: Blackwell).

Erskine, A., 2005, "Unity and Identity: Shaping the Past in the Greek Mediterranean," in E. Gruen (ed.), *Cultural Borrowings and Ethnic Appropriations in Antiquity* (Stuttgart: Steiner), 121–136.

*Erskine, A. (ed.), 2010, *Roman Imperialism* (Edinburgh: Edinburgh University Press).

Feeney, D., 2005, "The Beginnings of a Literature in Latin," *Journal of Roman Studies* 95, 226–240.

Ferrary, J.-L., 1988, *Philhellenisme et impérialisme: Aspects idéologiques de la conquête romaine du monde hellénistique* (Rome: Ecole française de Rome).

Ferrary, J.-L., 1997, "The Hellenistic World and Roman Political Patronage," in P. Cartledge, P. Garnsey, and E. Gruen (eds.), *Hellenistic Constructs: Essays in Culture, History, and Historiography* (Berkeley: University of California Press), 105–119.

Fine, J., 1936, "Macedon, Illyria, and Rome, 220–219 BC," *Journal of Roman Studies* 26, 24–39.

*Flower, H. (ed.), 2004, *The Cambridge Companion to the Roman Republic* (Cambridge: Cambridge University Press).

Franke, P., 1989, "Pyrrhus," in F. Walbank et al. (eds.), *The Cambridge Ancient History*, 2nd ed., vol. 7.2: *The Rise of Rome to 220 BC* (Cambridge: Cambridge University Press), 456–485.

Fuks, A., 1970, "The Bellum Achaicum and its Social Aspect," *Journal of Hellenic Studies* 90, 78–89; repr. in id., *Social Conflict in Ancient Greece* (Jerusalem: Magnes), 270–281.

Gabrielsen, V., 1993, "Rhodes and Rome after the Third Macedonian War," in P. Bilde et al. (eds.), *Centre and Periphery in the Hellenistic World* (2nd ed., Aarhus: Aarhus University Press), 132–161.

Gabrielsen, V., 2000, "The Rhodian Peraia in the Third and Second Centuries BC," *Classica et Mediaevalia* 51, 129–183.

Gebhard, E., and M. Dickie, 2003, "The View from the Isthmus, ca. 200 to 44 BC," in C. Williams and K. Bookidis (eds.), *Corinth: The Centenary, 1896–1996* (Princeton: American School of Classical Studies at Athens), 261–278.

Gilliver, C., 1996, "The Roman Army and Morality in War," in A. Lloyd (ed.), *Battle in Antiquity* (Swansea: University Press of Wales), 219–238.

Giovannini, A., 1969, "Les origines de la 3e guerre de Macédoine," *Bulletin de correspondance hellénique* 93, 853–861.

Giovannini, A., 1970, "Philipp V, Perseus, und die Delphische Amphiktyonie," *Ancient Macedonia* 1, 147–154.

Giovannini, A., 1988, "Review Discussion: Roman Eastern Policy in the Late Republic," *American Journal of Ancient History* 9, 33–42.

Giovannini, A., 2001, "Les Antécédents de la deuxième guerre de Macédoine," in R. Frei-Stolba and K. Gex (eds), *Recherches récentes sur le monde hellénistique* (Bern: Peter Lang), 97–113.

Golan, D., 1985, "Autumn 200 BC: The Events at Abydus," *Athenaeum* 63, 389–404.

Goldsworthy, A., 2000, *Roman Warfare* (London: Cassell).

Grainger, J., 1996, "Antiochus III in Thrace," *Historia* 45, 329–343.

*Grainger, J., 1999, *The League of the Aetolians* (Leiden: Brill).

*Grainger, J., 2002, *The Roman War of Antiochos the Great* (Leiden: Brill).

Green, P., 1990, *Alexander to Actium: The Historical Evolution of the Hellenistic Age* (Berkeley: University of California Press).

Griffith, G., 1935, "An Early Motive of Roman Imperialism (201 BC)," *Cambridge Historical Journal* 5, 1–14.

Gruen, E. (ed.), 1970, *Imperialism in the Roman Republic* (New York: Holt, Rinehart and Winston).

Gruen, E., 1973, "The Supposed Alliance between Rome and Philip V of Macedon," *California Studies in Classical Antiquity* 6, 123–136.

Gruen, E., 1974, "The Last Years of Philip V," *Greek, Roman, and Byzantine Studies* 15, 221–246.

Gruen, E., 1975, "Rome and Rhodes in the Second Century BC: A Historiographical Inquiry," *Classical Quarterly* n.s. 25, 58–81.

Gruen, E., 1976a, "Class Conflict and the Third Macedonian War," *American Journal of Ancient History* 1, 29–60.

Gruen, E., 1976b, "The Origins of the Achaean War," *Journal of Hellenic Studies* 96, 46–69.

Gruen, E., 1976c, "Rome and the Seleucids in the Aftermath of Pydna," *Chiron* 6, 73–95.

Bibliography

Gruen, E., 1981, "Philip V and the Greek Demos," in H. Dell (ed.), *Ancient Macedonian Studies in Honor of Charles F. Edson* (Thessaloniki: Institute for Balkan Studies), 169–182.

Gruen, E., 1982a, "Greek Πίστις and Roman *Fides*," *Athenaeum* 60, 50–68.

Gruen, E., 1982b, "Macedonia and the Settlement of 167 BC," in W. Adams and E. Borza (eds.), *Philip II, Alexander the Great and the Macedonian Heritage* (Washington, DC: University Press of America), 257–267.

*Gruen, E., 1984a, *The Hellenistic World and the Coming of Rome*, 2 vols (Berkeley: University of California Press; 1-vol. paperback ed., 1986).

Gruen, E., 1984b, "Material Rewards and the Drive for Empire," in Harris (ed.), 59–88.

Gruen, E., 1990, *Studies in Greek Culture and Roman Policy* (Leiden: Brill).

*Gruen, E., 1992, *Culture and National Identity in Republican Rome* (Ithaca: Cornell University Press).

Gruen, E., 1996, "The Roman Oligarchy: Image and Perception," in J. Linderski (ed.), *Imperium sine fine: T. Robert S. Broughton and the Roman Republic* (Stuttgart: Steiner = *Historia* Einzelschriften 105), 215–234.

Gruen, E., 2014, "Roman Comedy and the Social Scene," in M. Fontaine and A. Scafuro (eds.), *The Oxford Handbook of Greek and Roman Comedy* (New York: Oxford University Press), 913–936.

Habicht, C., 1956, "On the Wars between Pergamon and Bithynia," in id., *The Hellenistic Monarchies: Selected Papers*, trans. by P. Stevenson (Ann Arbor: University of Michigan Press, 2006), 1–21 (German original: *Hermes* 84, 90–100).

Habicht, C., 1976, "Ambrakia and the Thessalian League at the Time of the War with Perseus," in id., *The Hellenistic Monarchies: Selected Papers*, trans. by P. Stevenson (Ann Arbor: University of Michigan Press, 2006), 124–133 (German original: *Demetrias* 1, 175–180).

Habicht, C., 1997, *Athens from Alexander to Antony*, trans. by D. Schneider (Cambridge: Harvard University Press).

Hamilton, C., 1993, "The Origins of the Second Macedonian War," *Ancient Macedonia* 5, 559–567.

Hammond, N., 1966, "The Opening Campaigns and the Battle of Aoi Stena in the Second Macedonian War," *Journal of Roman Studies* 56, 39–54.

Hammond, N., 1967, *Epirus* (London: Oxford University Press).

Hammond, N., 1968, "Illyris, Rome and Macedon in 229–205 BC," *Journal of Roman Studies* 58, 1–21.

Hammond, N., 1988, "The Campaign and Battle of Cynoscephalae in 197 BC," *Journal of Hellenic Studies* 108, 60–82.

Hammond, N., 1989a, "The Illyrian Atintani, the Epirotic Atintanes, and the Roman Protectorate," *Journal of Roman Studies* 79, 11–25.

Hammond, N., 1989b, *The Macedonian State: The Origins, Institutions, and History* (Oxford: Oxford University Press).

*Hammond, N., and F. Walbank, 1988, *A History of Macedonia*, vol. 3 (Oxford: Oxford University Press).

Harris, W., 1971, "On War and Greed in the Second Century BC," *American Historical Review* 76, 1371–1385.

*Harris, W., 1984, *War and Imperialism in Republican Rome, 327–70 BC* (2nd ed., Oxford: Oxford University Press).

Harris, W., (ed.), 1984, *The Imperialism of Mid-Republican Rome* (Philadelphia: Pennsylvania State University Press = Papers and Monographs of the American Academy in Rome, vol. 29).

Harrison, T., 2008, "Ancient and Modern Imperialism," *Greece and Rome* 55, 1–22.

Helliesen, J., 1986, "Andriscus and the Revolt of the Macedonians, 149–148 BC," *Ancient Macedonia* 4, 307–314.

Hill, H., 1946, "Roman Revenues from Greece after 146 BC," *Classical Philology* 41, 35–42.

Bibliography

Hölbl, G., 2001, *A History of the Ptolemaic Empire*, trans. T. Saavedra (London: Routledge).

Holleaux, M., 1921, *Rome, la Grèce et les monarchies hellénistiques au IIIe siècle avant J.-C.* (Paris: de Boccard).

Holleaux, M., 1928, "The Romans in Illyria," in S. Cook, F. Adcock, and M. Charlesworth (eds.), *The Cambridge Ancient History*, 1st ed., vol. 7 (Cambridge: Cambridge University Press), 822–857.

Holleaux, M., 1930, "Rome and Macedon; Rome and Antiochus," in S. Cook, F. Adcock, and M. Charlesworth (eds), *The Cambridge Ancient History*, 1st ed., vol. 8 (Cambridge: Cambridge University Press), 116–240.

Hopkins, K., 1978, *Conquerors and Slaves* (Cambridge: Cambridge University Press).

Hopkins, K., 1980, "Taxes and Trade in the Roman Empire (200 B.C.–A.D. 400)," *Journal of Roman Studies* 70, 101–25.

Hopkins, K., and G. Burton, 1983, "Political Succession in the Late Republic (249–50 BC)," in K. Hopkins, *Death and Renewal* (Cambridge: Cambridge University Press), 31–118.

*Hoyos, D. (ed.), 2012, *A Companion to Roman Imperialism* (Leiden: Brill).

Isaac, B., 2004, *The Invention of Racism in Classical Antiquity* (Princeton: Princeton University Press).

*Kallet-Marx, R., 1995, *Hegemony to Empire: The Development of the Roman Imperium in the East from 148 to 62 BC* (Berkeley: University of California Press).

Kashtan, N., 1982, "L'impérialisme romain et la ligue achéenne (200-180 av. J.-C.)," *Ktema* 7, 211–220.

Kirigin, B., and M. Vickers, 2009, "Ancient Greeks in Croatia," in *Croatia: Aspects of Art, Architecture and Cultural Heritage* (London: Frances Lincoln), 20–31.

Korn, G., 1973, "An Apollonian Embassy to Rome," *Latomus* 32, 570–574.

Kostial, M., 1995, *Kriegrisches Rom? Zur Frage von Unvermeidbarkeit und Normalität militärischer Konflikte in der römischen Politik* (Stuttgart: Steiner).

Kuntić-Makvić, B., 2002, "Les romains et les grecs adriatiques," in N. Cambi, S. Čače, and B. Kirigin (eds.), *Greek Influence along the East Adriatic Coast* (Split: Književni Krug), 141–150.

Lampela, A., 1998, *Rome and the Ptolemies of Egypt: The Development of Their Political Relations, 273-80 BC* (Helsinki: Societas Scientiarum Fennica).

Larsen, J., 1935, "Was Greece Free between 196 and 146 BC?," *Classical Philology* 30, 193–214.

Larsen, J., 1936, "The Treaty of Peace at the Conclusion of the Second Macedonian War," *Classical Philology* 31, 342–348.

Larsen, J., 1937, "The Peace of Phoenice and the Outbreak of the Second Macedonian War," *Classical Philology* 32, 15–31.

*Larsen, J., 1968, *Greek Federal States: Their Institutions and History* (London: Oxford University Press).

Lazenby, J., 1978, *Hannibal's War* (Warminster: Aris & Philips, 1978).

Le Bohec, S., 1987, "Demetrius de Pharus, Scerdilaidas, et la ligue hellénique," in P. Cabanes (ed.), *L'Illyrie meridionale et l'Épire dans l'antiquité* (Paris: de Boccard), 203–208.

Lendon, J., 1997, *Empire of Honour: The Art of Government in the Roman World* (Oxford: Oxford University Press).

Le Rider, G., 1992, "Les clauses financières des traités de 189 et de 188," *Bulletin de correspondance hellénique* 116, 267–277.

Linderski, J., 1995, "Ambassadors Go to Rome," in E. Frézouls and A. Jacquemin (eds.), *Les relations internationales: Actes du Colloque de Strasbourg, 15-17 juin 1999* (Paris:), 452–478; repr. in id., *Roman Questions*, vol. 2 (New York: David Brown, 2007), 40–60.

Linderski, J., 1996, "Cato Maior in Aetolia," in Wallace and Harris (eds.), 376–408.

Lintott, A., 1972, "Imperial Expansion and Moral Decline in the Roman Republic," *Historia* 21, 626–638.

Lintott, A., 1993, *Imperium Romanum: Politics and Administration* (London: Routledge).

*Lintott, A., 1999, *The Constitution of the Roman Republic* (Oxford: Oxford University Press).

Low, P., 2007, *Interstate Relations in Classical Greece: Morality and Power* (Cambridge: Cambridge University Press).

Ma, J., 2000, *Antiochos III and the Cities of Western Asia Minor* (Oxford: Oxford University Press).

Mackay, P., 1970, "The Coinage of the Macedonian Republics, 168-146 BC," *Ancient Macedonia* 1, 256–264.

MacMullen, R., 1991, "Hellenizing the Romans (2nd Century BC)," *Historia* 40, 419–438.

Magie, D., 1939, "The 'Agreement' between Philip V and Antiochus III for the Partition of the Egyptian Empire," *Journal of Roman Studies* 29, 32–44.

Mandell, S., 1989, "The Isthmian Proclamation and the Early Stages of Roman Imperialism in the Near East," *Classical Bulletin* 65, 89–94.

Mandell, S., 1991, "Roman Dominion: Desire and Reality," *Ancient World* 22, 37–42.

Marasco, G., 1986, "Interessi commerciali e fattori politici nella condotta romana in Illiria (230–219 a.C.)," *Studi classici e orientali* 36, 35–112.

Mattingly, H., 1997, "Athens between Rome and the Kings, 229/8 to 129 BC," in P. Cartledge, P. Garnsey, and E. Gruen (eds.), *Hellenistic Constructs: Essays in Culture, History, and Historiography* (Berkeley: University of California Press), 120–144.

May, J., 1946, "Macedonia and Illyria (217–167 BC)," *Journal of Roman Studies* 36, 48–56.

McDonald, A., 1967, "The Treaty of Apamea (188 BC)," *Journal of Roman Studies* 57, 1–8.

McDonald, A., 1981, "Studies on Ancient Macedonia," in H. Dell (ed.), *Ancient Macedonian Studies in Honor of Charles F. Edson* (Thessaloniki: Institute for Balkan Studies), 243–254.

McDonald, A., and F. Walbank, 1937, "The Origins of the Second Macedonian War," *Journal of Roman Studies* 27, 180–207.

McDonald, A., and F. Walbank, 1969, "The Treaty of Apamea (188 BC): The Naval Clauses," *Journal of Roman Studies* 59, 30–39.

McDonnell, M., 2006, "Roman Aesthetics and the Spoils of Syracuse," in S. Dillon and K. Welch (eds.), *Representations of War in Ancient Rome* (Cambridge: Cambridge University Press), 79–105.

McGing, B., 2010, *Polybius' Histories* (Oxford: Oxford University Press).

McShane, R., 1964, *The Foreign Policy of the Attalids of Pergamum* (Urbana: University of Illinois Press).

Meadows, A., 1993, "Greek and Roman Diplomacy on the Eve of the Second Macedonian War," *Historia* 42, 40–60.

Mellor, R., 1975, ΘΕΑ ΡΩΜΗ: The *Worship of the Goddess Roma in the Greek World* (Göttingen: Vandenhoeck and Ruprecht).

Mellor, R., 2008, "*Graecia Capta*: The Confrontation between Greek and Roman Identity," in K. Zacharias (ed.), *Hellenisms: Culture, Identity, and Ethnicity from Antiquity to Modernity* (Aldershot: Ashgate), 79–125.

Meloni, P., 1953, *Perseo e la fine della monarchia macedone* (Rome: L'Erma di Bretschneider).

Mendels, D., 1998, *Identity, Relgion and Historiography: Studies in Hellenistic History* (Sheffield: Sheffield Academic Press).

Momigliano, A., 1975, *Alien Wisdom: The Limits of Hellenization* (Cambridge: Cambridge University Press).

Morgan, M., 1969, "Metellus Macedonicus and the Province Macedonia," *Historia* 18, 422–446.

Bibliography

Mørkholm, O., 1967, "The Speech of Agelaus at Naupactus in 217 BC," *Classica et Mediaevalia* 28, 240–253.

Mørkholm, O., 1974, "The Speech of Agelaus Again," *Chiron* 4, 127–132.

Murray, W., 2012, *The Age of Titans: The Rise and Fall of the Great Hellenistic Navies* (New York: Oxford University Press).

Nicolet, C., 1976, *Tributum: recherches sur la fiscalité directe sous la république romaine* (Bonn: Habelt).

North, J., 1981, "The Development of Roman Imperialism," *Journal of Roman Studies* 71, 1–9.

Oakley, S., 1993, "The Roman Conquest of Italy," in Rich and Shipley (eds.), 9–37.

Ogden, D., 1999, *Polygamy, Prostitutes and Death: The Hellenistic Dynasties* (London: Duckworth).

Oost, S., 1954, *Roman Policy in Epirus and Acarnania in the Age of the Roman Conquest of Greece* (Dallas: Southern Methodist University Press; repr. New York: Arno, 1975).

Oost, S., 1957, "Amynander, Athamania, and Rome," *Classical Philology* 52, 1–15.

Oost, S., 1959, "Philip V and Illyria, 205–200 BC," *Classical Philology* 54, 158–164.

Paltiel, E., 1979, "The Treaty of Apamea and the Later Seleucids," *Antichthon* 13, 30–41.

Petrochilos, N., 1974, *Roman Attitudes to the Greeks* (Athens: Saripolos).

Petzold, K.-E., 1971, "Rom und Illyrien: Ein Beitrag zur römischen Aussenpolitik im 3. Jahrhundert," *Historia* 20, 199–223.

Petzold, K.-E., 1992, "Griechischer Einfluss auf die Anfänge römischer Ostpolitik," *Historia* 41, 205–245.

Petzold, K.-E., 1999, "Die Freiheit der Griechen under die Politik der *nova sapientia*," *Historia* 48, 61–93.

Pfeilschifter, R., 2005, *Titus Quinctius Flamininus: Untersuchungen zur römischen Griechenlandpolitik* (Göttingen: Vandenhoeck and Ruprecht).

Poláček, A., 1971, "Le traité de paix d'Apamée," *Revue internationale des droits de l'antiquité* 18, 591–621.

Pollitt, J., 1978, "The Impact of Greek Art on Rome," *Transactions of the American Philological Association* 108, 155–174.

*Pollitt, J., 1986, *Art in the Hellenistic Age* (Cambridge: Cambridge University Press).

Potter, D., 2012, "Old and New in Roman Foreign Affairs: The Case of 197," in Smith and Yarrow (eds.), 134–151.

Raaflaub, K., 1996, "Born to be Wolves? Origins of Roman Imperialism," in Wallace and Harris (eds.), 273–314.

Raditsa, L., 1972, "Bella Macedonica," in H. Temporini (ed.), *Aufstieg und Niedergang der römischen Welt* 1.1 (Berlin: de Gruyter), 564–589.

Raeymaekers, J., 1996, "The Origins of the Rivalry between Philopoemen and Flamininus," *Ancient Society* 27, 259–276.

Rawlings, H., 1976, "Antiochus the Great and Rhodes," *American Journal of Ancient History* 1, 2–28.

*Rawson, E., 1985, *Intellectual Life in the Late Roman Republic* (London: Duckworth).

Reiter, W., 1988, *Aemilius Paullus, Conqueror of Greece* (London: Croom Helm).

*Rich, J., 1976, *Declaring War in the Roman Republic in the Period of Transmarine Expansion* (Brussels: Latomus).

Rich, J., 1984, "Roman Aims in the First Macedonian War," *Proceedings of the Cambridge Philological Society* 210, 126–180.

Rich, J., 1989, "Patronage and Interstate Relations in the Roman Republic," in A. Wallace-Hadrill (ed.), *Patronage in Ancient Society* (London: Routledge), 117–136.

Rich, J., 1993, "Fear, Greed and Glory: The Causes of Roman War-making in the Middle Republic," in Rich and Shipley (eds.), 38–68.

Rich, J., 2008, "Treaties, Allies and the Roman Conquest of Italy," in P. de Souza and J. France (eds.), *War and Peace in Ancient and Medieval History* (Cambridge: Cambridge University Press), 51–75.

Rich, J., 2011, "The *Fetiales* and Roman International Relations," in J. Richardson and F. Santangelo (eds.), *Priests and State in the Roman World* (Stuttgart: Steiner), 187–242.

Rich, J., and Shipley, G. (eds.), 1993, *War and Society in the Roman World* (Abingdon: Routledge).

Richardson, J., 1975, "The Triumph, the Praetors, and the Senate in the Early Second Century BC," *Journal of Roman Studies* 65, 50–63.

Richardson, J., 1979, "Polybius' View of the Roman Empire," *Papers of the British School at Rome* 47, 1–11.

Richardson, J., 1986, *Hispaniae: Spain and the Development of Roman Imperialism, 219–82 BC* (Cambridge: Cambridge University Press).

Richardson, J., 2008, *The Language of Empire: Rome and the Idea of Empire from the Third Century BC to the Second Century AD* (Cambridge: Cambridge University Press).

Rosenstein, N., 1993, "Competition and Crisis in Mid-Republican Rome," *Phoenix* 47, 313–338.

Rosenstein, N., 2008, "Aristocrats and Agriculture in the Middle and Late Republic," *Journal of Roman Studies* 98, 1–26.

Rosenstein, N., 2011, "War, Wealth, and Consuls," in H. Beck et al. (eds.), *Consuls and "Res Publica": Holding High Office in Republican Rome* (Cambridge: Cambridge University Press), 133–158.

*Rosenstein, N., 2012, *Rome and the Mediterranean, 290 to 146 BC* (Edinburgh: Edinburgh University Press).

*Rosenstein, N., and R. Morstein-Marx (eds.), 2010, *A Companion to the Roman Republic* (Oxford: Blackwell).

Roth, J., 2009, *Roman Warfare* (Cambridge: Cambridge University Press).

Rowland, R., 1983, "Rome's Earliest Imperialism," *Latomus* 42, 749–762.

Rubinsohn, W., 1988, "Macedonian Resistance to Roman Occupation in the Second Half of the Second Century BC," in T. Yuge and M. Doi (eds.), *Subordination in Antiquity* (Leiden: Brill), 141–158.

Russell, A., 2012, "Aemilius Paullus Sees Greece: Travel, Vision, and Power in Polybius," in Smith and Yarrow (eds.), 152–167.

*Sabin, P., H. van Wees, and M. Whitby (eds.), 2007, *The Cambridge History of Greek and Roman Warfare*, 2 vols. (Cambridge: Cambridge University Press).

Sacks, K., 1975, "Polybius' Other View of Aetolia," *Journal of Hellenic Studies* 95, 92–106.

Šašel Kos, M., 2002, "From Agron to Genthius: Large-scale Piracy in the Adriatic," in L. Bracessi and M. Luni (eds.), *I Greci in Adriatico*, vol. 1 (Rome: Hesperia), 137–155.

Scafuro, A., 1987, "Prusias II of Bithynia and Third Party Mediation," *Historia* 36, 28–37.

Scholten, J., 2000, *The Politics of Plunder: Aitolians and Their Koinon in the Early Hellenistic Period, 279–217 BC* (Berkeley: University of California Press).

Sciarrino, E., 2004, "A Temple for the Professional Muse: The *Aedes Herculis Musarum* and Cultural Shifts in Second-century Rome," in A. Barchiesi, J. Rüpke, and S. Stephens (eds.), *Rituals in Ink: A Conference on Religion and Literary Production in Rome* (Stuttgart: Steiner), 45–56.

Scullard, H., 1945, "Charops and Roman Policy in Epirus," *Journal of Roman Studies* 35, 58–64.

Scullard, H., 1973, *Roman Politics, 220–150 BC* (2nd ed., Oxford: Oxford University Press).

Seager, R., 1981, "The Freedom of the Greeks of Asia from Alexander to Antiochus," *Classical Quarterly* n.s. 31, 106–112.

Seibert, J., 1995, "Invasion aus dem Osten: Trauma, Propaganda oder Erfindug der Römer?," in C. Schubert and K. Brodersen (eds.), *Rom und der griechische Osten: Festschrift für H. Schmitt* (Stuttgart: Steiner), 237–248.

Sherwin-White, A., 1977, "Roman Involvement in Anatolia, 167–88 BC," *Journal of Roman Studies* 67, 62–75.

Sherwin-White, A., 1980, "Rome the Aggressor?," *Journal of Roman Studies* 70, 177–181.

Sherwin-White, A., 1984, *Roman Foreign Policy in the East, 168 BC to AD 1* (London: Duckworth).

Shimron, B., 1972, *Late Sparta: The Spartan Revolution, 243–146 BC* (Buffalo: State University of New York).

Shipley, G., 2000, *The Greek World after Alexander, 323–30 BC* (London: Routledge).

Smith, C., and L. Yarrow, (eds.), 2012, *Imperialism, Cultural Politics, and Polybius* (New York: Oxford University Press).

Smith, R., 1981, "Greeks, Foreigners and Roman Republican Portraits," *Journal of Roman Studies* 71, 24–38.

de Souza, P., 1999, *Piracy in the Graeco-Roman World* (Cambridge: Cambridge University Press).

Starr, C., 1938, "Rhodes and Pergamum, 201–200 BC," *Classical Philology* 33, 63–68; repr. in id., *Essays on Ancient History* (Leiden: Brill, 1979), 205–211.

Steinby, C., 2007, *The Roman Republican Navy from the Sixth Century to 167 BC* (Helsinki: Societas Scientiarum Fennica).

Swain, J., 1940, "The Theory of the Four Monarchies: Opposition History under the Roman Empire," *Classical Philology* 35, 1–21.

Texier, J.-G., 1975, *Nabis* (Paris: Les Belles Lettres).

Texier, J.-G., 1976–7, "Un aspect de l'antagonisme de Rome et de Sparte a l'époque hellénistique: l'entrevue de 195 avant J.C. entre Titus Quinctius Flamininus et Nabis," *Revue des études anciennes* 78–79, 145–154.

Twyman, B., 1986, "Philip V, Antiochus the Great, the Celts, and Rome," *Ancient Macedonia* 4, 667–672.

Twyman, B., 1993, "Roman Frontier Strategy and the Destruction of the Antigonid Monarchy," *Ancient Macedonia* 5, 1649–1656.

Twyman, B., 1999, "Cotta's War against Philip V," *Ancient Macedonia* 6, 1277–1284.

Veyne, P., 1975, "Y a-t-il eu un impérialisme romain?," *Mélanges de l'École Française de Rome (Antiquité)* 87, 793–855.

Walbank, F., 1938, "ΦΙΛΙΠΠΟΣ ΤΡΑΓΩΙΔΟΥΜΕΝΟΣ" *Journal of Hellenic Studies* 58, 55–68.

*Walbank, F., 1940, *Philip V of Macedon* (Cambridge: Cambridge University Press).

Walbank, F., 1941, "A Note on the Embassy of Q. Marcius Philippus," *Journal of Roman Studies* 31, 82–93; repr. in id., *Selected Papers: Studies in Greek and Roman History and Historiography* (Cambridge: Cambridge University Press, 1985), 181–192.

Walbank, F., 1942–4, "Alcaeus of Messene, Philip V, and Rome," *Classical Quarterly* 36, 134–145; 37, 1–13; 38, 87–88.

Walbank, F., 1949, "Roman Declaration of War in the Third and Second Centuries," *Classical Philology* 44, 15–19; repr. in id., *Selected Papers: Studies in Greek and Roman History and Historiography* (Cambridge: Cambridge University Press, 1985), 101–106.

Walbank, F., 1963, "Polybius and Rome's Eastern Policy," *Journal of Roman Studies* 53, 1–13; repr. in id., *Selected Papers: Studies in Greek and Roman History and Historiography* (Cambridge: Cambridge University Press, 1985), 138–156.

Walbank, F., 1977, "The Causes of the Third Macedonian War: Recent Views," *Ancient Macedonia* 2, 81–94.

Walbank, F., 1993, "Η ΤΩΝ ΟΛΩΝ ΕΛΠΙΣ and the Antigonids," *Ancient Macedonia* 5, 1721–1730; repr. in id., *Polybius, Rome, and the Hellenistic World: Essays and Reflections* (Cambridge: Cambridge University Press, 2002), 127–136.

Wallace, R., 1990, "Hellenization and Roman Society in the Late Fourth Century BC," in W. Eder (ed.), *Staat und Staatlichkeit in der frühen römischen Republik* (Stuttgart: Steiner), 278–291.

Wallace, R., and E. Harris, (eds.), 1996, *Transitions to Empire: Essays in Greco-Roman History, 360–146 BC, in Honor of E. Badian* (Norman: Oklahoma).

Wallace-Hadrill, A., 1988, "Greek Knowledge, Roman Power," *Classical Philology* 83, 224–233.

Wallace-Hadrill, A., 1998, "To be Roman, Go Greek: Thoughts on Hellenization at Rome," in M. Austin et al. (eds.), *Modus Operandi: Essays in Honour of Geoffrey Rickman* (London: Institute of Classical Studies), 79–91.

*Wallace-Hadrill, A., 2008, *Rome's Cultural Revolution* (Cambridge: Cambridge University Press).

Walsh. J., 1993, "Bones of Contention: Pharsalus, Phthiotic Thebes, Larisa Cremaste, Echinus," *Classical Philology* 88, 35–46.

Walsh. J., 1996, "Flamininus and the Propaganda of Liberation," *Historia* 45, 344–363.

Walsh. J., 2000, "The Disorders of the 170s BC and Roman Intervention in the Class Struggle in Greece," *Classical Quarterly* n.s. 50, 300–303.

Wardman, A., 1976, *Rome's Debt to Greece* (London: Elek; repr. London: Bristol Classical Press, 2002).

Warrior, V., 1981, "Livy, Book 42: Structure and Chronology," *American Journal of Ancient History* 6, 1–50.

Warrior, V., 1988, "The Chronology of the Movements of M. Fulvius Nobilior," *Chiron* 18, 325–376.

Warrior, V., 1992, "Intercalation and the Action of M'. Acilius Glabrio (cos. 191 BC)," in C. Deroux (ed.), *Studies in Latin Literature and Roman History* 6 (Brussels: Latomus), 119–144.

Warrior, V., 1996a, *The Initiation of the Second Macedonian War: An Explication of Livy, Book 31* (Stuttgart: Steiner = *Historia* Einzelschriften 97).

Warrior, V., 1996b, "Evidence in Livy on Roman Policy prior to War with Antiochus the Great," in Wallace and Harris (eds.), 356–375.

Waszink, J., 1960, "Tradition and Personal Achievement in Early Latin Literature," *Mnemosyne* ser. 4, 13, 16–33.

West, S., 1984, "Lycophron Italicised?," *Journal of Hellenic Studies* 104, 127–151.

Wiemer, H.-U., 2004, "Der Beginn des 3. Makedonischen Krieges: Überlegungen zur Chronologie," *Historia* 53, 22–37.

*Wilkes, J., 1992, *The Illyrians* (Oxford: Blackwell).

Will, E., 1972, "Rome et les Séleucides," in H. Temporini (ed.), *Aufstieg und Niedergang der römischen Welt* 1.1 (Berlin: de Gruyter), 590–632.

*Woolf, G., 2012, *Rome: An Empire's Story* (New York: Oxford University Press).

Yarrow, L., 2006, "Lucius Mummius and the Spoils of Corinth," *Scripta Classica Israelica* 25, 57–70.

Zanker, P. (ed.), 1976, *Hellenismus in Mittelitalien*, 2 vols. (Göttingen: Vandenhoek and Ruprecht).

Ziolkowski, A., 1986, "The Plundering of Epirus in 167 BC: Economic Considerations," *Papers of the British School at Rome* 54, 69–80.

Ziolkowski, A., 1993, "*Urbs Direpta*, or How the Romans Sacked Cities," in Rich and Shipley (eds.), 69–91.

INDEX